THE DIGITAL CITY

econ pol mgmt educ human' crime

economy
political
mgmt
education
human nature
criminal aspect

CRITICAL CULTURAL COMMUNICATION

General Editors: Jonathan Gray, Aswin Punathambekar, Adrienne Shaw
Founding Editors: Sarah Banet-Weiser and Kent A. Ono

The Digital City

Media and the Social Production of Place

Germaine R. Halegoua

NEW YORK UNIVERSITY PRESS

New York

NEW YORK UNIVERSITY PRESS
New York
www.nyupress.org

References to Internet websites (URLs) were accurate at the time of writing. Neither the author nor New York University Press is responsible for URLs that may have expired or changed since the manuscript was prepared.

Library of Congress Cataloging-in-Publication Data
Names: Halegoua, Germaine R., 1979–   author.
Title: The digital city : media and the social production of place / Germaine R. Halegoua.
Description: New York : New York University Press, [2018] | Series: Critical cultural communication | Includes bibliographical references and index.
Identifiers: LCCN 2019012048 | ISBN 9781479839216 (cl : alk. paper) | ISBN 9781479882199 (pb : alk. paper)
Subjects: LCSH: Cities and towns—Technological innovations. | Smart cities. | Digital media. | Place marketing.
Classification: LCC HT153 .H328 2018 | DDC 307.76—dc23
LC record available at https://lccn.loc.gov/2019012048

New York University Press books are printed on acid-free paper, and their binding materials are chosen for strength and durability. We strive to use environmentally responsible suppliers and materials to the greatest extent possible in publishing our books.

Manufactured in the United States of America

10 9 8 7 6 5 4 3 2 1

Also available as an ebook

CONTENTS

Introduction

How do you figure out how to travel somewhere that you've never been before? When I asked 108 people this question in 2015, 96 percent said that they used some sort of global positioning system (GPS) to help them find their way. Many of the respondents explained the process: you search for the address of a location and then type it into the search function on a mobile map or GPS-enabled device, and route options to your destination appear on the screen. You're the blue dot or the red dot, and the device tracks your movement as the position of your avatar traverses across the map. The majority of participants described this process as convenient, easy, necessary, awesome, and a time (and life) saver. One participant responded to the question simply: "God bless Google Maps."

Every day, millions of people turn to small, possibly handheld screens and location-aware devices to search for destinations or receive recommendations for places to visit and then dutifully follow the step-by-step instructions provided until the journey is complete. We don't consciously reflect on these activities as they're happening and probably don't associate these practices with placemaking or constructing a sense of place. Most attempts to understand navigation behaviors construe them as digital processes that distract users from fully experiencing or knowing the places they travel through. Or computing one's location is held up as an example worthy of critique or comparison to the good old days of paper maps, knowing directions by heart, or asking a friend or passerby for help. Although studies that focus on digital wayfinding might suggest otherwise, if we take account of the lived experiences, the practices of doing, and the ways in which digital wayfinding makes the world around us meaningful, then digital navigation is entirely about placemaking and placeing oneself in space.

Notions that digital media dissociates users from place stem from frameworks employed by scholars and critics to understand media consumption in shared spaces. Early scholarship addressing human-computer interactions with place tended to foreground human *versus* machine relationships. Public uses of media were understood as enacting processes of alienation, abstraction, and distraction and as spatially disembedding. All forms of media at one point or another have been categorized in this disparaging manner. Similar to the long-standing perspective that reading books or magazines on public transportation is a strategy for negotiating street sociability or limiting encounters with strangers, Shuhei Hosokawa referred to the "cassette recorder for headphone listening" (a.k.a., the Walkman) as an "urban strategy."[1] He noted that the listener "seems to cut the auditory contact with the outer world where he really lives" in order to revel in the "perfection of his individual zone of listening."[2] This impression of a "partial loss of touch with the here and now" was identified by Margaret Morse as a result of watching television, using freeways, or frequenting malls.[3] Around the same time, Joshua Meyrowitz famously noted that electronic media refigured "situational geographies" of daily life and dissociated physical place from social place—until media users were left with "no sense of place."[4] A decade earlier geographers had been concerned with the flattening of place and place-based experience that media encouraged. Edward Relph argued that media transmitted "an inauthentic attitude toward places," which encouraged a sense of "placelessness" that he described as "a weakening of the identity of places to the point where they not only look alike but feel alike and offer the same bland possibilities for experience."[5]

In more recent work on digital and mobile media technologies, scholarly perspectives have broadened to recognize more positive associations between digital media and experiences of place. Humans and machines are not as readily perceived as mutually exclusive categories and are not treated as separate considerations for designers of everyday experience as they once were.[6] People are observed to work *with* technologies in order to move through and experience places. As Rowan Wilken notes, we use mobile media to negotiate our engagement with the places we inhabit, and Scott McQuire argues that the contemporary urban experience is uniquely defined by the pervasiveness of digital media within cities, which leads to new contexts for the production of public space.[7] However, in discussions of distracted, disruptive, or poor negotiations of digital media, space and place are still evident. McQuire also notes that digital media paradoxically both place and displace users. For example, Michael Bull has argued that MP3 players provide users with increased control and orchestration of their experience of time and space in urban environments.[8] Through personal technologies such as the portable music player or mobile phone, users are able to create a "privatized auditory bubble" that encapsulates a personal, curated space composed of one's own music collection. However, like the boom box, Walkman, and other preceding mobile media, the personal bubble that Bull describes has been interpreted by some critics as a dissociative enclave that allows users to "shut out everyone around you. . . . [The device is] a personal accessory that allows the oblivious to live in their own world."[9] These paradoxes of presence reverberate in scholarly literature in that technology users are popularly recognized as hyperconnected members of "lonely crowds" or exist "alone together."[10]

Other scholars and journalists have noted that digital media themselves are a distraction: from work, from social interaction, from our everyday conditions of existence, or from any space that is not behind a screen. The distracted glance has been described as the ontology of digital media. As Debra Benita Shaw notes, "cyberflaneur" has emerged as a term to describe a Web 2.0 or mobile media user who moves through space in a series of unfocused and circuitous movements with "a kind of detached inquisitiveness about fellow citizens and their social status."[11] This type of distracted and detached inquisitiveness produced by the intersections of media and urban space has also been read as inherently commercial. Robert Luke suggests that the ubiquitous "phoneur" fills city streets: a postmodern subject who is situated within the "space of flows" of commodity and desire and whose actions and identity are composed through the logic of mobile capital and mobile technologies and services.[12]

In this book, I aim to illustrate and analyze the ways in which the exact opposite processes are observable: many different actors are actually using digital technologies and practices to re-embed themselves within urban space and to create a sense of place—or the recognition of a space as an individually or collectively meaningful location—for themselves and/or others. Although there are copious socially constructed technopanics, cautionary tales, and science fiction narratives around the potential for digital media to dissociate or liberate us from the confines

[handwritten margin note: one aspect of ecological model]

of physical locations, we've lacked careful attention to the ways people actually use digital media to become placemakers. Contrary to these scholarly and colloquial narratives of dissociation or distraction, creating and controlling a sense of place is still the primary way that we connect with our environments, interact with others, and express our identities. However, the tools and methods that people appropriate to produce and perform place are more plentiful, are more dependent on code, and may appear more diffuse, more fragmented, and potentially more difficult to recognize. As this book will illustrate, people from various sectors of society with distinct roles to play in the social and physical production of urban environments employ digital media in their personal and professional placemaking practices. The case studies analyzed in this text are entry points for disambiguating these digital placemaking practices and interpreting what it means to make place now.

The examples highlighted in this book are not gathered from obscure corners of the digital landscape. Rather, they comprise routine and seemingly unremarkable practices that will be familiar to readers of all digital backgrounds and literacies. Readers might live in or might have visited the cities mentioned on these pages, might have read or heard about some of these projects in major news outlets, might have used some of the applications and services mentioned, and might have participated in some of the activities analyzed in this book but have never thought about them as "placemaking" practices or as producing meanings of place and space. In fact, like many scholars, journalists, and cultural critics, readers of this book might have even entertained the opposite perspective.

The Digital City offers a new theoretical framework for thinking about our relationships to digital media by reconceptualizing common, mundane digital interactions as placemaking activities. This framework is expressed through two main arguments. *First,* I argue that by reading digital media through the lens of "place," we gain a more holistic and nuanced understanding of digital media use and non-use, processes and decisions around their implementation and adoption, and our relationships to digital artifacts and infrastructures. *Second,* I argue that people consciously employ digital media (such as mobile phones, wireless and fiber-optic networks, ubiquitous computing and navigation technologies, and location-based social media) to take account of their social and physical positions within urban space and to create and negotiate a new sense of place within rapidly changing media landscapes and socio-spatial relationships.

My interpretation of what place is and how place is experienced through digital media has been shaped by David Morley's prompting in *Home Territories: Media, Mobility, and Identity*: "We must ask how, in a world of flux, forms of collective dwelling are sustained and re-invented."[13] Drawing on social constructionist as well as phenomeno-logical approaches to place, I recognize that most urban places are experienced in flux. Places are perpetually coming into being as they are socially constructed and reconstructed by institutional and cultural forces. People and places are constantly moving and changing; their rhythms, circulations, and differential mobilities shape urban space, urban life, and their relationships to other places within global flows and networks of exchange. But the meaning and significance of places are not perpetually deferred. As David Harvey and many other geographers have noted, placemaking entails creating a deep, albeit temporary, sense of permanence, pause, or investment in fixity within the forces and scapes that shape spatiality.[14] This book investigates the digital tools and situations embraced by urban populations for creating temporary permanence. The individual chapters of this book present representative cases of how different actors use digital media to exploit the possibilities for circulation and change while alleviating the challenges and risks of social, economic, and physical mobilities (from personal movement to globalization). These actors use digital media to negotiate creating stable places of belonging while being in flux. In all cases, the populations mentioned in this book attempt to shape emotional attachments with(in) urban environments by re-placing the city as unique, desirable, familiar, or knowable through assorted digital media forms.

What I call "re-placing the city" is the subjective, habitual practice of assessing and combining physical, social, and digital contexts in order to more fully understand one's embeddedness within urban places and to reproduce a unique sense of place through the use of digital media affordances. By recognizing the intersecting conditions that shape urban development, mobilities, and the affective relationships that connect us to place, urban planners, government officials, corporations, develop-ers, artists, and community activists—as well as urban residents and travelers—reproduce layered, seemingly abstract urban environments as rooted, humanized places once more. People with disparate positions of social power, access to resources, and digital literacies engage digital media to turn the spaces in which they find themselves into the places in which they "dwell."

The concept of re-placing the city is not meant to signify that the city is being replaced, as in exchanged for something else. Instead, the practices of re-placing highlighted and analyzed in this book are akin to the lived experiences and performances of what Anthony Giddens describes as "re-embedding."[15] Similar to re-embedding, re-placing is a set of practices that manage the seemingly fragmented or overwhelming conditions that the networked urban subject experiences and routinely acts within, then re-embeds these conditions within meaningful spatial and temporal contexts. As other scholars have described, contemporary urban environments are intricate nodes and accumulations of local and global flows as well as shifting sites of development and renewal, and they have become spaces reconfigured by software and screens, digitized data repositories, algorithmic politics, and ambient information. The concept of re-placing is not a disruptive break from previous understandings of how people use digital media to coordinate and express socio-spatial relations but an extension. Rather than locatability, findability, or perpetual contact, re-placing prioritizes placemaking as an interpretive framework used to understand how and why actors negotiate and harness the discourse and affordances of digital technologies to adjust to changing principles and conditions of making and being in place. Digital practices, from installing broadband networks to taking selfies, can be understood as acts of re-placing the city because of the ways that these activities seek to combine physical experiences and imaginative constructions of both place and digitality to create meaning, value, and attachments to socio-spatial geographies—situating oneself and others within rapidly changing urban environments through the meaning and implementation of digital technologies and practices.

Re-placing the city emerges as a series of tactics and strategies to negotiate the pervasiveness of digital media in public space, with shifts in the situations, audiences, and conditions under which people experience and incorporate place into daily life. These activities occur at different scales and sites and are performed by diverse populations, through the use of myriad digital media technologies. However, processes and practices that can be categorized as re-placeing share common characteristics. Most commonly, re-placeing can be recognized in the intention and/or perceived experience of digital media use. All forms of re-placeing the city aim to adjust the "situational geographies" of social life to reproduce space as a familiar, stable, or knowable place. Through digital media use, place becomes an inhabited and meaningful location where a person or community could potentially belong. The specific practices, artifacts, and outcomes of re-placeing the city differ drastically based on habitus, access and literacy with digital media, and socioeconomic experiences of place. Among some populations, the by-products of re-placeing may be photographs shared on a social network site or archived data collected through self-quantification software; in other cases, the outcomes might be a public art project or even the creation of an entire city. But the intention—harnessing digital media to create meaningful places and build emotional attachments to particular locations—remains the same.

Mobile technologies in particular have been thought to transform person-to-person and person-to-place relationships in a variety of ways.[16] Throughout the 2000s, mediated activities beginning with prefixes like "geo-" or titles such as "locative" or "location-based" entered mainstream lexicons. Consumer markets offered a steady increase in prosumer GPS, cartography, sensor, and tracking technologies that privileged mediated visions of space and place. The rendering of people, goods, and services as more "locatable" became a technological reality and was discursively constructed as desirable as well. Slogans for portable GPS equipment encouraged potential customers to "Track what you love" and "Go everywhere, find everything." Over the past ten years, consumers have been offered a plethora of digital tools to support a sense of geospatial empowerment that aided their interpretation and experience of increasingly complex and extroverted urban spaces.

For urban digital media users and non-users, these digital technologies are no longer ideologically or practically "new," but mundane. In many urban environments some form of mobile media and/or digital infrastructure has been incorporated into the habits and rhythms of urban life. Rob Kitchin and Martin Dodge's code/space and coded spaces are routine and expected; people maintain intimate and collaborative relationships with and through these spaces—we keep coded objects close to our bodies and use them to manage our homes, to connect with loved ones, and to help us make decisions about where to go and what to do there.

Previous modes and tools for placemaking are indelibly linked to communication and media technologies that feel or appear intimate or personal as well. Printed artifacts for placemaking such as journals, scrapbooks, photo albums, and postcards as well as placemaking practices like decorating a room or a yard account for personal presence and taste but also tangibly and asynchronously communicate and archive the meaning of place for one or a few other people. Lee Humphreys has astutely analyzed the ways in which documenting everyday life on social media is similar to analog forms of media accounting.[17] Comparable to the use of media accounting in the formation of Humphreys's qualified self, the places produced through digital media are representations of place that we create to be consumed. Although the forms of documentation (photographs, written accounts, videos) and motivations for making place are replicated and remediated in digital placemaking practices, the perceived affordances and uses of digital media intervene in the process and type of constituted place.

The sense of place constructed through these analog tools and modes of communication articulate individual or personal experiences, place attachments, and place identities as momentary pauses that are witnessed and subjectively described, reinforcing phenomenological theories that place *is* pause. In contrast, the sense of place produced through social media posts, real-time cartographies or check-ins, or routinely updated blogs reinforces a sense of place as mobile in its instantaneity, mutability, replicability, and cocreation. As Judith Butler suggests in regard to gender performativity, place also does not gain authenticity from intrinsic essential qualities alone but is a product of repeated and habitual actions, utterances, and behaviors. Nicky Gregson and Gillian Rose come to a similar conclusion, suggesting that space can be "citational, and itself iterative, unstable, and performative."[18] Expanding on this perspective, I argue that the citational, iterative, and flexible performativity of place is forefronted in practices of re-placeing as the affordances of digital media echo these qualities. The perceived affordances and discourses of digital media texts and technologies emphasize the performativity of place, as places are continually reproduced and recontextualized on distinct platforms and by multiple communities.

In her insightful study of expat communities, Erika Polson analyzes how transnational professionals engage in a combination of online and offline activities to create a flexible or "mobile sense of place" or an emotional attachment to the places in which they temporarily reside.[19] In addition to a sense of place that is constituted through individual mobility, re-placeing reinforces a "mobile sense of place" in the circulation or mobility of articulations of place that are collaboratively constituted by people harnessing imaginations of networked flows and/or connecting through digital networks. The mobility in sense of place refers to the movement of people and devices across places but also to the movement of coded data and knowledge about place and the assumed speed and mobility of digital networks. Instead of pause, the places produced by all forms of re-placeing are restless and conditionally under construction. The uses and discourses that shape digital media texts and technologies as interactive and mutable, mobile and flexible, and as entities that are governed by and propel global flows encourage the perception of place as participatory and performative. In this way, the extroverted "global sense of place," or place as a unique but open-ended constellation of social relations that Doreen B. Massey elaborated on in the 1990s (but whose existence, she noted, stretched centuries before), is the foundational condition for digital placemaking. Through practices of re-placeing the city—from creating smart cities to posting status updates— place becomes more evident as something that we do. Place becomes recognizable as a performative process. *fundamental aspect of ecosystems*

Place as Performative

As Tim Cresswell argues, the theory of place that researchers adopt in their work is both ontological and epistemological; it shapes how they understand what exists and ways of seeing and knowing existents.[20] To understand the meaning of place, I rely on theories from human geography and cultural studies primarily. While I draw on Yi-Fu Tuan's disambiguation and general distinctions of place and space, I also refer to feminist and critical cultural geographers' and cultural studies scholars' engagement with place and place-based experiences throughout this book.[21] These theorists question connections between place as rooted or as bounded, focus on lived experiences of place, and complicate perceptions of "home" as they relate to meaning making, power, exclusion, and practice. At the heart of my arguments is an understanding that place is both always already there *and* always becoming.

Most notably, Tuan has circulated the idea that place and space are two distinct entities that are composed of idiosyncratic interactions and activities. "Space" is conceptualized as a plane of abstract mobilities and scientific rationality and as an arena of logistic economic flows where geometric and scientific analysis can be applied. "Place" concerns dwelling and the rootedness of lived experience and human reactions. Frequently, place is equated to home or to feeling at home in the world. Lynda H. Schneekloth and Robert G. Shibley utilize the term *querencia* to describe a place on the ground where one feels secure and draws one's strength, "having and loving a place, not because it is abstractly or universally understood as unique, or even supportive, but because it is yours. It is intimate and known, cared for and argued about."[22] According to these interpretations, querencia derived from place does not emanate directly from its descriptive qualities or characteristics but comes from personal attachments and feelings of ownership or groundedness in particular locations. As the above quote implies, these powerful feelings of querencia or belonging in place are regarded as positive and are initiated by people who have generated their own meaning of place from the ground up. However, this is only part of the perspective on place and placemaking that I observe in the case studies that follow.

Practices of the social production of space are often segmented into two encompassing categories: productions initiated by those at the apex of social hierarchies and productions and practices initiated from below. For Michel de Certeau, these types of social-spatial practices are known as "strategies" and "tactics" respectively. Corporate, military, governmental, or scientific actors who possess both the will and the power to carve out a space of their own for logistical purposes implement strategies. Strategies are strategic in that these actors gain territory, a base, or a delimited place of its own power from which to interact with possibly subversive or targeted others. On the other hand, "the space of a tactic is the space of the other . . . an art of the weak."[23] Tactics play with the provided structures of place, often in creative, fluid, and sometimes ephemeral ways and convert space as meaningful and purposeful within the everyday lives of ordinary people. Even as the concepts of place and space have been taken up in information and communication studies, media studies, and design, space as strategic and place as tactical echo these de Certeauian connotations and associations.

In general, the social construction and experience of place are regarded as somehow romantic and resistive as compared to the social construction or strategic experience of space. Making place is often linked to making home or making oneself feel at home, thus creating an intimate site from which we interpret and interact with the rest of the world. This connection is reasserted in studies of digital media too. "Placing," as Dourish and Steve Harrison describe it, is fundamentally concerned with how humans make themselves at home with the use of technology.[24] In this interpretation, the concept of place stands in for feelings of comfort, intimacy, and groundedness that are composed by familiar and repeated interactions over time, qualities that are reminiscent of how a sense of place is understood colloquially. Place is often reified as potentially and most likely evocative, poetic, and at the very least as Tuan's "field of care." A sense of place is reminiscent of other romanticized terms like local, homeland, intimate, and nostalgic. However, this is not where I begin.

Expanding on institutional concepts of placemaking, re-placeing is practiced by individuals as well as collectives and in ways that do not always work to augment social value and community pride in a place. Instead, re-placeing the city also includes economic, industrial, or strategic practices around making place and constructing "valued" places with digital media. Thus, re-placeing can occur in the hands of a pedestrian carrying a mobile phone across town as well as in the plans for expansive smart cities that are constructed over several years, and it may reveal implicit power hierarchies that govern placemaking and breed experiences of inequity as well as belonging.

Drawing on feminist geographers' and cultural studies interpretations of place, I focus on the fact that emotional attachments and psychological connections to place and home can relate to negotiating difference or can even be traumatic or make one uneasy. The stories we know and tell about places can be stark and gut wrenching, awkward or uncomfortable. In our attempts to socially produce, to know, and to experience place, we might be working to create a sense of place that is uniquely exclusive, specifically oppressive, commodified and branded, while also being inviting and domestic. In these cases, tactics are noted as tools used to cope, make do, or resist logics and experiences of place in the face of strategic social practices that might try to ignore, silence, or co-opt tactics and their productions.

Theories and practices of placemaking less frequently recognize the *strategic* in the production of place. Strategic practices are typically reserved for abstract, economic, or scientific space or social productions that tactical placemakers need to contend with, that tactics or use work to undo. This book brings attention to the ways that place is constructed both strategically *and* tactically by digitally connected people and places in motion. For example, gentrifiers, real estate developers, and municipalities rely on and rework preexisting meanings, collective experiences, and representations into highly visible reproductions of place. Placemaking or place remaking becomes strategic, economic, rationally organized, and purposely implemented in the service of redevelopment. In the case of re-placeing, the strategic production of place may appear less violent in its totality and force but is equally an exercise of dominant power and knowledge. Strategic placemaking with digital media exclusively performs place in a way that resonates with and invites in those who are already networked and already recognized as politically and socially powerful.

While place is powerful, it is also constructed through power relations. In *In Place/Out of Place*, Cresswell recognizes that place identities are created by the powerful as well as those who resist or transgress established meanings of places and subvert expectations of places in contradictory and conflicting ways. The meaning of place is a constant terrain of struggle where power and polysemy based on situated knowledges, differential mobilities, identity, and difference (race, class, gender, sexuality, disability, etc.) are at play. As Cresswell's approach suggests, there should be a concern for "the way place works in a world of social hierarchies."[25] In other words, place is "social space,"[26] where constantly evolving relationships, exchanges, and disruptions call attention to the relations of power that construct and reconstruct these spaces over time. When places are interpreted as social spaces that are perpetually reproduced and debated and are potential sources of *querencia*, places and the power to make place become akin to an event or process that can indicate one's position in a social order. In addition, because of these connections to social and cultural capital, people have always been invested in the way that places are performed and practiced. My interpretation of place and placemaking are very closely related to these human geographers' and urban theorists' perspectives on place: that place is made concrete and meaningful through practice. However, I claim that digital media have become an integral part of this practice. Digital media technologies, discourses, and practices are new tools with which to construct locational capital or the social value derived from connecting oneself to certain places, which becomes embodied in spatial habitus.

As Pier Carlo Palermo and Davide Ponzini observe, placemaking, or efforts to create more livable places with meaningful connections for residents, has become increasingly prevalent in community organizing and professional discourses as these groups have seen the concept of place as depleted, threatened, or in need of regeneration or renewal.[27] The speed and scale of globalization have been underscored as prime culprits that lead to spatial fragmentation, lack of community cohesion, and the creation of urban environments that lack a quality of life and the "spirit of place." These perspectives imply that the augmented mobilities of Arjun Appadurai's scapes have disrupted our collective sense of place and left people unsure of how to live within conditions and boundaries that seem more flexible and fluid. However, this perspective approaches place as container rather than as a process and eschews the power-geometries of place. These power-geometries, which emphasize that place is polysemic and that places accrue significance based on our social positionalities and interactions, are overtly performed through digital modes of communication.[28] Through digital media people express not just where they go and what they do there but who they are.

The pervasiveness of digital platforms and networks in structuring social relations and communication has made individual and collective acts of placemaking more observable, conscious, and shareable. The identifiable artifacts, acts, and intentions for re-placeing space can be understood as intersections of place and performativity: the collective and individual performances that compose places, the ways that place is used to perform identities (of people as well as locations, corporations, government entities, etc.), and place as the manifestation of social practice. By seeing the world as a network of meaningful places, or by allocating place as a central lens or question in our inquiries about the world around us, we begin to understand lived experience as well as social hierarchies and topographies differently—and not always in a flattering light.

The intersections of performance and place through digital media draw attention to the poiesis, or active making, of place. Approaching place as a performative process investigates both the final work created and the process of construction: the crafting, guiding principles of composition, and a place's "function, effects, and uses," which might include economic systems, labor relations, and location within a larger culture.[29] Poetics as poiesis, or "making," have come to be understood as taking into account the critical and the creative without necessarily privileging one over the other.[30] However, poiesis as "making" is often inseparably intertwined with and often obscured by "making sense of" in terms of the treatment of space and place in the humanities. Focusing on the making of place in terms of performance and performativity encourages an eye toward the minute yet perceptible movements and expressions of production as culturally significant factors in the way place is built, experienced, and interpreted. Just as the unphotographable polysemy of Clifford Geertz's "wink" is derived from its acting out (its performance) and contextualization within webs of culture, so is the case with status updates and geo-coded texts, mobile phone and digital infrastructure use, and mobility tactics in place. All are in need of thick description to be understood, and all are communicative, cultural performances that express or make visible subjective experiences of participation, marginalization, and differential power in the social production of urban environments.

Re-placeing the City

Even before the "spatial turn," it has been the responsibility of the humanities to make sense of place in representational and artistic texts, documented expressions and artifacts of lived experiences, and cultural geographies and migrations and their role in shaping identities, hierarchies, and texts.[31] However, the study and activities of place*making* also reveal ways in which people manage and document human experience.

Making places, and the places produced, can be read as sites where the expression and documentation of human experience happen and are contested. These performances are creative and critical, controlling and resistive, symbolic and tangible, poetic and traumatic, and they are always about the inscriptions of power, bodies, and meaning within place. The practices and people that produce spaces and places are not singular, cohesive, or complementary, nor is there a unique essence or single "authenticity" of place to be uncovered.

Shaw recognizes performativity in connection with the city street as a site of posthuman urbanism, which is "a performance of everyday reality attuned to the potential for rearticulations of space which new techno-scientific ontological configurations ironically promise."[32] This "potential for rearticulations of space" and place—which is promised by and through digital media infrastructure, texts, exchanges, and use and the practices of doing and struggling with these rearticulations—is the focus of re-placeing the city. If we want to understand what particular places mean to people, as experienced through interfaces of digital media, we have to look at what people *do* within these places to make sense of them.[33] As Etienne Wenger would argue, we would also have to understand what people experience in the doing.[34] The intent of this book is not to discredit or further examine the assumption that postmodern society has produced "thinned out places" or the "disarray of place" but to identify and analyze how digital media are tools in the imaginative work that goes into making urban place and the processes and outcomes of this labor.[35]

More recently the term "digital placemaking" has surfaced in popular, institutional, and scholarly literature. Digital placemaking has been generally understood as the intersection of placemaking practices with social media. The Project for Public Spaces created a Digital Placemaking program in 2010, which they define as "the integration of social media into Placemaking practices, which are community-centered, encouraging public participation, collaboration, and transparency."[36] In this model, social media becomes a way to listen to people and communities and to incorporate grassroots efforts and perspectives into conversations and initiatives about placemaking and place-based civic engagement. Other perspectives on digital placemaking have noted instances where digital media can encourage play, storytelling, place

discovery, and social engagement through shared and/or collocated experiences or memories.[37] Games, 3-D modeling, and social media have
been used in processes of participatory design and urban planning.[38]
Amid the integration of "big data" within all types of analyses along with
data-driven placemaking, open-source placemaking, the understanding
of the city as an application programming interface (API) or platform,
and the automatic collection of data related to urban patterns and environments, a more quantitative conception of digital placemaking has
emerged as well.

ecosystem

In response to these interpretations, the concept of re-placeing introduced in this book offers a more cohesive baseline of what digital
placemaking means: the use of digital media in cultivating a sense of
place for oneself and others. This framework for understanding processes of placemaking alongside imaginations and actual use of digital
media recognizes that experiences and expressions of place guide the
activities of digital media users and designers and allows for critiques
of digital media use within ongoing processes of making place. The
designed and perceived affordances of digital media, the politics of
these systems, and familiarity with hardware and software become instrumental in the production and experience of re-placeing. Perhaps
more importantly, one's perceived relationship and lived experience
in regard to these affordances, how they work or don't work to one's
advantage, and how they are made relevant as meaningful forms of
connectivity in everyday life are essential components in re-placeing
processes. A study of re-placeing not only establishes the ways in which
digital media act and are acted upon in the performance of place but
also reveals diverse and contradictory comprehensions, negotiations,
and productions of urban place. If the power of placemaking is derived
from its "world-making" potential, then re-placeing is doubly powerful
as it takes this potential into account as well as the politics and subjectivities produced through discourses of digital media technologies
and empirical use.

"Re-placement," "re-place-ing," "re-placeing," or related variations of
this term appear in humanities and social science writings that do not
focus on digital media in any way. These terms materialize in studies
concerned with the location and relocation of people, activities, artifacts, monuments, and memories as well as the reinterpretation and

re-presentation of a city's image or the meaning of a city in the public consciousness.[39] Re-placeing has even been implied in previous literature on technology, space, and place. Harrison and Dourish famously suggest that researchers and designers should "re-place space" in digital media design and analyses of computer-supported cooperative work; instead of space, it should be a sense of "place" that frames interactive behavior.[40] In another widely read study, Mizuko Ito uses the term "re-placement" in the title of her book chapter about mobile phone use among Japanese youth.[41] These youth were not liberating themselves from the boundedness and stronghold of place or reveling in frictionless anytime, anywhere connectivity; rather, Ito points to ways in which the integrity of existing places and social identities were not eroded or bypassed but incorporated into and structured by the power-geometries of place. In these cases, re-placement refers to the persistence of place within digital and mobile media use, but they do not examine *how* processes of redoing or reproducing a sense of place through digital media manifest, who participates, why, and under what circumstances this participation might happen. What I aim to investigate through re-placing the city are the discursive, cultural, and political practices of (re)doing place with digital media. The prefix, "re-," recognizes the constant reproduction and remaking of place over time as well as the act of reproducing place as remediated through digital media.

While algorithms construct situations that might direct a sense of place such as "digiplace," "software-sorted geographies," "software-supported spatialities," "the automatic production of space," and "code/space,"[42] this book focuses on the ways in which people engage with the representation of code through screens and experience digital infrastructure rather than study the software and engineering behind code. Re-placing investigates digital media as interfaces, intermediaries, or "points of transition" and translation between place and placemaker as well as platforms upon which the processes, contexts, and performances of place are enacted and experienced.[43] Re-placing can be read as an opportunity to analyze the digital interfaces of placemaking that tend to be effaced in the service of ubiquitous computing and user friendliness and to critique the ideologies that are sutured to digital media by different actors in constructing a sense of place.[44] In re-placing the city, the habitual or strategic placemaking practices and forms of digital media employed differ depending on the tensions, situations, and environments that a person is embedded within or trying to negotiate. The case studies and examples presented in this book focus on some of the ways in which people construct certain locations to be lived in in meaningful ways through mundane and professional digital practices—where encoding and decoding place meet binary code. The politics, discourses, and imaginations of digital media are engaged with on the levels of implementation processes, use and non-use, the construction and expression of locational capital, and the reproduction of the "city as platform" for digital services, technologies, and networks.

2nd ed.

Methodologically, my selection of sites follows the tradition of multisited ethnographies and multiple-case-study design—where sites are defined by the human relations under analysis—as well as more recent interpretations of "fieldsite as network."[45] The selection of case studies was primarily driven by the types of practices and digital media employed in placemaking and, secondarily, by the particularities of the places themselves. Each chapter presents a different model of re-placeing the city based on the impetus and media utilized: big data and the Internet of Things for an efficient city; fiber-optic infrastructure for a connected city; navigation technologies for a familiar city; locative and social media for a sense of belonging in the city; and the sidelining of digital media in the production of a creative city. To follow or "contour" re-placeing as a cultural practice and to illustrate its breadth, I've selected global cities (major metropolitan areas), emerging cities (cities built from scratch), and understudied cities (secondary and small cities) as well as mobile and online practices and texts that are not fixed to a single physical location. The book begins with digital placemaking primarily shaped by global flows and ends with hyperlocal practices of creative placemaking and personal social media use.

Through five examples of digitally mediated urban life—smart cities in Asia, the Middle East, and Europe; digital infrastructure projects in large and midsize US cities; globally adopted locative media projects and platforms; digital navigation practices among US-based populations; and National Endowment for the Arts–funded "creative placemaking" initiatives—I show how various actors employ digital technologies to reproduce abstract urban spaces into inhabited places with deep meanings and affective attachments. This book expands practical and theoretical understandings of how urban planners envision and plan cities with digital technologies in mind, the role of urban communities in shaping the affordances of digital urban networks, and the expressions and narratives that are produced by individuals through mobile phone and web-based projects and services.

Overview of the Book

The remainder of the book critiques practices of digital placemaking and the types of places and affective attachments that are produced, by and for whom, and at what cost. Each chapter in this book engages with concepts and practices of placemaking as re-placeing through different performances of place by actors from various positions within social hierarchies and scales of practice. Although placemaking, digital or otherwise, may involve myriad perspectives and activities, it has been continually connected to community empowerment and efficacy, fostering social interactions and exchanges, and strengthening place identity. Placemaking activities have also been related to cognitive mapping, or constructing images of cities in order to make certain cities or certain locations within cities more legible and uniquely recognizable from inside and outside those locations. They encourage play, discovery, and exploration within particular locations as well as improve spatial education and literacy in regard to planning processes and spatial practice. The chapters that follow analyze the ways in which these conceptions intersect with digital media and are experienced, augmented, or disrupted through practices of re-placeing.

To investigate lived relationships between urban places, people, and digital technologies, I consider the work of those who professionally program urban space (such as urban planners, architects, and public officials) as well as the experiences of those who live within it. By comparing top-down plans, regulations, and actions with bottom-up practices and texts, this book works toward a more informed understanding of the production of urban spaces within networked societies. The implementation of digital technologies has increasingly placed the power to reorganize or reproduce space into the hands of the public, who are increasingly routine technology users. While at times the practices of these networked urban subjects mesh with the visions and designs of urban planners, architects, technology designers, and public officials, there are also perpetual tensions between everyday users' understandings of their own mediated urban experiences and the plans of those who design connected spaces and technologies.

All the examples in this book involve interrogations and critiques of privilege, typically in terms of those who use digital media to produce and access a sense of place. Privilege in this case might manifest in regard to access, technological literacy, social and economic hierarchies, and relations of power and control of global, municipal, and local interactions. The case studies in this book also draw attention to the production of place despite access to or engagement with digital media—by those who choose to opt out or do not occupy advantageous positions within local and global power-geometries. Regrettably, research related to urban and community informatics and studies of infrastructure and digital cities too often ignore issues of non-use of digital technologies. Analyses of non-use or opting out of digital technology use, particularly in terms of navigation technologies, municipal Wi-Fi, and fiber-optic cable projects are intertwined with discussions of digital media participation. In this way, *The Digital City* extends understandings of the reasons behind non-use of digital media and digital infrastructure as well as what non-use can tell us about the social production and understanding of place in the digital era. In terms of power to produce a sense of place, this book interrogates examples where the meaning of place is generated from a variety of positions simultaneously: planners, architects, politicians, and developers as well as activists, artists, and populations with little or no consistent or convenient internet access.

Chapter 1 engages the process of re-placeing on a global scale, examining how top-down imaginations of the built environment are coupled with digital media to express particular paradigms and plans for urban forms and urban experiences. The chapter identifies and analyzes a global trend of planning, designing, and constructing "smart-from-the-start" cities. In this particular model of smart city, digital media technologies and infrastructures are planned in tandem with the buildings, roads, and other municipal services that will compose the urban environment. As a result, professionals are charged with the burden of having to construct these cities as "places" from scratch as well. Several examples of this type of urban form have emerged over the past few decades, from Masdar City in the United Arab Emirates to PlanIT Valley in Portugal and South Korea's extensive network of ubiquitous cities, or U-cities projects (cities that universally embed ubiquitous computing opportunities into the built environment). This chapter analyzes some of the ways in which planners, developers, municipal officials, and technology designers employ digital infrastructures and technologies to replace the city as a unique, inhabited, user-friendly urban place instead of an abstract space of advanced capitalism or "spatial fix." Based on press releases, legal documents, and interviews conducted with smart-city executives, planners, technology developers, and residents, this chapter offers a humanities-centered analysis of the spatial inscriptions of strategic imaginations of urban futures and digital media.

In chapter 2, I analyze debates about re-placeing at the municipal scale. A key focus of this analysis is how different models of infrastructure deployment create visible geographies of digital inclusion and exclusion. I investigate the practice of re-placeing the city from the perspective of those who plan and implement digital infrastructure projects, municipal officials who oversee them, and the people who benefit from them as well as those who opt out of or are excluded from these efforts. Through the example of Google's Fiber for Communities project in Kansas City, Kansas, and Kansas City, Missouri, I illustrate how processes of digital infrastructure implementation reveal polysemic experiences of the city as a place. Through interviews and participant observation of Google Fiber deployment and digital inclusion efforts in Kansas City, I offer an analysis of how infrastructure installation as urban renewal replaces the city and highlights conflicting affective experiences of infrastructure. This chapter investigates how digital connection is perceived as relevant among populations with differential mobilities and socioeconomic statuses and distinct experiences and attachments to home and the cities in which they live.

Through questionnaires with 210 navigation technology users (e.g., GPS, digital maps, and mobile navigation systems) and interviews with ten navigation technology users, chapter 3 identifies the ways that users understand their own spatial relations, conditions of and tactics for mobility, and embeddedness within urban space. One of the most common engagements with GPS is through online mapping tools and mobile navigation technologies,[46] yet we know very little about how these technologies are incorporated into everyday life, how they shape spatial relations, influence cognitive mappings of urban space, and contribute to the formation of a sense of place. Many scholars and critics have understood digital navigation technologies as enacting processes of alienation and abstraction and the disembedding or distancing of the digital media user from place. In contrast to popular assumptions about the distracted perception of space and place encouraged by digital navigation technologies, this chapter analyzes the ways in which navigation technology users are developing wayfinding strategies that reframe their image of the city, alter perceptions and practices of mobility, and re-embed themselves within urban environments.

Digital media texts, practices, and mobile technologies tend to represent and rescue the practice of "passing by" and particular ontologies or ways of being in the city. Chapter 4 examines how digital traces produced through locative media and geo-location technologies can be read as performative rather than precise and highlights some of the ways that cultural studies and humanities scholars can add value and insight to discussions of locative and location-based social media. Several of the projects discussed in this chapter make legible what is normally invisible, surface personal and/or collective memories and ontologies, and incorporate digital stories and situated knowledges into the practice of moving through the city. These examples evidence re-placeing the city by urban residents or travelers at the scale of the street. The chapter begins with a brief examination of the ways in which people utilized early (and now defunct) locative media projects and continues with an analysis of more recent incarnations of location-based social media to examine shifts in digital storytelling and performances of place that are evident in these projects. Check-in and location-announcement services such as Foursquare and photographic social media such as Instagram are analyzed through participatory observation and textual and discourse analysis to understand how people imagine and express their sense of place through these services.

In the final case study, practices related to re-placeing the city are investigated from the perspective of those who professionally program and fund placemaking activities in the United States as well as the locales that receive this funding and support. The chapter explores the role and potential of digital technologies and practices in "creative placemaking" efforts. Through an investigation of organizations, artists, and cities that have undertaken creative placemaking projects, I evaluate the ways in which digital technologies and practices are imagined and implemented to "animate public and private spaces, rejuvenate structures and streetscapes, improve local business and public safety, and bring diverse people together to celebrate and inspire."[47] In addition, I offer reasons that digital technologies and practices are *not* being associated with and incorporated into creative placemaking endeavors.

Throughout these chapters I encourage the reader to consider digital placemaking in terms of how people employ digital technologies and practices in the performativity of place. I urge readers to reconsider their own mundane or professional uses of digital media in regard to placemaking and to directly reflect on the ways in which we become placemakers through our digital media use and non-use. In identifying and analyzing the power-geometries involved in re-placeing the city, this book suggests methods for investigating digital placemaking and moments when we should become more attuned to the places we create.

1

The Smart City

Strategic Placemaking and the Internet of Things

Debates about the smart city as innovative or disruptive have gained momentum as more cities that claim to be "smart" are built or retrofitted across the globe. Proponents of smart-city development emphasize the role of technology in "smart growth," improved public service, efficiency, entrepreneurial competitiveness, and quality of life.[1] However, suspicion about the "datafication" of urban processes, the monitoring and surveillance of urban populations, and the eagerness of municipal governments to regard information and communication technologies as "solutions" for perceived urban problems fuel these debates. A striking addition to smart-city conversations is the global trend of planning, designing, and constructing a city from scratch with extensive digital communications networks and infrastructures in mind.

Several examples of smart-from-the-start cities have emerged over the past decade, from South Korea's extensive network of ubiquitous cities, or U-cities (cities that universally embed ubiquitous computing opportunities into the built environment), to Neom in Saudi Arabia, Konza Techno City in Kenya, and Dholera in India. These "cities of the future" don prefixes such as "smart," "intelligent," "digital," and "ubiquitous" to indicate their distinction from less digitally integrated and data-driven urban environments. In some cases, digital media technologies and infrastructures are designed even before buildings, roads, and other municipal services are conceived or break ground. In all cases, the populations that will utilize these buildings and networks have yet to move in. As a result, professionals are charged with the burden of constructing these cities as "places" anew without the participation or input of residential communities.

Michael Batty summarizes the smart-city debate, in part, as such: "There is a sense, but only a sense, in which the form of the city is being divorced from its functions."[2] There is this sense of divorce because it is undoubtedly difficult to imagine and explain how the installation of sensors and infrastructure and the collection of data about almost every aspect of everyday life will transform the city. But it is no more than a sense because of the strategic placemaking efforts on the part of smart-city developers to construct these locations as attractive places to be lived in in meaningful ways.

This chapter identifies and critiques some of the ways in which planners, developers, municipal officials, and technology designers deploy and narratively construct digital infrastructure and digital media in order to reproduce smart-from-the-start cities as unique, inhabited, user-friendly urban places instead of abstract "spatial fixes" for advanced capitalism. My analysis focuses on how discourses and understandings of place are inscribed in the design and implementation of smart-city technologies, the construction of the built environment, and the decisions around the branding and promotion of the city as a social space. Based on press releases, legal documents, scholarly and popular literature, and interviews conducted with smart-city executives, architects, and technology developers, this chapter offers an analysis of the processes and challenges of constructing a smart-from-the-start city as an urban place.

The examples presented in this chapter highlight re-placeing as a series of top-down, strategic placemaking practices and ideologies that attempt to create a sense of place for target audiences rather than doing so in dialogue with pre-existing communities. Although placemaking is often understood in terms of engagement or citizen participation, re-placeing the smart city resembles an imposition or dictation of the qualities of place. In these examples, planners and developers utilize digital media discourses and infrastructures to create a sense of place for future residents within urban spaces that are currently under construction. While these specialized zones are still abstract entities in the process of becoming actually existing locales, the people and organizations responsible for their existence attempt to exploit "new media" to generate a sense of uniqueness and character for these cities on the rise. The places that have been created reveal certain myopic understandings of urban space and urban life and of how practices of re-placeing do not necessarily adhere to typical models of placemaking in terms of interaction between planners and residents. In addition, this case illustrates that reproducing a space as a familiar place of dwelling does not always yield an inclusive or socially stimulating environment.

The following sections focus on the physical and discursive development of three highly publicized smart-from-the-start cities—Songdo, Masdar City, and PlanIT Valley. In addition to exploring the outcomes and potential outcomes of smart-city development, this chapter begins with imaginations and rhetorical blueprints for these cities and concludes with a discussion of how processes of re-placeing are strategic and simultaneously construct and misunderstand the city as a field of care. In particular, this chapter focuses on practices of re-placeing by transnational developers and state governments in the making of global cities with imagined inhabitants. The placemaking processes analyzed in this chapter highlight that in the social production of smart cities, the showroom and demo space in addition to the screen and the street become active sites of re-placeing.

Common Characteristics and Discursive Constructions

In January 1995, coinciding with the steady rise of the term "smart" as a descriptor of cities and technologies, *New York Magazine* published an article about the etymology of the word "smart" and its changing meaning over time within the English language. The author notes that to the Brits the term refers to people and artifacts that are "modish" and "so relentlessly *with it*" but that the word also "contains a flick of the lash at those of us who don't qualify."[3] In American parlance, smart connotes "an active and engaged intelligence" that is different from brilliant, clever, brainy, or bright. The *Oxford English Dictionary* of the 1990s supported this interpretation, adding that smart meant "capable, adept, quick at devising, learning, looking after oneself or one's own interests." Unlike other forms of intellect or knowledge, smart is practical; it's applied on the ground; it's about utilizing information and surrounding stimuli for one's benefit, assessing a situation and available resources, and manipulating them to one's advantage. As the article is careful to note, to be smart requires "the stamina to be perpetually on and in full command . . . fast thinking, good memory, adaptability, nerve, and a feel for the moment."[4] It is out of this etymological context that the term and concept of "smart city" is popularized. However, as a concept and term, "smart city" was used well before its 1990s incarnation.

Preceding the mid to late 1990s, a "smart city" referred to a city that was fashionable, attractive, or fast-paced and applied to sophisticated, complex, expansive metropolises that served as centers or switching points for economic, political, or cultural activities. Some articles referred to the smart cities of the 1940s as "nerve centers" or technologized coordinating centers for the flow of goods, services, communications, and people.[5] Cities referred to as "smart" at the beginning of the 1900s, like Chicago, New York, Paris, London, and Singapore, also implemented technologies that networked people and places in ways that afforded more efficient services to residents or convenient exchange across urban space: subway systems, highway systems, telephone lines, and waste management and utility systems. The residents who lived in these cities were said to share similar qualities with the cities themselves: they were en vogue, intelligent movers and shakers, on guard and one step ahead with fingers on the pulse of progress. Smart citizens were often contrasted to "country bumpkins," who were framed as constitutive others in their lack of access to knowledge, culture, speed, and progress.

Throughout the 1990s, particularly in the late 1990s, there were numerous articles published in academic, popular, and trade journals that described the "smart city" as a "cybercity," "information district," "telecity," or "city of bits," cities where "new media become woven into the fabric of urban life."[6] These articles also referenced the development of specific urban areas such as media districts or media quarters, televillages ("telecottages" or "wired villages" were also common terms), international business districts, electronic villages, and silicon alleys. In regard to what the integration of digital media into the everyday routines of smart-city residents might feel like, one newspaper article about Japanese efforts to create smart cities imagined:

> On the way home from work, a businessman will learn from a computer in his car where traffic is heavy and take a different route. With a hand-held control, he will then unlock the door of his house, turn on the lights and start the water for his bath. A housewife will use a computer to pay the bills, take a history course, flip through on-screen store catalogs, order products, buy theater tickets and get a dog license.[7]

The shifting meaning of "smart city" along these lines united urban planning and urban renewal with media technologies and practices and strategies for incorporating digital and mobile information and communication technologies (ICTs) within urban environments and urban life. In particular, new and expanded digital infrastructures like fiber-optic networks or broadband Wi-Fi in public spaces and ICTs fitted to preexisting transportation, communication, and utility infrastructures like smart meters, sensors, and video cameras were defining elements of 1990s smart cities.

The smart city is part of the trajectory in the ongoing evolution of the future of cities as envisioned through the lens of urban management and planning. Taylor Shelton, Matthew Zook, and Alan Wiig note the resemblance of current smart cities' technoscientific efforts toward cost-efficiency and entrepreneurism to past models and rhetoric of urban growth in times of austerity.[8] Amy Glasmeier and Susan Christopherson note that imaginations of the 1980s future city envisioned "intelligent," globally and internally networked urban spaces that utilized extensive and innovative transportation and communication infrastructures to enable rapid and cost-effective mobility and high-speed data transfers.[9] The value of speed, flexibility, and technology-oriented management in cultivating market-driven systems of urban competitiveness, which was also prominent in urban studies and planning literature of the 1980s, is read as foundational to more contemporary conceptions of the smart city. Rob Kitchin and others have positioned the smart city as an incarnation emanating from (among other origins) a shift toward neoliberal entrepreneurship within city management that shaped later visions of the globally competitive city, the sustainable city, and Richard Florida's brand of creative city.[10]

IBM, one of the technology companies leading smart-city development in the early 2000s (including Cisco and Siemens), uses "smart city" to describe "how various public services and infrastructure projects can be enhanced with information technology and data analysis."[11] Industry press outlets and urban and technology developers who are in the business of designing smart cities and implementing the technologies that make them smart note that these urban forms are defined by their ability, innovativeness, and agility in integrating intelligent devices of the Internet of Things in urban development and planning.[12] In all cases, smart cities are defined as places where digital media is aggressively integrated as infrastructure, software, and hardware; information is regarded as a necessary resource for coordinating technologies and actions; and data is collected, analyzed, and shared in the service of city management and responsiveness. In corporate documents, IBM elaborated on these essential qualities of the smart city as three *I*s "instrumented," "interconnected," and "intelligent."[13]

At present, smart cities and the people who plan them are categorized as visionary, but definitions and characteristics of smart cities vary. Scholars repeatedly use the term "nebulous" to describe the contemporary smart city as they sift through promotional materials that make disparate claims about the value and purpose of these cities. Vito Albino, Umberto Berardi, and Rosa Maria Dangelico have noted that the definition and use of the term "smart city" vary wildly as do the metrics for measuring "smartness" and the success of these urban spaces.[14] Being smarter might mean that the city knows more about itself and can adjust accordingly—that the city becomes more intelligent. Success might refer to the way a city gathers, analyzes, and utilizes information about itself. However, the authors note that the connotation of smart city has shifted from merely meaning that digital infrastructure and ICTs have been implemented in a city but that these ICTs are intended to optimize every urban system with the goal of enhancing everyday services and quality of life for its residents.[15] Smart-city development is bookended by a drive toward competitiveness through optimized efficiency, sustainability, and entrepreneurial incubation by being programmed and programmable, constantly collecting, analyzing, and making changes based on information. This conception positions contemporary smart cities within an extensive history of city management where municipal actors aim to make rational, informed decisions about urban space to maintain order and efficiency and foster economic growth and competitiveness in global and regional markets through technological and scientific developments.[16]

As Shelton, Zook, and Wiig, acknowledge, smart-from-the-start or greenfield cities built from scratch tend to be the exception rather than the rule.[17] Instead the authors recognize that most smart cities are mature cities that are retrofitted to be smart. I agree with Shelton, Zook, and Wiig that smart-city policies for actually existing cities are often "assembled piecemeal, integrated awkwardly into existing configurations of urban governance and the built environment." It is also important to recognize that the reason for this inelegant fit is that smart-city implementers unflinchingly adhere to dominant, corporate-driven imaginations of what a smart city should be and what information and communication technologies and data-driven and quantitative measurement systems can do for a city. Much of this imagination has been concretized through prominent and expensive smart-from-the-start developments in places like Songdo, PlanIT Valley, and Masdar City and has been circulated by a handful of technology-oriented corporations, industry consortiums, and early-adopter planners and city governments that participate in the maintenance of this imagination. Particularly revealing of dominant smart-city ideologies are the metaphors and understandings of the city that circulate within smart-city development materials—what these visions evoke and what they leave out. In the following section, I draw on promotional materials, internal documents, and conversations with smart-city developers to elucidate foundational elements and reiterated metaphors that indicate how practitioners and managers envision smart cities as concept and place.

Imagining Smart Cities in Practice

Technology designers, urban developers, and municipal officials often hail smart-city environments as advanced and upgraded in terms of safety, efficiency, transportation, economic development, sustainability, and overall responsiveness to urban structures, patterns, and demands. In all cases, digital infrastructure, software, and human-computer interaction is "baked into the master plan and initial design" from the outset.[18] Trade publications for urban planning practitioners publish resources and debates about how to leverage big data gathered through smart-city technologies, mobile phones, surveys and census reports, and municipal websites for planning decisions.[19] Articles featured in these publications inform planners and developers about the potential of wireless networks, cloud computing, and the Internet of Things to achieve smart-city goals. Cities that aren't yet smart, particularly large-scale cities, are recognized as spaces that might not be collecting or processing data effectively to make their cities more productive, pleasurable, and efficient.

In urban planning literature, the smart city is seen as an outgrowth and response to "new urbanism," or efforts to make dense, highly populated urban centers more "livable," "green," sustainable spaces that will support "smart growth." The linkage comes from the idea that the "key to sustainability is information," that by collecting and analyzing data about ongoing processes and interactions within urban environments, municipal organizations can make more informed decisions about how to regulate urban space.[20] By measuring elements like water and energy consumption, pollution, waste management, and climate, environmental stewards and smart-city proponents hope to understand sustainability and waste in complex systems to make cities more resourceful, ecological, and able to accommodate population and business growth and climate change safely and cost effectively. Data provides "intelligence" about systems and how layered systems interact. Sensors that measure variables—such as CO_2 emissions, greenhouse gases, energy and utility use within office buildings and residences, and transportation patterns—and report back to centralized and/or open-access websites and databases are common technology implementations in smart-city blueprints.[21] The abundance of LEED-certified buildings, green spaces, nonsmoking environments, public transport and biking infrastructures, and systems that recycle trash, water, and energy have led reporters and those branding these cities to note them as "eco-cities" that are devoted to sustainability.[22] Consumer products such as cars and amenities for residential buildings have begun to don the prefix "smart" to indicate their efficiency, innovative qualities, environmental consciousness, and size. For example, the micro "green" car, the "Smart City Coupe," entered the European market in 1998 and was produced in Smartville, a production facility in France, for use in congested city streets.[23]

The integration of digital media such as sensors, kiosks, smart cards, and internet infrastructure are also noted as ways to increase efficiency in government, public safety, education, and public services as well as to upgrade and "digitize the economy."[24] As an executive from Gale Corporation, the primary developers of New Songdo in South Korea, states, "We consistently advise that technology is the fourth utility—in addition to water, waste and energy—and is a crucial and fundamental element to ensure the environmental responsibility and economic success of the city."[25] The lure of the smart city for economic development has been noted as a way to attract and retain talent and business enterprises, to innovate and promote entrepreneurship, to provide digital and techno-logical resources for institutions that encourage and support economic growth, and to design networks and lifestyles that facilitate and stream-line the process of doing business in the city.

Beyond sensors and technologies embedded on the street to monitor and collect information about urban activity, smart-city infrastructure has also been noted to improve government and public-sector services. In particular, healthcare, emergency response systems, public safety, and education have been universally identified by smart-city developers as significantly upgraded by the planning and development of smart-city technologies. In developing countries, the vision of information and communication technologies for development is repeated in smart-city promotion.[26] For example, India's prime minister, Narendra Modi, promised to build one hundred smart cities across India to improve util-ity provision and to manage waste systems and energy consumption.[27]

Another common goal of smart-city development is to digitize and automate aspects of everyday life to make cities more livable and inhab-itable and to raise the overall quality of work and domestic life. Early on in their development, smart cities were discursively associated with contemporary versions of modernist "new town" movements or planned communities. Sharing the philosophy and planning strategies of post–World War II new towns that were once popular in the UK, Europe, and the United States, smart cities were urbanesque spaces that relocated people away from unhealthy or inefficient cities to autonomous, self-reliant districts that were built on undeveloped or underdeveloped land. Like new towns, smart cities offer residents their own, local options for recreation, entertainment, work, and commerce that promise a balanced social life and improved quality of life. New towns, like the smart cit-ies that followed, promoted a new, greener, more convenient, orderly, and apolitical form of urban life.[28] Stanley Gale of the Gale Corporation explained that he aimed to create a city where all people and processes were linked through ubiquitous computing, and information and com-munication systems that share information and are managed through a centralized system.[29] Developers of New Songdo coined a term for this living arrangement early on in their project development, even before any people had moved in: U-life, or ubiquitous life. Reminiscent of new town rhetoric, a spokesperson at Songdo U-Life notes, "So, when the city is accomplished we don't need to go outside [of the city]. Every function of the city will be provided within Songdo city. That's the aim of Songdo."[30] Technologies that serve this function are said to include mobile workforce automation, intelligent transportation, street light control, municipal utility monitoring, and street and building video surveillance as well as the provision of international schools and universities, parks, golf courses, malls, arts centers, convention centers, bars and restaurants, cafés, office buildings, and residences.[31] More recently developed smart-from-the-start cities have orchestrated digital systems to manage their versions of U-life such as the Urban Operating System™ and Place Apps in PlanIT Valley.

The symbolic power in the implementation of robust digital media infrastructure and services are thought to attract local residents, transnational business headquarters, research institutes, and universities as well as the transnational business and cultural elites that populate these institutions. To develop or become a smart city also means a repositioning of the city and its activities within regional and global networks of exchange and significance. As Tim Bunnell explains of the Multimedia Super Corridor in Malaysia during the 1990s, to build an "intelligent landscape," in partnership with or in the service of the state, repositions Malaysia within global networks, and this sort of strategic landscaping alters ways of seeing and being in the world.[32] Other cities that adopted aspects of smart-city development models such as implementing citywide, robust IT infrastructure also hoped to attract previously outsourced technology services in an effort toward job creation and economic growth.[33]

The discourses of "urban triumphalism," "sustainable urbanism," and "technoscientific urbanism" come together in the design and imagination of the smart city.[34] Why produce a place like this? This is a question that developers are frequently asked and have rehearsed answers for, but asking that question might not be as informative as asking what sense of place is produced in these projects. Which imaginations of "the city" are embedded within the blueprints and discursive constructions of this type of urban environment? And *how* do you make this place? What strategies are used to construct uninhabited or underinhabited cities as places to be dwelled in and to create emotional attachments to? What problems or challenges arise when trying to do so? Planners want the city to be victoriously innovative and prosperous and want to program these spaces to be sustainable and resilient, data-driven and technoscientific. However, developers also need to conceptualize how residents belong within these spaces, how people interface with the carefully designed environments and systems they've created, and what civilian experiences in this city might be. Aside from securing and maintaining financial backing, this is where the construction of smart-from-the-start cities becomes complicated.

Signs of Tech, Signs of Life

The technologies prototyped and implemented in smart cities indicate particular imaginations of place, community, and person-to-person or person-to-place contact. In theory smart cities are built on centralized communication and broadcast models—many different entities communicate to a central source, and that information is processed and broadcast out to individuals and institutions for surveillance of urban activity. However, as a 2009 brochure for Digital Media City (a smart-city district in Seoul, South Korea) notes, the goal of the smart city is to "create technology that puts man first." The technologies installed are imagined as synergies that bring together information and data about all observable aspects of everyday life. Several smart-city chief information officers (CIOs) and technology developers emphasize the roles that technologies and data will play in enriching and streamlining the "needs of the end user" and often refer to these technologies and socio-technical interactions as "cool." The technologies that are developed articulate a vision of the city as convenient, egocentric, individually responsive, and cutting edge.

In 2019 smart-city developers continue to propose technologies that mimic the platforms and devices that were prototyped and installed in smart-from-the-start cities in 2009. In 2009 South Korean U-cities slated a series of green, sentient, and networked technologies that resemble plans that are being promoted in smart cities and districts today. Green technologies such as charging stations for electric vehicles, smartcard- or sensor-activated bicycle rentals and recycling bins, and LEED-certified buildings equipped with "intelligent building systems" that were prototyped for Songdo now line the streets of cities across the globe. The once-innovative HomeNet systems that offer personalized services based on the collection and overlay of residential, medical, government, and commercial data are more commonplace uses of artificial intelligence along with sentient objects and RFID sensors that are installed throughout households and work and public spaces. Intelligent street lighting and ubiquitous internet connection for the efficient management and regulation of municipal infrastructure are typically the first networks slated for recent smart-city initiatives. Public digital kiosks where pedestrians can access bus schedules in real time, traffic and neighborhood maps, weather information, advertisements, and email are prevalent but are critiqued as eyesores on city sidewalks beyond Korea.[35] The technologies slated for smart-city streets and buildings are not necessarily specific to individual cities but are conceived of by transnational technology corporations to be packaged and sold within a variety of urban contexts. This development model is not particular to Songdo. For example, experimentation with self-driving cars and sensor-driven transportation systems have been unveiled in Masdar and other enclaved smart districts in order to be tested and resourced to other cities.[36]

ICTs are noted to improve quality of life by making the city and its buildings, government, services, and people more informed and responsive. Aside from primary functions such as lighting, transportation, internet access, and waste or water management, each technology is conceived of as a means to collect data. At-home and in-office digital concierge services often link to an Internet of Things where sentient objects compile profiles and patterns about users to alert them to changes in their environment or manage their environment based on personal preferences. As Gale, the Songdo developer, explains, "Imagine that a computer screen turns on by a simple voice command and reports the outside weather, the condition of the roads and traffic, or cultural events to kick off your day. It might sound like a scene from a science fiction movie, but New Songdo City will shape this 'future life.'"[37] The home or office space is transformed into a responsive, optimized place, personalized and managed through a centralized control center to maintain efficiency and convenience. Daily preparedness is distilled into data points about weather, traffic, and events and can be accessed on command.

In several smart cities, networked street-lighting systems not only are equipped with motion sensors for personalized and optimized electricity use but are outfitted with internet-connected cameras that collect images and report data on traffic flow, road and sidewalk use, and pedestrian activity. Digital kiosks (often described as extra-large iPhones) also collect data about the information accessed by passersby. The provision of Wi-Fi on public transportation and in public spaces doubles as an effort to monitor population numbers and mobility patterns. All these networked technologies report to a central command-and-control center operated by the city or a network management company like Cisco and can be queried by city officials and company employees as needed. Healthcare, education, climate, and customer service systems are all said to be streamlined or transformed through telemedicine, high-tech homework, and always-on, real-time notification for both customers and service providers.

In addition to similar technology implementation strategies across smart cities, a few common scenarios imagining how these technologies will be used are reiterated as well. These narratives originate in the demonstration spaces and public presentations of smart-city developers and technology designers but are continually reiterated by city officials, CIOs, and technology industry representatives. For years, common narratives about how ICTs might be utilized involved the use of smart technologies to locate lost children or property and to prevent or respond to accidents, inconveniences, or crime. Given that extensive critique and legitimation of smart cities revolves around surveillance, smart-city demos and promotion reframe surveillance within narratives of public safety. The consistent monitoring and control of traffic and pedestrian patterns, networked security systems, public lighting and utility infrastructure, 911 and 311 calls, and even drones are framed as beneficial to the safety and security of citizens. Digital systems monitor physical environments for diversions and incidents—robbery and assault, terrorist attacks, fire and traffic accidents, spills and blockages, overactive furnaces, or underactive snow plows—to produce more responsive agencies and first responders. Interfacing with data relies on a model of integrated, accumulated information about diverse urban infrastructural activities and depends on the ingenuity and motivation of intrepid citizens, civil servants, or start-ups to access and analyze automatically generated information. These actors are encouraged to look for inconsistencies in the data that indicate problems to be fixed.

The apps developed to interface with municipalities, smart-city technologies, and the data collected through these technologies also tell a significant story about how the union of digital media and space is envisioned. Apps and other smart-city interfaces promote access to information based on personal location and proximity to amenities and facilities. The cameras, sensors, and antennae that provide information to the apps are meant to inform and direct behavior accordingly: if there is a traffic jam, you should take another route; bring an umbrella with you because it's going to rain; the bus will be late, so try walking to a different bus line that's running on time. The apps that access this information construct the citizen as a customer and provide improved customer service while on the go. For example, the PlanIT app promises to bring the "dynamic, personalized, service-driven world of online retail to the physical space," providing an "improved customer experience" of the city and its facilities.[38]

Steve Lewis, CEO of Living PlanIT has compared his plan for smart-city development to the iPhone. During an interview with London's *Sunday Times*, he pulls out his iPhone to illustrate his vision: "In this [the iPhone] you have a bunch of gadgets and an operating system that makes it work efficiently. What we have done is taken the manufacturing techniques you see in this and applied them to a city."[39] The Urban Operating System for PlanIT Valley is modeled after not only the technological convergence of the smartphone but also the system of sensors and cloud computing that power Formula One race cars. Like sensors on a speeding car, the smart-city app is meant to provide mobile residents with information about their location in space and environmental conditions immediately. The comparison to a high-profile race car and constantly reversioned consumer technology creates a sense of how cutting-edge and integral PlanIT Valley developers interpret smart-city technology to be. Urban operating systems like Living PlanIT or the apps that are being created for the urban platform tend to support orchestrated urban life by providing controlled and predetermined access to data produced about air pollution, bus schedules, traffic flows, and restaurants nearby.

But as you walk the streets of a smart-from-the-start city, the streets and buildings often look like those of any other city. There are little gray-and-black boxes filled with sensors, antennae, or cameras mounted on buildings and lampposts, but these blend into the glass and steel architectures that support these structures. An intermittent button, kiosk, or digital screen indicates that technologically, something is happening there. From the street, there aren't many opportunities for intentional engagement or opting in to the technology that makes the city smart. Similar to how Edward Relph describes the modernist city, the streets resemble "a functionalist context for an efficient city."[40] Aside from the people who view and analyze the information collected by the sensors and cameras, most interactions are automated and are realized yet imperceptible. There is the vague promise of increased engagement with the city and with fellow citizens through digital media technologies, but only because you've been told that it's there.

Placemaking in Smart Cities

Smart-city developers readily engage in conversations about digital media and data accumulation for responsive environments rather than how digital media could enrich citizen experience or emotional attachment to urban space. The democratization of urban information through smartphones, web-based access to city data, and the sharing of urban information to augment social interactions occurs on a small scale or becomes the experience of a select few.[41] Critics have noted the ways in which the extreme coordination, management, and types of interconnection of smart-from-the-start cities lead to the creation of highly controlled, empty spaces that misunderstand the complexity, messiness, politics, and chaotic pleasures of cities.[42] I argue that part of the reason for this perceived misunderstanding lies in the interpretations of the city as place by smart-city developers.

Smart-from-the-start cities are intentional places. However, sense of place is rarely discussed in analyses of smart cities. In examining representations of smart spaces in blueprints, architectural models, and promotional materials, there are traces of how these urban developers, architects, and technology designers imagine and program the city to be lived in in meaningful ways. But meaningful for whom? What might living in these places entail and feel like for diverse urban populations? What type of maintenance and care do these types of places require and inspire? The following sections identify and analyze some prominent placemaking strategies and understandings of place exhibited in smart-from-the-start urban development.

The City as Place

At the Building Sustainable Cities Conference in 2010, Living PlanIT cofounder Steve Lewis repeated a question he was continuously asked after the plan for PlanIT Valley was announced. After it was decided that PlanIT Valley would be built in Portugal, reporters and fellow developers asked Lewis, "Why on earth would you be here? Why would you come to Portugal?" And to this, he answered: "Well, friends, this is not about Portugal. This is about innovating locally and replicating that innovation around the world."[43] After speaking about globalization and the potential profit of PlanIT technologies on the global market, he added another emphatic response to the Portugal question: "Why the hell not?!" This perspective that urban environments are interchangeable or that there is an inherent universality about urban structure and urban life or that a city (smart or not) can be both somewhere and anywhere creates a set of problems for the cultivation of a sense of place in smart-city development.

International researchers, developers, and consultants who are versed in the planning and organization of smart cities hail from across the globe and travel to distant locations to help local governments develop or retrofit smart cities. Scholars have noted the ways in which this combination of localized desire for smart-city development and dependence on mobile, foreign expertise replicates an entrenched trend of exporting urban expertise to developing countries in the service of acquiring global cachet and public attention for local cities.[44] The mobility and influx of transnational experts, urban developers, and technology companies is paired with the export of the cities themselves. Smart-from-the-start cities are designed to be replicable as a model for urban development in any context, but simultaneously they are meant to be unique. The goals of reach and replication situate these urban megaprojects as global digital products and contribute to a formulaic combination of tradition and innovation in architectural style, neighborhood layout, ownership, and city services management. The design and amenities of these cities recall familiar places, ones that transnational elites might have already lived in elsewhere but that also possess an ambient newness.

A critical entry point for understanding placemaking and discursive constructions of smart-city development is to recognize how smart-city developers, planners, and technology managers are literally and metaphorically understanding "the city" as a place, a site, and a concept. After listening to professional smart-city planners discuss their projects, several rhetorical patterns emerge. In general, cities are regarded as the sites that house the future of the world's population. The statistic that 70 percent of the world's population will be living in cities by 2050 is often noted in plans and presentations for smart cities. As Sam Palmisano, CEO of IBM, stated in a speech at the awards banquet of the Atlantic Council in 2008, "The integration point for civilization will be cities in the future."[45] However, cities are broken. They are represented as polluted and congested, unsanitary and mentally unhealthy, chaotic and dangerous, inefficient and uninformed environments. As one journalist covering smart cities observes, "If today's cities were living things, they would be monsters, guilty of guzzling 75% of the world's natural resources consumed each year."[46] This perspective is fueled by images of traffic congestion or congregations of unwieldy crowds that imply not just impending or actual overpopulation, but an abundance of entities and data points that need to be managed and ordered. Cities need to be fixed.

The exponential rise in urban populations and the space and resources needed to support these populations are strategically employed not only as explanations of imminent realities but as justifications for smart-city development. In order to adapt and accommodate increasing population densities and exchanges, cities need to be flexible and efficient governing entities and healthy in terms of sanitary living conditions and sustainability. The smart city is proposed as a blueprint, or "greenprint," for how cities can accommodate consistently increasing urbanization and population growth through the promotion of sustainable living.[47] Smart cities fit into and construct a narrative of development where they will

prevent and remedy catastrophic urban ills such as high-cost inefficien-
cies, climate change, and competition for natural resources that plague
contemporary cities. The city is constructed as a chaotic place in need of
"solutions," an industry term for any and all of a company's smart-city
technologies that can enforce algorithmic order. Transformation of the
city from a disorganized organism to a streamlined, responsive environment equipped with layers of controlled technological systems becomes
both the goal and justification for smart-city development.

At the most basic level, the city is thought of as an ecosystem where
different services, symbiotic relationships, and systems of exchange
work together to maintain the city. Repeatedly the city is referred to and
imagined as "complex," or the image of a city as "systems on top of systems" is invoked,[48] either as layers of networks or naturalized as living
organisms akin to the human body.[49] The smart city is often referred to
as a city with a brain, nervous system, eyes, and ears: it is an omniscient
and sentient place that sees, hears, locates, knows, and responds to residents. The city is a place where signals are sent out and where processing
and productive activities constantly and consistently happen.

For smart-city developers, the ecosystem of the city follows the UN's
"triple bottom line" definition of sustainability, an integrated approach
to city development that takes into account the interoperability of the
social, economic, and environmental factors.[50] The metaphor of a patchwork is often used to express these interconnected systems. The image of
a quilt, lattice, or pattern of squares is a reoccurring representation sym-
bolizing strength through coalescence of varied, select actors and op-
erations. Instead of the image of a cycle, where different entities within
an ecosystem not only support but sustain each other, the patchwork
maintains a distinction between each piece, allowing for the possibility
of the review or omission of one square or system without disrupting
the whole and the à la carte installation of smart-city services available
for sale.

The complexity envisioned within the city is extreme. Images of cities
that are rhetorically evoked or visually displayed alongside smart cities
are huge, global metropolises of past and present: ancient Rome, New
York, London, Shanghai, Tokyo, Hong Kong, Sydney, and Los Angeles.
Instead of designing for different levels of complexity, the smart-city
model conceives all cities as enormous and intricate in parallel ways

and in need of similar hardware and software. The Internet of Things, ubiquitous Wi-Fi connection, and "big data" collected through street-mounted and home-installed sensors, cameras, and antennae are perceived to work in the service of collecting information to "unite" and "harmonize" the interests of business, government, citizen, and environment.[51] Through these digital infrastructures, the assumed conditions of extreme complexity are to be maintained and orchestrated, not reveled in. The city is seen as a place to be operated and controlled and as an entity to make data-informed decisions about.

Alongside municipal representatives and urban planners, technology designers employed by corporations that specialize in smart-city development shape the character and structure of smart cities. As one Cisco smart-city designer explained, "This [Songdo] is the first time we are working with a developer to rethink how a city was going to be designed, built and, more importantly, operated. Our ICT master-plan experts literally intertwined with Gale's team to think how buildings could be a little more smart."[52] This interaction among planners not only cultivates an image of the city as data informed but suggests that the city can be transformed by data, that the city can respond to "intelligence" about itself. The strategic placemaking practices of smart-city developers construct a version of urban life and human behavior that is readily observable and can be seen, known, and monitored through digital technologies. Technology industry representatives denote a preference for listening to and orchestrating human activities that can be measured. By doing so, technology companies also define the affordances of smart technologies in terms of storage, processing, and display rather than participatory or interactive functionality. Although the city is framed as a place in need of improved organization, it is also a place that can be ordered through service provision, systems management, more extensive monitoring and data analysis, and more efficient infrastructure, which is how smart-city technology companies frame the affordances of the digital technologies they sell.

Managing urban complexity through technology is also linked to the promise of improving "quality of life," an elusive and yet all-encompassing phrase that has been a mainstay in discussions of smart-city benefits. Quality of life projects include dedicated spaces for education (international schools and universities), retail (malls and commercial districts), leisure and entertainment (bars, restaurants, and parks), culture (museums and art and music venues), and convention and business enterprise as well as residential living spaces. Improving quality of life has also signified the union of built environments, green spaces, and ICTs in order to make life "easier," "safer," "more convenient," or "more enjoyable" and to solve problems that hinder pleasurable urban living. All smart-city ICTs and ubiquitous computing opportunities are focused on improving quality of life in a fashion that differs from the environments that lie outside the city. In comparison to adjacent metropolises or districts, the planning and zoning of smart cities appear distinct (often with different architectural styles and more green spaces) as these cities directly cater to cosmopolitan foreigners providing carefully orchestrated density and recognizable conveniences.

One of the promotional pamphlets produced by the architects of New Songdo appears to be an attempt to ward off expected critiques. It begins by describing what the city is not: "Songdo is not an architect's utopia; it is not a developer's playground; it is not an engineer's machine; nor is it a governmental planning document."[53] It is a city intended to "help position South Korea at the commercial epicenter of north Asian regional markets," and it will house approximately fifty thousand native and non-native Korean residents.[54] In promotional materials like the two-part book series published by KPF in 2004, the architects and developers frame New Songdo as awe inspiring, "a perfect city" put together piece by piece, composed of fragments. The centerfold displays an illustrated timeline of the city's development and design process that maps planning milestones onto major world events and US and Korean elections, inscribing the grandiose significance of the project. United States president Bill Clinton's reelection coincided with the beginning of the landfill for Songdo City; the formation of the joint venture between KPF, Gale International, and POSCO E&C overlapped with the election of Mayor Ahn; the US invaded Iraq as financing was secured, and groundbreaking occurred at the same time as the Athens Olympics.

The timeline, detailed descriptions of the construction process, photographs of construction cranes draping a skyline of glass-and-steel skyscrapers, and images of the city's development imprinted throughout these booklets mimic time-lapse photography and contextualize urban newness through a sense of rapidly changing history and progress. The booklets and other promotional documents relay a narrative of cultivation and momentum and the completion of the herculean task of building a city out of sand and sea. The newness of these cities is reframed as a benefit instead of ahistorical. The fact that the city was designed with contemporary populations and needs in mind is used as a selling point to contrast these places against other great cities, which are positioned as grand but outdated. Smart-city architecture echoes this narrative, as each city has at least one skyscraper or otherwise-iconic building that symbolizes strength, prowess, recovery, persistence, or leadership into an exciting future. Memorable skylines are carefully planned to create a "pronounced and recognizable visual identity."[55]

Concurrently, smart-from-the-start cities are compared to Hong Kong, Shanghai, Delos, Lubeck, Hamburg, Sydney, New York, Venice, Amsterdam, and other American, European, and Asian trade cities. However, promotional materials assure that the smart-from-the-start city only borrows the best elements and design characteristics of each. The architecture and design of smart cities rely on the social and cultural connotations that borrowed designs provoke in name and in style. For example, in Songdo the Convention Center closely resembles the Sydney Opera House, the park in the center of the city is called Central Park (New York City), a desirable residential area at the edge of the park is called the Loop (Chicago), a section of the city with narrow alleys and a density of galleries, shops, and theaters is known as Kasbah (North Africa), and Park Avenue (New York City) is home to financial and business centers.

In addition to architectural and rhetorical references to real and imagined places, the place of the smart city is also thought of as a "crucible," a "petri dish," a "living laboratory," a "test bed," and a "proving ground," pioneering experiments in fragile yet robust ecosystems where a plethora of intricate systems and services intertwine: transportation, healthcare, government, energy, commerce, education, security, utilities, food, and water. As a Siemens manager explained in 2013, the company sought out a presence within Masdar City because it offered a "real life environment to test new technologies and see how they respond in a concrete urban context."[56] Or as Living PlanIT's promotional video states, cities are innovation places where technologies are "developed, perfected, and experienced."[57] Through the implementation of smart technologies, cities become testing grounds for "applied urban data science."[58]

In addition to a space for experimentation, the city is also recognized as a showroom. After technologies are tested and implemented, the city serves as a "permanent showroom,"[59] and residents become demonstrators of how technologies can be integrated into everyday life. Conferences, conventions, summits, and web portals often serve as accessories to promote the sale and display of the smart-city technologies that are implemented. As Federico Cugurullo accurately describes, event attendees listen to policy leaders and environmental experts talk about the necessity of becoming more equipped to handle the effects of climate change and overpopulation before attendees break for lunch and walk among smart technologies in the corridors or on the streets outside the conference building. Both the city-as-showroom and the showroom itself become sites of re-placing.

Making Place for Business and Everyday Life

Putting Place to Work

Attempts to woo businesses to establish enterprises, outposts, or headquarters within smart cities include some common promises within special economic zones: tax incentives, state-of-the-art infrastructure, high-tech hardware and ICT services, and available real estate and labor pools. Smart-from-the-start cities incorporate placemaking strategies that evoke images of cities that are built to and for work, with the support of a free economic zone and the convenience of a campus city. Digital media and infrastructure are used to show that this place "works" in more ways than one: it functions like a well-oiled machine and is the ideal location to incubate ideas and get work done.

Songdo is described as a place with an "exciting, bustling core," where clusters of economists, researchers, policy makers, and business leaders gather to establish headquarters, take advantage of the Incheon free economic zone, and reposition Korea within the global economy. It is a city of synergy. It is a place of openness to free trade, foreign transactions, and network technologies and is a logistical hub for regional and global flows. A "gateway," a "conduit," a "link," a "connector," a "mixing chamber," and a "hub" with an open door "welcoming foreign businessmen, exchanging technicians, students, and all manner of fortune seeker."[60] The architects promote the city as a literal and figurative "halfway zone" or a "filter." Geographically the city is half island, half mainland; symbolically it's framed as a hybrid place of local and global cultures and a mix of traditional, recognizable, and futuristic facilities. It is sold as a magnetic place that people are drawn to, where they enjoy staying and working: a dense, bustling market and trade city with pleasant gardens around the city's edges. There are clusters of innovation centers but also familiar amenities and facilities imagined for foreigners from businesses, knowledge economies, or innovation enterprises: international schools, medical centers, luxury housing and hotels, convenient public transportation, and easy access to downtown or the airport as well as nearby international restaurants and meeting spaces.

Each smart-from-the-start city emphasizes its city center as a core that reflects the city's overall meaning and significance. In Songdo, the city places educational institutions at the epicenter of two major neighborhoods while cultural institutions are located next to the iconic convention center on the coast. KPF notes that the central placement of these institutions "reflects the Confucian values of Korean society and the desire to strengthen cultural ties to other nations."[61] Masdar places the Institute of Science and Technology at the center of the city, which symbolically locates Masdar as an "innovation engine," incubator, and think tank. In the city's visitors guide, key places of interest for tourists include incubators, office buildings, the knowledge center, and research institutes. As promotional materials explain, "The institute is Masdar City's nucleus, which extends a spirit of innovation and entrepreneurship throughout the city."[62] The proximity of university institutions, research and development institutes, and innovation and entrepreneurship accelerators within the same neighborhood is heralded as a way that urban planning might help with economic development and "accelerate breakthrough technologies to market."[63] In addition, the first commercial property to be completed in Masdar was the Incubator Building, which houses more than 360 start-ups and more established companies.

Smart cities claim that they are the "perfect place" to "nurture new ideas" and test out new technologies.[64] Robust infrastructure and ubiquitous, free Wi-Fi create a place where work gets done: over lunch, in the park or plaza, at home, in the office, and in between. The claimed strategic logistical location of a city like Masdar, Songdo, or PlanIT Valley is framed as a characteristic that not only grants access to other global or regional business districts but also creates a place where a "like-minded business community" comes together.[65] The type of place that is fostered in these innovation districts is one where people from different cultures who speak different languages unite around a shared interest in business and entrepreneurship. Smart cities are framed as places of commonality, "joint venture," partnership, and cohabitation around a common cause: profit, progress, and economic development. Because of this, the smart city is not only a place filled with services and support for business enterprise; it is more than a business-friendly environment but a business-supportive *community*. Those cities are built around the concept of fostering a business community in an environment where the people who live and work there are surrounded by innovation and are equipped with all they need in close proximity. Like the campuses designed for the Silicon Valley tech sector, smart cities encourage employees to come to work and stay at work, providing everything they need on the premises. The corporation and citizen are united in these cities: partners in Masdar City, such as Siemens and GE, have become citizens as they claim and rent the property where their buildings are located.[66]

Quality of Life

Aside from branding itself as having zero waste and zero carbon (or at least low waste and a minimal carbon footprint) and being a hub for global business activities, there are other environmental characteristics promoted to attract residents and businesses and to create a unique sense of place in smart-from-the-start cities. Masdar emphasizes that its architecture is designed to create shade from the desert heat. Songdo publicizes its green spaces and safe, uncongested pedestrian walkways. PlanIT Valley advertises the convenience of personalized responsive environments, especially in promoting its plan for approximately 450 sensors per person.[67]

In terms of quality of life, smart cities tout themselves as self-sufficient, as places where a wide range of activities are accessible in close proximity. All spaces are green, energy efficient, safe, and walkable, with amenities and attractions conveniently located. Cities offer a variety of

residences to choose from in order to take advantage of these activities: garden apartments, canal houses, high-rises with park views, or dense areas of low-rise, mixed-use buildings. Descriptions and endless lists of amenities and activities portray the city as an all-inclusive, eco-friendly space composed through the logic and rhetoric of new-town politics. A defining element of the smart-from-the-start city is "access." Just as the business community enjoys access to services, support, and talent to cultivate their enterprises and encourage entrepreneurship, residents enjoy proximate, unfettered access to any social service or experience they might desire. However, these desires are typically limited to "quality of life projects" that structure leisure time and activities within prescribed spaces such as the mall, the golf course, the park, or cultural and business activities hosted at the convention center.

Although new-town rhetoric permeates promotional materials on Songdo, Masdar, and PlanIT Valley, there are specific textual maneuvers to dissociate smart cities from previous portraits of planned cities (like Levittown and Brasilia) that have negative connotations. The rational design of modernist new towns that govern and organize urban behavior are associated with projects like Le Corbusier's Radiant City or Unite d'Habitation, metaphors and images that are repeated and revised in smart-from-the-start city marketing materials. After distinguishing smart-from-the-start cities from Le Corbusier's designs, the developers and planners of Songdo draw a comparison: "Like the ocean liner, or the human body, Songdo is designed as an organic whole. . . . It completes a picture of modern life."[68] The impression is that the city, although organized, retains mobility and some potential to adapt or respond to changing environmental conditions.

Developers aim to represent the city as planned, but not too planned. One placemaking strategy emphasizes heterogeneity, not just of activities offered but in architectural styles and planning practices. Heterogeneity is utilized in the service of mimicking forces of time and historicity. Planners and architects vary architectural styles, building densities, landscapes, and zoning regulations to imitate the organic development of a city over time instead of a planned urban space that has been constructed in ten to twelve years. Websites and promotional documents exhibit images of these varied landscapes, street widths, and structures, with contrasting neighborhood visual styles or juxtapositions between the smart-city landscape and homogenous, modernist architectural styles. Images of brutalist buildings are often crossed out to emphasize this visual dissonance. KPF calls this strategy creating a "varied diet" for residents.

To emphasize this "varied diet," Songdo is mentioned alongside references to the imagined cities of Italo Calvino. The last page of KPF's master plan for Songdo is a lengthy, bolded pull quote from Calvino's *Invisible Cities*, signifying a connection between Songdo and Esmeralda, an open trade city with networks of intersecting canals and streets. Above all, Esmeralda is a city whose residents are "spared the boredom of following the same streets every day" because they have endless combinations of routes to explore.

In Masdar and PlanIT Valley, references to mixed use and heterogeneity of architectural styles, spaces, and retail options imply, less allegorically, that residents' varied options within the cities mean that they will be stimulated by their physical environments. Promotional materials and descriptions of Masdar's master plan emphasize Foster and Partners' design principles of providing a variety of low-rise, high-density residences.[69] Foster and Partners, led by the "Mozart of Modernism," Norman Foster, known for his glass-façade skyscrapers and open-plan spaces,[70] tries to distinguish the Masdar plan as having an "educational focus" within a one-of-a-kind, sustainable city. Masdar has been branded as a zero-carbon eco-city that (like Songdo) combines the traditional and the modern in terms of architecture, technology, and culture. The aerial view of the master plan for the city resembles the intricate, interconnected patterns of Islamic art tiles or a series of latticed *mashrabiya* (traditional oriel windows that create perforated shadows), which are prominent fixtures in the Masdar Institute and are often the focal image in brochures and websites.

The developers promote Masdar as familiar yet innovative, complex but clean, and cool, literally. Masdar "combines ancient Arabic architectural techniques with modern technology" and uses nature to its advantage, harnessing the sun's rays to create solar energy and capturing winds to keep residents cool. The diversity of architecture styles and architectural forms is linked to "creating the diversity of any major, modern city."[71] In a brochure to attract potential lessees and residents, the developers claim that the shaded "pedestrian-friendly districts and public spaces encourage a sense of neighborhood" and "wellbeing of the community." The unique elements that promote place attachment are presented as eco-friendly, including building facades made with green building materials, rapid public transit options, and solar energy and wind tower infrastructures.

Tensions in Smart-City Placemaking

Although they lived in a trade city of flowing water and interconnected streets, the residents of Italo Calvino's Esmeralda had uneasy relationships with the city they inhabited. The same might be true for residents of smart-from-the-start cities. Newspaper and magazine articles that cover smart-cities trends and the excitement around the cutting-edge, digitally connected cities being constructed around the globe are tempered by the question "Do we really want to live in them?"[72] Smart-city developers have reluctantly cited problems in attracting residents, talent, and businesses to their fabricated urban environments. These professional placemakers have noted issues in producing these cities as places where people who are familiar with the amenities and social life of urban environments would like to live. For example, Songdo has been critiqued as a "consciously planned, somewhat artificial city with a modern functionalist face," and because of this, it will be challenging to reinvent it as "lively and attractive."[73] Even Songdo's developer, Stanley Gale, concedes that the character of a city like Songdo will be difficult to cultivate from scratch. He emphasizes the role of urban programming and planning in constructing even the most mundane, seemingly organic elements of urban culture: "We know that right now we are not funky. We need artists, internet entrepreneurs, fashion designers, so we are building incubator spaces in the city to try to get the mix right. You can't manufacture grit, but you can encourage it."[74] The placemaking problems identified by smart-city planners, of creating physically integrated and culturally vibrant locations, have also been ongoing challenges for developers of knowledge and innovation spaces. Interviews that Surabhi Pancholi, Tan Yigitcanlar, and Mirko Guaralda conducted with policy makers and planners showed that innovation-space developers continually struggle with similar issues in the design of residential areas and public spaces and in fostering a sense of community and informal networks for interaction among residents.[75]

In their current form, smart-from-the-start cities like Songdo, Masdar, and PlanIT Valley fulfill policy initiatives of technology development and global entrepreneurship but tend to disregard urban experience, community efficacy, and social interactions in their construction. The social networks and cultural variation that lead to the success and sustainability of urban spaces has not emerged organically in smart cities but is being planned and orchestrated by people other than the residents themselves. As Jonathan Thorpe, CIO for the American developer Gale International, observes,

> It's the occupants who make a city. . . . You're trying to create a diversity and a vitality that organic development creates, in and of itself, so it's a challenge to try and replicate that in a masterplan setting. At the same time, with a masterplan you have the ability to size the infrastructure to make sure the city works—now and in 50 years' time.[76]

As this quote evidences, there is a reiterated duality in the imagined role of residents in the production of urban place. On one hand, people and public engagement are viewed as integral to the character and functioning of the smart city, but on the other hand, urban life is viewed as a set of activities that can be orchestrated and understood through urban programming and computer code. A stated benefit of programmed urban life is commonly framed in terms of smart growth and flexibility over time—infrastructures and services can be designed to accommodate urban growth and increasing complexity.

In 1997 the International Centre for Communications and other private planning organizations were already voicing concern about interurban digital divides: cities that are not equipped or motivated to engage with digital technologies and practices "risk being consigned to geopolitical obsolescence before they even know what hit them."[77] Thus, there is an urgent need for smart-city planning services. Adam Greenfield has criticized the smart city as urban form and urban imagination partially based on the narratives that technology developers and managers like IBM, Intel, Cisco, Samsung, Siemens, and various telecoms have created. Greenfield and others have pinpointed the seamless integration of ubiquitous digital networks that monitor and survey citizens, sometimes without their knowledge or consent, as components that make smart cities both highly networked and notoriously undemocratic.[78] Smart cities, particularly those built from scratch, are read as neoliberal, corporately owned and/or operated (often in partnership with municipal governments), centralized enterprises that hail the citizen as a consumer rather than a producer or contributor. The role and presence of citizens is reactive; they are quantifiable users of the city, and their prescribed agency is limited.

Edgar Pieterse traces a "stylized urban development trajectory" in urban planning that idealizes a rational, top-down design to create modern, vertical, gleaming, networked, and ordered urban spaces.[79] This trajectory moves away from informal urban activities and encounters toward orchestrated, controlled, and regulated interactions where those monitoring the city feel as if they have the right to intervene in the lives of millions of people because they can. According to this argument, developers and technologists rarely pause to question whether having access to the movement, records of exchange, and traces of citizen activity legitimizes this access. The stylized, strategic imagination of urban interactions is the vision that drives placemaking in smart-city development: citizens and their activities are data points and points of data collection that compose the city and need to be managed to transform the city into a smarter place.

In addition, the term "community" is evoked but is rarely directly applied to the smart city. Smart-city planners and government officials mention community engagement or efforts to develop a community after people move in, or they use the term "quantified community" (to describe a place where residents contribute streams of data about the city).[80] At conferences and during conversations with smart-city developers, community engagement is noted in retail terms and is regarded as "service provision" or "customer service." Business communities are the most frequently mentioned communities, which is related to the assumption that even though business people might arrive from assorted countries, speak different languages, and work for different companies, they are all interested in the same activities and hybrid lifestyle. In this sense, community is framed in terms of homogeneity rather than collaboration and care. Benefits of community are couched in terms of amenities that coordinate living en masse or of large populations living in close proximity: passive and intelligent building systems for energy and water consumption, smart transportation networks, retail opportunities, and a mix of tenants. Instead of community, the term most readily referenced in regard to people living together as a collective is "social." "Social" tends to be defined by categories such as conveniently accessed amenities like restaurants, shops, and public transportation—cultural (meaning local) and neighborhood identity, public safety, and responsive and efficient public services.

Streets and street sociability have been quintessential elements of urban life. Urban studies theorists have discussed the city as a theater of social action—interactions among familiar and not-so-familiar strangers, crowds with blasé attitudes, sidewalks as spaces of social cohesion, and a sense of belonging. Jane Jacobs suggests that cities utilize strategies of "zoning for diversity" or including mixed-use buildings, defined sidewalks, and short blocks with corners for congregating to help create vibrant, interactive communities. Diversity and interfacing with diversity, which have consistently been regarded in urban studies as essential characteristics of urban life, are introduced within the smart city as diversity of services and architectural styles, but not necessarily in terms of sociability. A diversity of buildings and architectural styles is often mentioned in relation to building height and a mix of traditional and contemporary design rather than pertaining to the use of these edifices or in regard to the shape of sidewalks or street ways. Diversity of architectural styles, while significant for their symbolic and aesthetic power, is limited in encouraging community building or street sociability. Likewise, technology in the smart city is imagined as doing what modernist architecture and rationalized design practices intended to do: tame the street and control the behavior of the urban citizen. As Scott McQuire succinctly observes in *The Media City*, "In streets designed primarily for circulation, the flaneur's 'art of strolling' has no place."[81] Smart-city streets are designed for flow, efficient circulation, monitoring and quantification, and momentum, not pausing or wandering. According to urban theorists and practitioners, much of what makes a space into a place is the dwelling, lingering, strolling, and staying put for a while. In the smart city, this type of lingering has moved from the streets to discrete green spaces like parks, retail spaces, plazas, or restaurants. Masdar claims that public plazas have been "activated" to encourage people to spend time in them. Songdo envisions green spaces and walkways along canals that are "infused with life and activity" through commercial spaces such as shops and markets.

In smart-from-the-start cities there is a contradiction between the placemaking practices evident in the technologies implemented and the placemaking strategies resonant in the design of physical spaces. Planners and developers have made concerted efforts to disavow centralized, rational, homogenously planned cities in their physical design (with discursive moves away from Le Corbusier and toward Esmeralda) but reinstate a sense of ordered place through digital design. Parks and retail spaces provide a sense of activity but are disconnected from the claims of what the digital "smartness" of the city will do for residents' sense of place. Images in promotional materials depict 3-D models with people gathering to sit on ledges and in atriums, but these ideal residents are not directly engaged with the technologies of the smart city. Designated, public places of dwelling in the city are also depicted as the places where smart-city technology is not directly felt or observed. These physical places look like ordinary spaces, separated from the sensors and networks that are intended to gather data on traffic and mobility. The invisibility of ubiquitous computing interfaces might be taken too literally; because interactions with technology cannot be seen, they are not pictured.

Sensors and code enable seamless, efficient travel through urban space as a responsive environment—"a symphony of effortless efficiency."[82] This efficiency is also in direct contradiction with the programming of physical space. The programming of public parks and walkways asks pedestrians to linger and ogle the work of renowned architects at the same time that the technologies designed for urban home and street life encourage people to move along. The streets that are lined with smart lighting, smart waste and water regulation, cameras and wireless networks that monitor traffic flow and pedestrian activity, and the digital concierge services in homes and offices urge people to connect with distant services and information and then be briskly on their way. While the green spaces and gathering places are inviting, with grandiose architecture in some cases, the streets themselves are mundane. Unlike the green gathering places in the middle of walkable neighborhoods, the digital technologies proposed and implemented nearly work in opposition to public space—segmenting and hailing urban populations into individual users with personalized, data-driven needs that necessitate continuous mobility. Smart-city technologies maintain and direct flow and monitor strangers while physical spaces are carefully programmed to support communal dwelling and interaction among diverse users of the city in shared spaces.

Planning documents and presentations repeatedly recognize that people are at the center of vibrant cities, but when cities are being built from scratch, designers struggle to integrate people into smart-city development. Technologies for the end user are like concierge services—they position the citizen as a consumer, user, or client rather than as a community member or collaborator in the production of the city as place. A key element that's underestimated in smart-city placemaking is digital media for triangulation, or the process by which some external stimulus provides a linkage between people and prompts strangers to talk to one another.[83] Instead, smart cities exhibit the opposite: digital kiosks for individual use, data and information for responsiveness accessed through smartphones, or individual monitors in domestic spaces. Citizens are empowered as managers who maintain order in personalized ways—they manage their relationships to infrastructure, on-call public services, and relationships with their environment or other people.

The People Problem

Attracting Residents

After spending nearly a year in Masdar, Cugurullo calls the smart city a "nonplace." He adjusts Marc Augé's definition to describe the city as a "spatial entity bereft of an organic society . . . a space where identity is suspended, and little or nothing is left for emotional relations."[84] Other critics of smart cities emphasize this idea in different ways, calling these spaces overly planned and orchestrated to the point where they lack the ability to evolve or to produce interesting friction, dynamism, and serendipity.[85]

Interviews with smart-city developers and advocates reveal a reiterated concern and challenge for smart-city development. More than technical challenges—such as creating robust infrastructure to handle data sharing; developing hardware and software to process, store, and analyze gathered data; and managing the scale of smart-city development—the key challenge for smart cities is the people who live in them. Guruduth Banavar, the vice president and chief technology officer of the global public-sector business at IBM, notes that a significant challenge is "getting citizens fully engaged in all transformations that take place."[86] He continues to explain that "the hallmark of a smart city is having the right people, in the right numbers, working the technology in the right way."[87] However, as vacancy rates in smart-from-the-start cities indicate, the "right" people may be few and far between. In 2013 it was reported that less than 20 percent of commercial office space in New Songdo was occupied.[88]

Although Songdo was designed with the intention of being an international business district and attracting transnational corporate headquarters, many Korean nationals are moving in. Upper- and upper-middle-class Koreans tend to read Songdo as an upscale urban development project for comfortable, green living, not necessarily as a place for commercial enterprise and ubiquitous computing. One resident describes that living closer to neighbors and to an expansive central park has improved her quality of life.[89] However, the high commercial vacancy rates and the high-rise residential buildings that are slow to reach capacity lack the density that would make the proximity, abundance of services, and data-accumulating technologies that are built for complexity meaningful. Although Masdar City officials and developers have justified recent building expansions by claiming that all buildings are "fully tenanted and occupied," possibly due to an overflow from nearby Abu Dhabi, reports from residents and visitors suggest that low vacancy rates are not equated to active street life. Masdar, which was originally planned for fifteen hundred businesses, forty thousand residents, and ten thousand more commuters, only had one hundred people living on-site as of 2013.[90]

One *Wall Street Journal* reporter describes a similar situation after a visit to one of India's smart-from-the-start cities in 2015, which has been under development for nearly ten years:

Of the two office towers, the first is about 50% occupied and the second one is empty. . . . 1.6-million-square feet of office space had been completed. Part of one building was occupied. A data center for telecommunications was also ready, as were a fire station and a school. The rest of the area was mainly empty. Construction was under way for a hospital and other facilities.[91]

However, the city manager reports that the city has already sold "nearly 14 million square feet to developers or companies in buildings not yet built. It will be another four to five years before the first phase of the city—now covering only a fifth of the originally planned area—will get going."[92] This narrative of ever expanding, magnificent ghost towns that have yet to reach their potential or cannot be evaluated yet because "it's too early to tell" has become a signature sense of place among smart-from-the-start cities. There is a paradox to this expansion that questions where the demand for these office buildings, residences, and cities as a whole are coming from.

Bugs in the System

The idea that a city should be a place of experience and local identity before it is formally programmed abrasively contrasts the vision of digital media systems as systems of responsiveness and governmentality. In particular, urban planners and technology developers struggle with mapping smart-city promises, rhetoric, and "symbolic power" onto local needs, social affordances, and lived experiences of urban space.[93] Jennifer Gabrys has interrogated the construction of the citizen and citizens' roles in smart cities. She highlights the ways in which citizens become "citizen sensors" or sensing nodes whose modality of citizenship and agency is reduced to monitoring and managing data.[94] Accompanying this construction of citizens as data producers and sensing beings is also the idea of the smart citizen as disruptive. Aside from issues with attracting people to smart cities, the idea that there are "right" types of people and proper uses of these systems looms large. At a recent smart-cities event hosted by IBM, one of its engineers joked that the company "tends to look at the pipes and then people come along and destroy all our nice optimized systems."[95] Similar statements from planners and engineers appear in trade publications that describe smart-city residents and potential residents as either tech-savvy technology industry workers or entities that both produce and upset the flow of information and urban services within the city.

In planning documents, public presentations, and conversations with smart-city developers, people are viewed as bugs in the system: drosophila, worker ants, and glitches within digital and physical designs and implementations. Smart-city residents are understood as drosophila, or early adopters that test new technologies and services. Residents are also understood as worker ants producing the data that informs the city about itself and the data that should inform and adjust their own behavior. Planning rhetoric situates users as customers rather than as civic-minded actors to the point that people are not wholly envisioned as agents within the urban ecosystem but as sensing nodes and data points that interact with it.

If digital urban technologies are seen as "solutions," then one of the "problems" is people. Discipline and governmentality of human behavior are maintained through citizen "operatives" generating, monitoring, and reflecting on data that is collected through ubiquitous technologies to create and maintain efficient, "productive infrastructures" and make "informed, responsible choices."[96] IBM and other companies have argued that this form of centrally administered, corporate-controlled smart cities with limited community and citizen input is just the first stage of smart-city development. However, human behavior remains the biggest variable in the seamless integration of technologies and the efficient functioning of the smart city. People are meant to contribute to and monitor data as behavior generated within these systems. If people actively try to participate in or influence the system, they are no longer a variable; they are the bugs.

Strategic Re-placeing

As illustrated by the programming of place through master plans and the construction of the role of the citizen as both bug and operator, smart cities are actively framed as particular types of places. Whether they are seen as a vision of the future of cities, sustainable "new town" environments, or curated places for flows of innovation and capital, what makes smart cities unique is the promise of transformation and responsiveness through digital infrastructures. In all cases, the city is constructed as a place filled with problems for which corporations, governments, data scientists, and technology developers have digital solutions. The promise of place does not come from the bottom up through civic and community engagement but is orchestrated and designed from the top down. The poetics at work at this most abstract level of re-placeing the city occurs in the showroom, with its models and demos, where no citizens inhabit any of the displays. At this scale of strategic placemaking, where people are quite literally absent from the social production of place, we see that re-placeing the city—in the manner of affording a "sense of place"—actually requires citizens to participate and inhabitants to contribute. Smart-city use by residents brings out the incongruences and absences in smart-city imaginations and implementations, such as contradictions between designs for physical and technological spaces and the need to incorporate residents as placemakers.

The strategic transformation of place envisioned for smart cities is what people who observe and participate in their construction find both appealing and appalling. According to the Project for Public Spaces, an organization founded on the ideals of sociologist William H. Whyte, "what makes a great place" is a combination of "sociability," "uses and activities," "comfort and image," and "access and linkages." Smart cities echo these categories in terms of what they measure but not necessarily in the activities and behaviors that they support. Songdo, Masdar, and PlanIT Valley excel in the "access and linkages" category, which consists of descriptors such as walkability, convenience, proximity, legibility, and connectedness. Smart-city developers work tirelessly to create a sense of "comfort and image," but "uses and activities" and "sociability"—which encompass authenticity, stewardship, vitality, interaction, cooperation, and pride in place—are perpetual speed bumps on the road to smart-city innovation and attractiveness. Scenarios for use and outcomes of smart-city interaction are limited: locating an object or person that's been lost, finding the best route, accessing on-call information and communication, making use of convenient and responsive services and facilities. Future residents are considered beta testers for new technologies and target markets for digital infrastructure, products, and services rather than active participants in re-placeing the city.

Although smart-from-the-start cities are under construction and will continue to be in development for years to come, the socio-technical imaginaries—collectively envisioned and attainable futures for social life and social order—are reflected in the design and implementation of these scientific and technological projects.[97] Most applicable to smart cities is Sheila Jasanoff and Sang-Hyun Kim's suggestion that socio-technical imaginaries simultaneously "describe attainable futures and *prescribe* futures that states believe ought to be attained."[98] Imagination, in this case, acts as a force of defining and anchoring state-sponsored or private-public visions for urban society within technological projects. Instead of engaging in a game of "catch-up," smart-city development carves out a place in the global arena that aims to secure a city's or region's status as a capital of digital innovation, now and in the future. Smart-from-the-start cities create a purpose, an iconic physical space, and a research and development sandbox and showroom to encourage domestic monopolies and start-ups to diversify and innovate.

The vision of ubiquitous digital infrastructure and computing opportunities includes municipal and state-sponsored imaginations of social order and economic and technological development but often excludes the citizen and grassroots understandings of social life and urban computing culture. As Palermo and Ponzini note, real estate developers conceive and construct urban spaces based on long-standing, codified models and canons for urban development. Models such as the Garden City or Radiant City, which have been critiqued by Jane Jacobs and William H. Whyte as decidedly antiurban, resurface in smart-city planning. Furthermore, the authors argue that in professional planning practices for real estate development, placemaking is shaped by rational and utilitarian logics that prioritize instrumental goals and exchange value over other design values and ethics.[99] The imaginative blueprints and funding processes that lead to the construction of these cities reiterate assumptions that reinforce centralized control over the development and use of ubiquitous computing in conjunction with traditional assumptions and models of urban design. These representations of space promote universality and uniformity in lieu of citizens' diverse imaginations and experiences of technologies and cities.

These circulating socio-technical imaginaries for urban space showcase a tendency toward harnessing digital media and infrastructure in the name of strategic development and place promotion. The main attribute that produces the elaborate construction sites of Songdo, Masdar, or PlanIT Valley as unique "places" is the fact that they are *smart* cities. The harnessing of ubiquitous computing as a concept (even before this concept is developed and implemented) can be read as an act of placemaking, of constructing an abstract space as a particular place through the formation and harnessing of technology and technological discourses.

By employing the rhetoric of ubiquitous computing, big data, and the Internet of Things and articulating this rhetoric within a particular urban environment, top-down players in the construction of smart-from-the-start cities are re-placing the yet-to-be-constructed city. Smart-city technologies, as defined by developers and planners, are being strategically utilized to discursively transform a construction lot into a "place." The imagination of ubiquitous computing as a public service and modality of civic engagement based on sensing and monitoring data and efficiently rationalizing urban life is a particular brand of urban future and urban technology made legible through practices of placemaking.

If we read these strategic placemaking processes through Henri Lefebvre's terminology, re-placing smart cities is related to obscuring spaces of domination for these environments to appear less like abstract space and more like spaces of appropriation. In the case of smart-from-the-start cities, spaces in the service of advanced capitalism, globalization of capital and economic processes, and corporate and state power are disguised as places in the service of human needs through the incorporation of digital infrastructure and services. However, the ways in which digital technologies are being incorporated into these environments actually reinforce the smart city as a "space of domination" and do not echo the human needs and practices of "spaces of appropriation," as the incorporation of technology either excludes or awkwardly delimits citizen participation and agency in its formation. The re-placing of smart-from-the-start cities and the ways in which they are used as models for other cities illustrates how the social production of place does not always include people "on the ground" in its construction of rooted, bounded environments as well as the complications that arise from not doing so.

Conclusion

While smart cities lack universality in terms of their definition, there are similarities in their strategies for placemaking. There is the potential for grassroots placemaking in a tactical sense as more residents move in and the expected density (which is a key aspect of the smart cities' social and communication aspects) is reached. However, it cannot be ignored that a certain sense of place and imagined urban experience have been designed into these cities already.

In smart-from-the-start cities there is a contradiction between placemaking strategies initiated through technologies and the placemaking strategies coded into the design of physical spaces. Designers make concerted efforts to disavow the image of centralized, rational, homogenously planned cities in their physical design, but they reinstate this sense of ordered place in their digital design. Whereas the physical environment is programmed to be stimulating and intricate yet open, the instrumented technology that manages and organizes this complexity maintains and monitors the fragile ecosystem. While smart-from-the-start cities tend to be somewhat progressive in their programming of the physical urban environment, creating open and mixed-use spaces in which people can congregate and interact, the technology does not exist in a symbiotic relationship to these activities. In fact, many of these technologies oppose these ideals, segmenting and hailing urban populations as individual users with personalized, data-driven needs. As these smart-city models and the international players who have monopolized their development continue to expand their reach, the imaginations of urban place embedded within smart-from-the-start cities are exported without question.

What is evident in their planning documents, interviews, and public presentations is that smart-city developers struggle with how to put people first. Amid constant calls for more citizen participation and civic engagement to be designed and invited into smart-city plans, I argue that some of this transition necessitates changing the ways developers and technologists think of cities as places and their assumptions about how people live in them. Smart-city developers and designers need to reconsider the city as a "field of care" in order to recognize and cultivate the "affective bond between people and place."[100]

Places, like people, have character. In describing the character of places, Tuan notes two contrasting (but not mutually exclusive) aspects: a place can command awe through its sublime construction or natural beauty, or a place can evoke affection due to the emotional attachments and associations a person has to a given location. At present, dominant smart-city forms and strategies tend to command awe among elites without generating feelings of belonging, emotional attachments, or a sense of place more widely. The question of how to make smart cities socially attractive remains a recognized issue for developers. While smart cities are smart, they are also *cities*. Although the lure of technology might engage technophiles, how these technologies are employed to enrich urban life will have more lasting effects. Social aspects of urban life are often reduced to terms that resemble customer service and convenience. The city and its amenities aim to be acceptable, recognizable, or convenient rather than stimulating or lively.

The formalization of the "social" that is evident in assumptions about urban life and the design of smart-city technologies works against the informal character of the city, which is what should give it character. The orchestration of hipness, creativity, and grit works against the community-generated character of a city.[101] The suggestion attempts to solve, simplify, and straighten out the messiness and dynamism of everyday urban life though digital media—re-placeing certain types of complexity with digital proxies.

Strategic placemaking constructs an image of the city in the service of corporation and government and as a place to be, or that can be, ordered through service provision, systems management, extensive monitoring, and data analysis. What is too often forgotten in smart-city development is that community and civic engagement rely on different interests, constraints, mobilities, needs, and uses of space as well as communion. Difference is flattened in the conception of place of the smart city. People are thought of as anonymized data points responding to technologies that encourage them to use the city in similar, efficient ways. If heterogeneity carries over into the design of digital technologies, it is evident in the personalization of technology use, not the type of imagined user or interpretive flexibility of the services offered. The overarching illusion of universal use that is envisioned by smart-city designers shapes the image of the smart city as a place where neighborhoods are thought of as homogeneous and communities are conceived of in terms of imagined homophily.

The need to preserve and create new opportunities for serendipity, spontaneity, and sociability within cities has been advised by a variety of researchers and architects.[102] However, the need to consider culture and community alongside technology has been problematic in the smart city. Developers need to consider the cultural aspects of intended innovation from the outset, not as an afterthought.[103] They need to rethink placemaking strategies, situate and extend public participation, and reconsider how people and human behavior become legible in smart-city systems. The functionalist view of the city as place that is currently articulated through strategic re-placing can shift to consider flexibility and difference as urban values—the city as a ballet as well as an ecosystem, a theater as well as a laboratory, recognizing urban constraints as well as convenience—by focusing on how people make place as well as data.

2

The Connected City

Digital Infrastructure and Urban Transformation

In 2015, four years after the neighboring cities of Kansas City, Kansas (KCK), and Kansas City, Missouri (KCMO), bested the competition to host Google Fiber for Communities' one-gigabit experimental fiber network (more commonly known as Google Fiber),[1] I sat around a table with representatives from eleven different local nonprofit, philanthropic, and governmental organizations. We were gathered at the Kansas City Public Library to brainstorm digital inclusion needs and strategies for Kansas City communities. The people seated at the table were among the 250 participants at the first Digital Inclusion Summit in Kansas City. Participants offered insightful observations from their interactions with inner-city residents on the "wrong side" of the digital divide. A representative from a regional food bank proposed the analogy that access to internet connection was like access to food: it's not access to food that's the problem—food is all around us—it's affordability; people can't afford good, healthy food. She continued to explain that the communities she assisted had internet access points, but there was a high cost for the "good" kind of connection. A representative from a community support group noted the need to better understand the populations affected by digital divides. She suggested that people concerned with digital access gaps should work within neighborhoods to bring resources and training to where people in need resided. Other representatives mentioned that aside from affordability, Kansas City needed to improve computer and internet literacy. The observations continued in a rapid flow: we needed to understand internet connection as a fundamental right; we needed more resources and labor devoted to these issues; we needed to join forces; we needed a culture shift; we and the corporations that provided internet connection needed empathy.

I sat at this table, and many others, where people had discussions about the disparities of internet connection in Kansas City and the organizations determined to alleviate these inequities. During these discussions, one place was mentioned more often than public libraries, YMCAs, community centers, city government services, public schools, church basements, and computing centers: the McDonald's on Prospect Avenue near East Truman Road. This McDonald's served fast food to a neighborhood population where the median household income and percentage of bachelor's degrees was significantly below the state average. The neighborhood surrounding the McDonald's had high unemployment rates; the percentages of black, Hispanic, and foreign-born residents were significantly above average; and it was within walking distance of at least one high school.

The fast-food restaurant was where the high school students went after school to buy fries or a Coke, to socialize, and to do their homework. It was known among area parents, kids, and community activists that the high school students hung out there because the McDonald's was the only place with a free wireless connection that was accessible after school and was a relatively safe walk between the school and students' homes—an oasis in what community activists called "a digital desert." This McDonald's, and the high school students that frequented it, resided in a neighborhood that didn't qualify for Google Fiber. Although the fast-food restaurant filled the role of a makeshift community center, it didn't fit within Google's initial mandate to offer affordable connection to nonprofit and public institutions under the Community Connections program. At the beginning of 2016 two nearby neighborhood schools, a museum, a community center, and a few office buildings were waiting for installation of Google's high-speed network. The McDonald's, however, still had not signed up.[2]

People without a stable at-home internet connection experience place differently. Not only because they lack access to information, literacies, or opportunities afforded by a consistent, reliable digital connection but because they need to search out stable internet connection hubs in a variety of public spaces. Without an internet connection at home, they face a distinct set of constraints and employ different tactics for connecting to the internet while mobile. I spoke with many Kansas City residents who relied on nonplaces, in-between spaces that doubled as internet hot spots: churches, retail spaces, fast-food establishments, and parking lots all became internet providers. Digital inclusion activists repurposed the city in similar ways, transforming abandoned gentlemen's clubs, office building lobbies, social services reception areas, libraries, and community centers into digital hubs. The McDonald's on Prospect Avenue was one of these places, but not the only one. However, the image of this fast-food outlet as an internet node for students trying to finish their homework before their Coca-Colas ran dry was striking because it was so antithetical to the gigabit network that the city had heavily publicized and to other Kansas City residents' experiences and expectations of internet connection and place. Even housing and urban development secretary Julian Castro referenced the image of this makeshift internet café in his announcement of the Google Fiber and ConnectHome initiatives that would provide free service to select residents in low-income housing: "For families here, at West Bluff, the days when young folks had to research a paper using the Wi-Fi at McDonalds, or research a paper using a library computer, are over."[3]

The arrival of Google Fiber in KCK and KCMO in 2011 provided increased momentum and renewed impetus for alleviating digital divides based on cost, access, education, and computer literacy. Although the implementation of Google's high-speed network in KCK and KCMO called attention to digital divides and the organizations determined to alleviate them, the initiative also exacerbated inequalities and sociocultural differences inscribed in the geography of these cities. Many of these differences were sparked by discussions of internet connection, or lack thereof, but were articulated through connections to place and place-based communities. Google and the municipal officials who solicited the company's network desired to re-place the city through the deployment of digital infrastructure in ways that echoed smart-city development and place-branding strategies. However, in contrast to the greenfield cities analyzed in chapter 1, these midwestern cities were not planned as smart-city hubs from the outset but were retrofitted with digital connection in the service of urban renewal and urban transformation. Although strategic, the processes of re-placeing occurring in these cities were not void of inhabitant engagement. Instead, the practices of re-placeing initiated by municipal officials and corporate executives existed in tension with certain Kansas City communities' experiences of place, digital infrastructures, and internet access.

Residents who chose not to sign up for Google's network maintained different relationships to the city, which influenced how they interfaced with municipal and corporate re-placing efforts. Conceptions of community, neighborhood, and home and the labor and language of digital inclusion promoted by Google conflicted with smartphone-dependent and low-income populations' realities of urban life and internet access. Although the cost of broadband has been a serious concern for Kansas City residents who lack home connections, other cultural and socioeconomic factors influenced decisions about what sort of internet access to sign up for and whether to sign up for service at all.

In this chapter, I argue that in the case of Google Fiber, as well as interactions with digital infrastructure networks more generally, experiences and attachments to urban place influence how and why people opt in to and opt out of certain digital infrastructures and services. As previous studies have shown, the choreography of lived experience, space, and time plays an important role in understanding infrastructure.[4] But how does a preexisting sense of place in Kansas City contribute to the construction and understanding of a digital network like Google Fiber? How were concepts like community, home, and connection activated in Google's plans and actions? And how did these articulations relate to sense of place within the neighborhoods and populations they were trying to reach? To answer these questions, I monitored the development of Google's Fiber for Communities (Google Fiber) in Kansas City, Kansas, and Kansas City, Missouri, (the first test-bed cities for the project) through press releases and news outlets, reports from government officials, statements from digital inclusion organizations and local technology entrepreneurs, and discussions on social media and blogs from participants and residents of Kansas City since the project was announced in 2010. I've attended cabinet meetings hosted by the mayor's office, digital inclusion and infrastructure meetings led by the public libraries and local activists, and nonprofit computing and digital literacy classes. I've met with start-up collectives and innovation teams and conducted formal and informal interviews with Google employees, Google Fiber volunteers, and digital inclusion activists and residents. Drawing on this material, I show how relationships between digital infrastructure and place have implications for activism, the politics of digital media adoption, and the social life of digital media infrastructure.

Jonathan Donner has argued that focusing on the heterogeneity of experiences "after access" can shed light on the work that still needs to be done in terms of digital development and inclusion.[5] Ultimately, what emerges in this chapter is an "after-access" story—what happened after some people obtained certain types of internet access and others did not as well as after internet access was granted more broadly. The case of Google Fiber is not only a study of top-down efforts to re-place the city in the name of economic development and "progress" but also a study of how experiences of place and differential mobilities govern how populations imagine and interact with socio-technical systems of internet access. By focusing on the linkages between digital infrastructure and placemaking, I highlight assumptions about socio-spatial relations that are designed into urban broadband infrastructures and explore how the ideologies and materialities of these initiatives configure a sense of belonging to the city by hailing some populations while excluding others.

Infrastructure Matters

How processes of exchange such as mobility, communication, and circulation are enabled by technical forms and social structures is as important to consider as the messages being communicated or the services and people moving through these systems. The mundane manifestations of media infrastructure represent a serious set of social decisions, policy goals, industrial exchanges, and, sometimes, contentious imaginations and desires for urban space and urban life. Telephone wires, cable lines, broadcast networks, and wireless systems often coalesce around matrices of negotiations between top-down and bottom-up sensibilities, needs, and visions of the future.

Digital infrastructures include a wide range of technologies and processes, all of which are structures and social arrangements that lie beneath the surface of digital applications and interactions. Infrastructures are defined by their designed and perceived affordances, but they are also given meaning by our experiences and discursive constructions of these affordances, our interactions with the social practices and design decisions that go into implementing social and technological substrates. Our experiences of infrastructure orient and position people within social hierarchies and political and economic structures as well as orchestrate interactions and access to information. As Brian Larkin observes, infrastructures carry with them technological, ideological, and socializing processes. Infrastructures that "enable the movement of other matter" also embody a sense of collective fantasy, desire, and possibility.[6] Consequently, digital media infrastructures serve as sites in which to examine how differently empowered actors understand their place within society through assemblages and interactions with the access and distribution of material and with cultural networks and systems.[7] Several of the essays in Lisa Parks and Nicole Starosielski's anthology *Signal Traffic* bring these relationships to the fore in examples of how Palestinians experience uneven political geographies through everyday mobile phone use or how the policing practices of cybercafé operators in Turkey influence public engagement with internet content and temper the power of national policies.[8] By relying on a definition of infrastructure as technical substrate, cultural practice, and structure that forms or reinscribes social collectives, the sections that follow explore experiences and imaginations of infrastructure that shape and are shaped by relationships to the meaning and value of urban place.

Parks also sees infrastructure as suggestive of "imaginaries" that provide insight into how they are managed and restricted, by and for whom, and how they organize or shape collective experience.[9] In addition to analyzing how infrastructures work and what they do, she suggests that more attention be paid to "infrastructural affects" and structures of feeling generated through routine and repeated material encounters with media infrastructures.[10] These affective encounters are not necessarily or exclusively material but extend to interactions with policy and culture that manifest through debates and practices around implementation models and the imagined use of media networks.

Critical media infrastructure studies reveal materialities and processes of distribution that may augment public attention and involvement in these networks; however, media infrastructures tend to become recognizable during moments of crisis, inaccessibility, reinvention, or maintenance.[11] I am interested in the gray zone between these moments—between "new" and "disrupted." The examples presented in this chapter are located not as glitches in the system but within ongoing critical moments where the inequity of implementation and innovation and the politics of "upgrading" become visible to those who are directly affected by this "improvement" and those who have created it through articulations of what digital connection means for urban space, how it will be implemented, who the network is for, and how various players' harness the middle of the network to exert power over processes of digital placemaking.

Infrastructural Imaginaries and Placemaking

Throughout the early 2000s municipal or citywide Wi-Fi and broadband networks were conceived of as similar to stadiums, convention centers, business, or entertainment districts in that they were ways to attract and retain talent, encourage tourism, and foster economic prosperity. Municipal leaders hoped that new media infrastructure would help promote their cities as competitive locations for economic development. Citywide networks could present an image of a city as forward thinking and tech savvy to target what Richard Florida calls the "creative class." As Sako Musterd and Zoltán Kovács observe, during the early 2000s strategies for place branding shifted from attempting to attract a wide audience to promoting creative environments for urban professionals.[12] City broadband and Wi-Fi networks meshed with this new philosophy and were leveraged as amenities to brand metropolitan areas as not only "hip" or "cool" but as centers of creative production and experimentation that encouraged civic engagement as well as local innovation. Public safety, government efficiency and response, and the provision of internet access as a public utility were recognized as factors promoted by a robust, affordable network infrastructure.[13]

Discourses surrounding Wi-Fi and municipal networks circulate from a variety of sources that legitimize municipal governments' drive toward metropolitan digital network implementation. As researcher and urban planner, Anthony Townsend declares, "Places that have it [Wi-Fi] will become special."[14] Popular and industry press, technology and innovation consultants, and scholarly literature reinforce the claim that municipal networks are necessary for urban and economic development, that hosting a widespread wireless network will magnify a city's value.[15] Recognized broadband industry analyst and community broadband advocate Craig Settles continually advises urban and rural communities to fund and build local broadband infrastructure, claiming that "superfast broadband boosts local economies, transforms education, improves healthcare delivery and increases local government efficiency."[16]

In addition to these discursive constructions, the benefits of municipal networks are most often framed as aiding both the affluent and the disadvantaged and providing additional opportunities for internet connection outside the home as well as public connectivity for residents who can't afford at-home connections. Gwen Shaffer finds that proponents of municipal Wi-Fi emphasize economic and social benefits from Wi-Fi implementation and frame these initiatives as augmenting quality of life for urban residents, tourists, and business owners while alleviating digital divides.[17] François Bar and Namkee Park outline similar motives for municipal involvement with internet service provision: connect city employees and services, entice businesses to locate downtown, render convention centers and other institutions more desirable and up to date, and ameliorate access divides.[18]

According to some reports, more than four hundred cities in the United States announced the prospect of building and funding municipal broadband and Wi-Fi services in their communities in the early 2000s.[19] In many cases stakeholders in municipal network deployment framed initiatives in terms of showing a commitment and investment in local communities as well as an investment in the future of a city as a whole. "Broadband optimism," or enthusiastic perspectives about the benefits and transformative powers of broadband, have radiated within municipal government circles espousing the idea that Wi-Fi can revitalize cities as better places to live, play, work, and do business while encouraging democracy and local empowerment.[20] By promoting the "public good" through the betterment of government services, access to information for richer educational and cultural experiences, and democratization of internet access, cities courting municipal Wi-Fi and broadband systems implied that urban centers would be transformed into more equitable, innovative, prosperous hubs of urban life. The promises of municipal Wi-Fi were both ambitious and grand, offering a "coming revolution that would transform sleepy old towns and cities into modern metropolises."[21]

Implementers and proponents of municipal digital infrastructure initiatives cultivate a particular sense of place for their cities, one that reframes the meaning of the city for internal as well as external audiences. Through mission statements, interviews, press releases, and public conversations, organizations involved in the discursive and tangible construction of municipal digital infrastructure participate in re-placeing the city. Often the city is framed as a site in need of renewal or revitalization at the same time that it is referred to as groundbreaking and as a model for how urban digital innovation works. For example, while government officials legitimized the need for Wireless Philadelphia, one of the most expansive urban Wi-Fi projects proposed in the early 2000s, through tropes of government inefficiency, need for increased government responsiveness, service provision, and public safety, it was also stated that "with the build out of this network the City of Philadelphia will be a national model for how to operate and economically leverage a broadband network for the benefit of its citizens."[22]

The language and purpose of digital inclusion and amelioration of the "digital divide" have been integral to discussions of urban transformation and re-placeing the city through Wi-Fi and broadband efforts. In order to justify, and in some cases "sell," the idea of municipal broadband to stakeholders, advocates publicly recognize inequities in terms of internet access, types of internet connectivity, and prohibitive costs of home internet and broadband connection. Although digital inclusion is a significant concern in cities with municipal Wi-Fi and broadband initiatives, researchers have suggested that highlighting digital divides was a calculated move on the part of governments and internet companies to justify why cities should play a role in internet service provision.[23] Municipal governments suggested that they were providing a civil service to residents by making internet access more equitable and affordable for those who had never been online and/or could not afford consistent internet access at home.

Couched in this idea was the chance for more robust civic engagement through economic development and potential profit-generation. Municipally sanctioned internet infrastructure was not a welfare service but a neoliberal enterprise that laid the groundwork for large-scale innovation and could encourage individuals to become entrepreneurs or at least more economically productive members of society. A stable, consistent, affordable internet connection could improve "quality of life" for those who fell on the wrong side of digital divides as well as provide more convenient services to those who were already networked. For those already connected, internet use was reimagined outside the home in spaces such as on the street, in coffee shops, in hotel lobbies, at convention centers and museums, during networking events, and in public spaces more generally. Ironically, these were the spaces where people without at-home connection might already congregate to access free Wi-Fi.

Scholars and critics have noted that many of these transformative, community-focused endeavors didn't play out as intended or were never implemented at all.[24] Municipal governments and network implementers claimed that digital infrastructure and the services it provided would engage citizens and increase local civic engagement and efficacy. However, several digital infrastructure plans that were orchestrated and approved by municipal officials didn't serve the needs and desires of local communities. Andrea H. Tapia and Julio Angel Ortiz suggest that not only did these municipal digital infrastructure projects fail, they also encouraged mistrust and damaged relationships between local governments and citizens.[25] Concurrent with the rise and fall of municipal, public-private broadband initiatives throughout the 2000s were the persistence of alternative, grassroots models of municipal wireless and broadband networks. Several of these initiatives emerged from discontented or underserved communities that recognized internet access as a necessary utility within their cities and towns.

The imaginations inscribed in municipal networks of the early 2000s represent the unique power of re-placeing efforts: the power of networked technology to promote place, the power to select and implement particular visions of technology into urban space, and the power that exists both at the ends and in the middle of the network—control over innovation, representation, infrastructure, and use. Mid-2000s municipal broadband efforts share several common characteristics in terms of placemaking efforts and implementation models with newer initiatives such as Google Fiber for Communities. Both sets of projects involved some form of public-private partnerships and plans to connect expansive urban areas anchored in cities with racially and socioeconomically diverse, geographically segregated populations in strong need of digital inclusion efforts. However, the particularities of place and the populations and governments that inhabit these places differ and illustrate the nearsightedness of a one-size-fits-all model of municipal wireless connection. As Laura Forlano recognizes, one model of Wi-Fi implementation cannot necessarily be transplanted onto another location.[26] Relatedly, Alison Powell and Leslie Regan Shade observe that grassroots internet infrastructures often echo or work in conjunction with other preceding community networks or networking projects.[27]

Place-based conditions shape the ways in which digital media infrastructures are implemented and used. In Kansas City and elsewhere, people consciously opt in to, or are more willing to adopt, services that mesh with their place-based identities and attachments and their perceptions of and interactions with place. The following case study of Google Fiber in Kansas City explores how disparate understandings of community, mobility, the meaning of neighborhood, and experiences of home (as they intersect with more traditional markers of digital divides such as socioeconomic status, education levels, and computer literacy) shape the meaning of particular media infrastructures and implementation models as well as how hierarchies of access to these infrastructures shape relationships to place. Although processes of infrastructure implementation are often overlooked as significant moments where a sense of place is produced, different implementation models and types of networked connection reproduce physical and social embeddedness within place. Network providers and residents construct and rely on their experiences and emotional attachments to place in their decisions about implementation, discursive constructions of infrastructure initiatives, and infrastructure use and non-use.

The Promise of Digital Transformation

In February 2010 Google announced that the company would build an experimental one-gigabit-per-second (gbps) fiber-optic network in a select number of US cities. The endeavor was dubbed Google Fiber for Communities and promised to provide residents and businesses with download and upload speeds up to one hundred times faster than any preexisting commercial service available in the United States. Cities interested in acquiring this high-speed network had approximately one month to fill out forms and organize campaigns to present a desire and need for Google Fiber services. The typically banal process of selecting sites for infrastructure implementation became an interactive spectacle. Participating cities created Facebook pages and YouTube videos, started petitions, and staged elaborate stunts to attract Google's attention. The mayor of Topeka, Kansas, officially changed the city's name to "Google, Kansas," for the duration of the month. The mayor of Duluth, Minnesota, swam in the bitter-cold waters of Lake Superior in the middle of winter, and not to be outdone, the mayor of Sarasota, Florida, swam with sharks. Madison, Wisconsin, eateries started serving Google Fiber–flavored ice cream and pizzas called "the Fibertron." Grassroots efforts organized by residents made national news as well. Grand Rapids, Michigan, staged a rally; Columbia, Missouri, orchestrated a flash mob; Highlands Ranch, Colorado, created a human "We Love Google" sign. By the end of the competition for Google services, the company had received more than one thousand requests from communities across the United States and nearly 200,000 more from individuals.[28] In March 2011 Kansas City, Kansas, was selected as the winner of the competition. In May 2011 the winning city was expanded to include the adjacent city of Kansas City, Missouri, as well.

Throughout the competition and selection process, Google promised urban transformations that would affect the economic, political, and social lives of cities. This "different kind of internet" could ameliorate digital divides, connect Kansas City schools, and make public services more efficient while jumpstarting technology innovation and start-ups, encouraging economic development, and fostering revitalization in underdeveloped urban areas. Eventually local entrepreneurs would collaborate with Google to "build products that [would] help improve our users' lives."[29] In videos released on YouTube, Google executives employed the construction of the railroads in the 1800s as a metaphor for the transformative growth that Google Fiber would provide in Kansas City.[30]

A few years after KCMO and Google began installing and activating the fiber network, Kansas City officials discursively re-placed Kansas City as a "smart city." The city composed a "digital roadmap,"[31] hired a chief information officer, convened task forces and advisory boards on digital media adoption, and selected a mayor's special cabinet on innovation. The mayor's office sponsored events in conjunction with start-ups in which tech entrepreneurs could discuss smart-city initiatives. On the city's official website, the municipality claimed that Kansas City was well on its way to "evolving into a Smart City," which it defined as a city that "uses communication networks, wireless sensor technology and intelligent data management to make decisions in real time about infrastructure needs and service delivery. 'A smart city is a dynamic city that makes living in a dense urban environment more civil and rewarding.'" This digitally networked city would also "improve the way people experience Kansas City" and "enhance the citizen experience" in terms of the efficiency of city services—in particular, traffic navigation and mobility.[32]

In 2015 the city solidified partnerships with commercial entities that would provide and manage key smart-city technologies: Smart + Connected Communities (Cisco), Wi-Fi (Sprint), lighting and video sensors (Sensity), traffic flows (Rhythm Engineering), digital kiosk implementation (City Post), and a "Living Lab" (Think Big).[33] During the first weeks of March 2016, immediately preceding the start of the NCAA Big 12 Tournament, which would bring thousands of visitors to Kansas City, two digital kiosks were installed along the recently operational streetcar route outside the Sprint Center, where the first basketball games would be held. The smart kiosks were introduced at one of the few public meetings to discuss smart-city and fiber-optic plans. Event participants immediately started tweeting to quote Kansas City's new CIO and the event speakers who introduced the benefits of this hardware, which would attract businesses to downtown Kansas City. How, exactly, was unclear, but attendees seemed convinced and enthusiastic about the kiosks' purpose and use.

Google Fiber and Kansas City made concerted efforts to frame broadband and smart-city initiatives as open and enriching for all residents and visitors. However, conversations and decisions about KCMO as a "smart city"—as well as meetings where input on what enhanced citizen experience and technology use would look and feel like—remained exclusive. Smart-city meet-ups and invitations for public input were geared toward those who were already connected to the internet and who were already incorporated into the burgeoning tech industry scene. Meet-ups and requests for public input were organized via Twitter and Facebook and/or were conducted via online survey or questionnaire.

Meetings hosted by the Office of Innovation—with promotional taglines like "Urban Momentum: Where Conversation Meets Innovation"—were announced via social media or email with no more than a week's or a few days' advance notice. These events were held at cocktail or craft beer bars (Ruins Pub, Double Shift Brewing, Border Brewing Company) and boutique coffee shops (Thou Mayest) and were followed by hors d'oeuvres in gentrified areas or arts districts. The conversations that occurred in these spaces between digerati, start-up and incubator directors, and regulars at smart-city, innovation, tech industry, and cabinet meetings were sometimes live tweeted, but the information presented at these events was rarely distributed otherwise. All photos and tweets that documented these conversations resembled public relations hype and self-promotion, with pictures of smiling or intrigued faces of attendees networking and drinking locally produced beer or tweets celebrating the "great conversations" happening at these events, without actually reporting the content of the discussions. The hours of smart-city and Google Fiber meetings and similar events prohibited certain members of the community from attending. Although open to the public, these informal meetings tended to start at 4:00 p.m. (although later events started at 5:00 p.m.) and were located far from lower-income neighborhoods.[34]

Exclusive, youthful, hip events that resembled "catching up" and socializing with libations in hand, rather than participatory planning and town hall meetings, were characteristic of public information sessions about smart-city and digital infrastructure developments. These events felt similar to the "cybersuds" and networking events that had taken place during the dot-com boom in New York City and San Francisco, where tech insiders and those hoping to break into the tech industry would go to talk shop, self-promote, and network.[35] After attending a few of these events, I was greeted by the same faces and noticed that everyone seemed to know each other a priori and that attendees used these informal gatherings as a chance to touch base about other related projects or upcoming events.

Although some of these events focused on Google Fiber's role in digital inclusion or smart cities, the people who could benefit most from these efforts were not included. After the first Urban Momentum meet-up, a few Kansas City residents of color and those outside the tech scene tweeted messages indicating that they had not known about the gathering and information session but would have liked to attend. Members of the Kansas City community requested to be notified of future events, and some lamented that they were not able to attend due to work schedules. Although these tweets and comments were liked or bookmarked by some participants and organizers, they generally went unanswered. In some cases, concerned residents pointed out the lack of people of color in photos from the Urban Momentum meet-ups. Cities with similar digital inclusion concerns and efforts toward digital innovation such as Detroit have hosted "DiscoTechs" or learning events where community members come together to discuss, discover, and learn more about "the impact and possibilities of technology within our communities."[36] Kansas City, however, chose to embrace fiber-network adoption and smart-city planning initiatives as economic development performed by "experts" rather than as an opportunity for civic engagement and community input.

The exclusiveness of these events echoed other outcomes of Google Fiber implementation. Similar to the interurban competition to win Google's network, Google adopted a participatory implementation model that encouraged residents to take an active role in soliciting Google's infrastructure in their neighborhood. The company divided KCK and KCMO into "fiberhoods" based on neighborhood delineations and zoning boundaries. To qualify for Google Fiber, fiberhoods had to preregister at least 5 percent of their residents with a ten-dollar registration fee within six weeks.[37] The first fiberhoods to sign up for Google Fiber had their $300 installation fee waived. Neighborhoods who signed up after the early-bird registration were required to pay a one-time, flat fee of $300 and received low-cost, high-speed internet service.

The fiberhood registration process collapsed "neighborhood" with "community" and framed the act of signing up as something that would not only benefit a single household but would benefit friends, family and Kansas City as a whole. Essentially, signing up for Google's services was framed as akin to doing a public good or community service. As an executive in a Google Fiber promotional video explained, "When you participate in the rally, not only are you bringing Fiber to your home, you're bringing Fiber to Kansas Citians that you care about."[38] Google monitored the progress of fiberhood preregistration via a color-coded map on its website. If a neighborhood was blanketed in green, then residents would be able to sign up for Google services. Yellow signified that the preregistration goal had not yet been achieved.

Levels of neighborhood involvement and investment varied. Several neighborhoods took to the call for participation with zeal. These neighborhoods' residents, composed of early adopters, technology enthusiasts, and self-proclaimed Google fans, worked alongside Google employees and volunteers to canvas their neighborhoods with yard signs emblazoned with Google's name and an image of a rabbit running with the wind at its back. These volunteers held information sessions and traveled door to door to recruit households to preregister. Google employees and volunteers also drove through neighborhoods with ice cream trucks, handing out Google-branded local gourmet ice cream and other treats for free. The company hired temporary employees through local third-party event-hosting companies to stage demos and hold happy hours, sandboxes, and information sessions at their Fiber Space in downtown KCMO or at colleges and neighborhood community centers, libraries, restaurants, block parties, and local event spaces.[39]

These events usually included large, interactive displays where attendees could interact with perky, energetic, and well-trained millennials showcasing Google networks and services such as Google TV. Employees guided potential subscribers through activities that allowed them to experience or see visualizations and stats about fiber upload and download speeds. The largest display was always a desk or platform where residents could sign up for Google Fiber and track their neighborhood stats to see whether they would reach their fiberhood quotas. Happy hours offered free food, beer and wine, coffee, and local music while daytime events geared toward families with children might offer "sweets, snacks, and face painting fun with the Fiber team."[40] Participants were required to provide their full name, home address, and email address and were invited to take free Google Fiber gear such as reusable water bottles and Google Fiber yard signs as souvenirs. In addition to information sessions and workshops, Google Fiber maintained a presence at major KCK and KCMO locations and community events to inform and register residents: Google Fiber lounges at the finish lines of organized runs (the Hospital Hill Run); a tent at the Crossroads Summer Block party; and presence at the Kansas City Pride Fest,[41] farmers markets, zoos, local festivals, fairs, parades, and holiday events. The Google Fiber events page read like a community events calendar. The company not only made a concerted effort to engage potential subscribers in places where they were already gathering as members of the larger Kansas City community, but Google also framed itself as part of this local community. The company's emphasis on the hyperlocal in its promotional materials and implementation model was striking. Employees and representatives regularly called upon the image, rhetoric, and role of Kansas City as a place with a certain culture, presence, and future in its plans and promotion of Google Fiber.

When I spoke to Google representatives involved in the Kansas City implementation process, they said that this participatory, community-based model was not just a gimmick. Google aimed to include people on the neighborhood level so that residents would feel a sense of ownership and control over the network. The participatory implementation model was intended to make people feel as if they were building the network themselves in cooperation with Google, that they were contributing to its growth and were part of the decision-making and implementation process as "community stakeholders." In addition, Google desired to welcome new people to the world of internet connectivity. As one representative mentioned, when the participatory model was introduced, Google Fiber organizers thought that providing accessible and affordable internet services was imperative. Access and affordability were initially regarded as the main barriers to internet adoption among lower-income households and households that had never been connected to home broadband services. But as many Google employees noted, by 2015 their "sense of that [was] changing." One of the reasons for this reinterpretation was based on the reactions of Kansas City residents during Google Fiber's initial implementation phase. The patterns of opting in to and opting out of high-speed infrastructure reveal that Google Fiber did not erase preexisting digital divides but actually rendered these divisions more visible.

Fiber for . . . Whom?

Although the place of Kansas City was often incorporated into Google campaigns in terms of the city's bright new digital future, its current sense of place was rarely referenced. While short quips about barbeque and jazz appeared in promotional videos announcing Google Fiber's arrival, images of the city and its residents were omitted from advertising campaigns. The specificity of Kansas City as an urban place was flattened along with any recognition of the city's history of racial segregation and redlining in inner-city neighborhoods. When the initial maps of the fiberhoods were released, the "before" and "after" Google Fiber images looked startlingly familiar to Kansas City locals. After the September 9 deadline, the maps on the Google Fiber website illustrated that not all Kansas City fiberhoods had met their goals. A closer investigation of the maps showed that historically wealthy and predominantly Caucasian neighborhoods met their preregistration targets while lower-income, predominantly African American neighborhoods did not. The divisions depicted on these maps echoed previous divides so exactly that even Troost Avenue in KCMO—colloquially referred to as the "Troost Wall," which has served as an economic and racial dividing line for decades—separated the western, green sections from the eastern, yellow sections, those who would receive fiber-optic cable (green) from those who would not (yellow).

Journalists' and citizens' investigations began to reveal that many of the households that did not participate in the preregistration process were also those that had never had internet access. Despite the fact that community groups specifically targeted these underserved households and disadvantaged neighborhoods, their participation rates were low. After receiving these results, community groups and Google employees traveled door to door or gathered at community centers and neighborhood events to help register residents, using gift cards so that the local school or community center could be connected by Google with no cost to residents through the Community Connections Program.[42] Neighborhood organizations and public libraries hosted "Get Us a Gig" initiatives where prepaid credit cards were handed out to residents to help them pay their registration fees and sign up for service. Some sign-up events were stationed outside stores that sold prepaid charge cards so that people with cash could stop by the store and buy a card in order to sign up. Google also started waiving or subsidizing construction fees for apartment buildings and attempted to lift barriers so that landlords could wire buildings.

Volunteers and Google employees working at these sign-up and registration events noted that it was "different" and "more difficult" to do

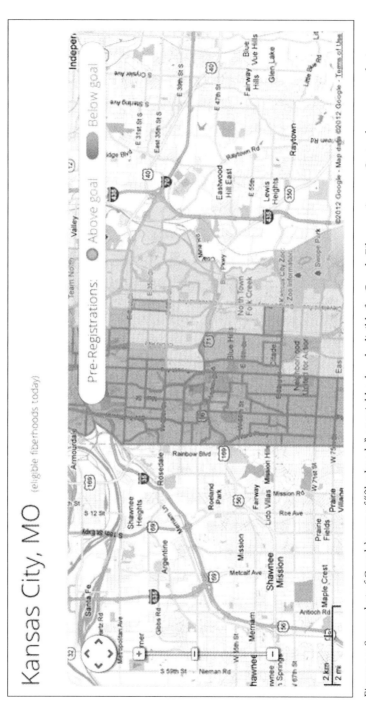

Figure 2.1: Screenshot of Google's map of "fiberhoods," or neighborhoods eligible for Google Fiber services, on September 13, 2012, during the initial preregistration stage. Screenshot by author from https://fiber.google.com/cities/kansascity/. Source: Google.

their job in KCK and inner-city neighborhoods in KCMO. The digital inclusion activists and grassroots organizers I spoke with found the emphasis on network speed in low-income communities to be a curious tactic. They questioned why employees emphasized network speed when close to 20 percent of the city's population did not have *any* internet connection at all. After the initial sign-up phase, employees explained to me how they adjusted "the pitch" and information that they provided about Google Fiber for different audiences. At happy hour events employees tended to emphasize speed as a main selling point and showcased Google Fiber infrastructure, gear, and services as emerging, innovative technologies. Google sign-up recruiters explained that "the speed argument" didn't resonate with populations that didn't already have internet access. Instead, employees emphasized the relevance and necessity of the internet for improving quality of life and opportunities for social, educational, and economic engagement. While Google Fiber representatives tried to express high-speed network connection as meaningful in terms of economic and social participation, the question of relevance left some community activists circumspect regarding Google Fiber in Kansas City: Fiber for "communities"? Really? Whose communities? How so?

Sense of Place, Infrastructure Adoption, and Non-use

Although studies of digital media platforms and practices tend to focus on people who participate in these services and technologies, research into non-use, opting out, media refusal, and strategies of disconnection have proliferated.[43] These studies have found that people maintain various understandings of the significance and purpose of the internet and digital connection in their daily lives and that many factors (not solely socioeconomic statuses, education levels, and demographic or geographic characteristics) contribute to their motivations to join, leave, or negotiate their levels and types of digital connection.

The case study of Google Fiber in Kansas City occupies a space in between media refusal (which Laura Portwood-Stacer describes as "conspicuous non-consumption") and digital access issues as they've been discussed in terms of "digital divides".[44] This is especially the case from the perspective of Kansas City residents who were being asked, recruited, and courted to sign up for an experimental fiber-optic network but chose not to subscribe or those who preregistered but chose not to activate the service. Google employees and internet activists in Kansas City observed that many people who already had internet service provision through another carrier tended to register for Google Fiber in order to qualify their fiberhoods or because they were interested. Many of these registrants were undecided about whether to change carriers and never paid the construction fee or never scheduled installation.[45]

In particular, the case of Google Fiber in Kansas City is akin to the refusal to take part in a digital infrastructure model that's perceived as exclusive or "not for us." These same populations were consciously adopting, or at least considering, digital infrastructure services that more directly meshed with their place-based identities and experiences. The remainder of this chapter identifies and analyzes how preexisting sense of place became linked to digital "infrastructural affect" for lower-income populations who opted out of Google Fiber in Kansas City.

"Relevance" and Experience of Place

After the statistics from the first round of sign-ups were reported, I spoke with a few Google employees about the outcomes. Google employees were concerned about the lack of registration within certain neighborhoods and were trying to understand some of the variables that accounted for the lack of fiberhoods on the eastern side of Kansas City. As one employee explained to me, "Six weeks is tough." The representative noted that the six-week span that Google had allotted for fiberhood registration was too short; there was too much to address and complete in six weeks. After surveying residents, a variety of reasons why people didn't register for Google services emerged, but the factor that stuck with Google employees, the Kansas City mayor's office, and digital inclusion activists was "relevance."

In 2012 Google and the Mayor's Bi-State Innovation Team presented a study about internet access and internet use that they had conducted with 3,219 residents in Kansas City. The main finding presented from the study was that "a lot of people in KC don't get online, even though they believe that internet connectivity is generally important to their livelihoods."[46] By "a lot of people," the research team meant even more than the national average. The study found that 25 percent of Kansas City residents surveyed did not have broadband access at home and that 17 percent claimed that they didn't use the internet at all.[47] In a survey conducted by the Kansas City Public School System, it was reported that 70 percent of students enrolled in public schools did not have internet access at home. Although schools sometimes provided tablets for student use, internet access was required to complete homework and assignments through online learning software.

Specifically, Kansas City residents noted that not using the internet was a major disadvantage for job hunting, accessing health-related information, and learning new information and skills. The 17 percent of residents who didn't use the internet on a daily basis were senior citizens, African Americans, people who had obtained a high school education or less, and those who earned less than $25,000 per year. The top two reasons for internet non-use coincided with findings from a previous Pew Research Center survey on adults nationwide: people either were not interested or didn't perceive the internet as being something they wanted or needed. In the Pew study, the researchers summarized interest and other issues, such as being "too busy" and regarding the internet as "a waste of time," as issues of "relevance." The Kansas City study did the same.[48] As one Google employee explained to me a few weeks after the survey was completed, a six-week sign-up period wasn't long enough to convince people that Google Fiber and high-speed internet were relevant to their lives.

Over the course of four years, I met many people who had qualms or concerns about signing up for Google Fiber. Some of these people ultimately registered for service, but many remained unsubscribed. Many residents I spoke with who already had at-home broadband service didn't want to bother switching service providers or were content with their service provision. Some people were dissuaded by the lengthy installation process and the time between registration and installation. Others were unsure of how switching to Google Fiber would improve their internet service since they didn't think that their internet activities required a lot of bandwidth or faster speeds.

However, in conversations with people who lived on the "yellow" side of the Kansas City map and who had never had a home broadband connection, it became evident that Google Fiber was perceived as a service that didn't imagine them as potential users in realistic and meaningful ways. This perspective, held by many residents in neighborhoods east of Troost Avenue, regarded Google Fiber as a service that would further network people and places that were already served and valued and were already catered to within the sectors that Google Fiber was intended to augment: education, government services, public safety, economic development, and innovation. Even before the green-and-yellow maps were published, many residents already felt that Google Fiber's presence and the fiberhood model would exacerbate existing place-based inequalities. These individuals and families decided that becoming a fiberhood was not a goal aimed at *their* neighborhood, community, or household. Although cost and affordability were definitely a concern for these residents, there was also the issue of "relevance" and how the internet mattered within their lived experiences as minority, economically disadvantaged populations in Kansas City.

Relevance was interpreted by public officials, Google employees, and digital inclusion activists to mean that people did not know what the internet could do for them or why they needed it. But in speaking with residents who attended computer classes at Connecting for Good (a local nonprofit that provides digital literacy classes and computers to low-income communities) who had signed up for alternative internet services from other providers and attended digital inclusion meetings at the public library, I found out that there was immensely more to this term. Community organizers insisted that resource-poor and economically disadvantaged people *did* understand the advantages of internet access. However, after budgeting to pay for rent, clothes, food, and utilities and coming up short each month, the internet looked a lot less "relevant." Aside from cost, there were other issues that emerged from conflicting imaginations of infrastructure upgrade and assumptions about internet use. When and how an internet connection becomes meaningful in daily life, the meaning of speed, and the (un)importance of at-home connection were all frameworks that shaped feelings of relevance for residents.

While I was sitting at a table with low-income residents, community and neighborhood organizers, and social service representatives, someone voiced an opinion that everyone immediately and emphatically agreed with. With a mix of emphasis and dismay, the activist and resident said, "We've been forced into online." She explained how social security, healthcare, job applications, exams and certifications, homework, and almost any other service she could think of were most "easily" accessible online and that communities were being "forced online whether they like it or not." Her comment framed the relationship between lower-income communities and digital technology as outsiders and bystanders. "Online" was something that happened to them, not something that they made happen, a situation that an outside authority had decided upon and imposed.

Relevance was not a feeling these residents cultivated for themselves; instead internet connection became meaningful to these users when they interfaced with institutions that demanded a certain type of internet use. People who relied on mobile and public Wi-Fi felt the relevance of the internet most pointedly in their interactions with institutional infrastructures. Although many residents paid for or regularly used the internet through mobile phones, they noted how job applications and government forms were not mobile friendly. These Kansas City residents were not faced with the decision of whether to use the internet or not; they knew that they had to. Instead, they dealt with the inability to join this digital revolution at the same level as other local communities but without the same resources, training, and tools. They felt pressured to participate in a system and services that didn't cater to them and didn't account for their infrastructural experiences or after-access connections in their transition to "online only." The fact that the city was upgrading digital infrastructure speeds and capacities was not read as an effort that would improve their lives but as one that reinscribed their marginalized status as internet users. When mobile-only Kansas Citians spoke about the lack of relevance of high-speed internet, they referenced their struggles to reconcile something that they knew was simultaneously incredibly important and seemingly unavailable to them. For many residents, the statistic about relevance that was repeatedly outlined in digital inclusion meetings and reports reflected a larger idea that an at-home, high-speed internet connection was the target internet connection for everyone, the relevant connection.

As residents who had never had internet access at home explained to me, the internet was still regarded as a luxury within their communities—because it was. The relevance issue was deeply linked

to understandings of the internet through the lens of economic avail-
ability and the workarounds or tactics developed to access the internet
outside of at-home subscription services. Paying for internet access
didn't make sense in economic terms, so much so that it changed the
terms of the debate and the perception of importance in one's daily life.
As Anita Dixon, vice president of the Mutual Musicians Foundation (a
storied institution on the east side of Troost Avenue), observed, there
was initial excitement around the prospect of the internet connection
that Google promised. However, once Google released its participatory
model for implementation and explained both the financial criteria as
well as the model for networking people based on collective interest
and ability to pay, excitement drastically waned. She explained, "We
knew that whoever sat at the table and said 'We're going to put the
little rabbit [Google Fiber logo] in front of your face and everything,
and everybody's gonna love it, and the billboards are going to be all in
the 'hood.' And after we got the message, *we got the message*. 'This is
not for you.'"[49]

In addition to affordability, other parameters contribute to internet
adoption. Certain environmental factors have been identified as being
correlated to, or at least variables in, low broadband adoption rates: living in public housing or in areas with vacant land or unoccupied buildings, lack of commercial corridors or business-improvement districts, or
low rates of owner-occupied housing. Architectural design and terrain
might also influence infrastructure deployment models, such as building height, altitude, and the presence of natural barriers such as trees
or mountains. Relevance can also be interpreted through environmental and geographic situations and experiences. Internet users and non-
users draw on the particularities of place and place-based experiences
to help them evaluate the relevance of internet technologies and services
in their everyday lives. For example, when I started attending some of
the classes and forums where people came together to learn about and
use computers and digital networks, sometimes for the first time, I was
struck by how environmental factors, place-based identities, and mobility became major influences in evaluating internet service provision.
Which networks underserved communities chose to subscribe to, or
why they might not subscribe at all, was shaped by how they navigated
and negotiated socio-spatial geographies within the city.

Sense of Place and Infrastructure Decisions

The Irrelevance of High Speed

On a sunny Friday morning I stood outside Reconciliation Services on Troost Avenue with seven students who were waiting for the building to be unlocked for the regularly scheduled Digital Life Skills class offered by the nonprofit Connecting for Good. The building was located directly adjacent to two bus stops and was surrounded by other social welfare and charitable organizations. We entered the open, windowed space, and the instructor, an African American woman in her early thirties, unlocked a closet and a cabinet and set up several laptops and one desktop computer to be used for class. Two other Connecting for Good members arrived and organized a station to sell low-cost routers and refurbished laptops and desktops to people who qualified. A few previous Digital Life Skills class participants stopped by to pick up their computers in addition to a woman with her child who was interested in an internet router.

The instructor chatted with regular attendees and introduced herself to the new students (half the class was composed of new students). She asked the returning students to turn on their computers and log on. She assured all students—there were now approximately ten of them seated in the lobby of the service center at tables that resembled lab benches—that she would guide them through whatever skills they wanted to learn. One man, already seated at a desk in the center of the room with a tablet, utilized the free internet connection while his companion took a seat with the rest of the class. The instructor walked from student to student, asking what they wanted to learn that day. Some returning students requested to work on typing or attaching files to emails, one hoped to become more familiar with Microsoft Office programs, and another person wanted to do some tutorials and take a test based on what she learned during the last class.[50] While the class was in session, several new students arrived and requested a variety of instructions: how to throw something away; how to fill out online job applications and upload a résumé to online job sites; how to attach documents and photos. At one corner of a table, the instructor taught a middle-aged woman about fonts, word processing, size and style options, highlighting, and style changes. At another table, the instructor showed an older gentleman how to do a Google search. Students seemed to make progress during their hours in class. A middle-aged man took a quiz on the skills he had acquired during the previous class, received an 80 percent, and wanted to high-five. A man who had begun the class by writing down search results from Google without following the search result links to the indicated websites began to look at the information on the web pages retrieved by his queries.[51]

The new students filled out their intake forms that included questions about demographic information, computer literacy, habits, access, and what skills they were interested in learning. The instructor quizzed them before they could touch a keyboard. What do you know about computers? What are some examples of endings to website addresses? There's dot-gov; what else is there? What can you attach to the computer (meaning hardware attachments like VGA adapters, USB devices, speakers, a mouse, a CD player, etc.)? Where are the computer ports? What gets plugged into computer ports? Which ones? She explained how ads on popular websites led to other websites, she warned them about scams and spam, and she told them that they should not click on everything they saw on screen because some sites were unsafe. The instructor explained that sites ending in dot-gov and dot-edu had padlocks in the URL window, which meant that it was OK to enter personal information. She reminded them that some sites wanted to steal information and passwords. She urged them to be careful and make sure to be safe online.

Watching students sit down in front of the refurbished laptops and desktops revealed the tentativeness with which they approached the computers and the fragility with which they handled them and tapped at the keys. Their actions suggested that they had minimal experience spending time with such consoles. In some cases, students arrived overwhelmed by the idea of using a computer and the internet. Some students felt that there was already too much information and too many skills they had not acquired and that they didn't know where to start. Several students explained that they didn't always view the broadband connection and computer consoles with wide-eyed looks of opportunity. Instead, their actions were sometimes hesitant, their faces filled with visible trepidation, exasperation, and the knowledge that not everyone in Kansas City convened with the internet in the same way. Although many of the students carried and used cell phones or smartphones with comfort and ease, the computer was an unfamiliar device and an object that produced anxiety and frustration in some instances. In all cases, the instructor focused on teaching basics rather than offering quick fixes and provided students with time, support, and access to tinker with computers with free, stable internet connections. Some students became frustrated with the class because there was something specific they wanted to know, such as how to open a Gmail account, and the instructor tried to teach them more than that: how email worked, how to attach a document, speed and storage rates, and what exactly a gigabit was.

Interestingly, a minimal amount of people used their time at the computers to surf the web or search for information online. Instead, their interactions with the web were via email (setting up accounts, learning to attach files, sending photos, downloading attachments) and online tutorials or quizzes about skills they'd acquired in Microsoft Word, general computer knowledge, or handling files on- and offline.[52] Two women came to class one day wanting to learn about uploading résumés and searching for jobs online. After a while, one of the students became frustrated and turned to her phone. She mentioned to her friend that she could do a lot of the tasks, such as searching for jobs, on her phone without having to worry about attachments. When the instructor came back around, the student abandoned her attempts to learn the web-based components of job applications and asked for Microsoft Word training instead. Having grown accustomed to the affordances of mobile phones and their apps, students were often reluctant to understand windowed interfaces and file attachments. Later, a low-income resident and educator explained to me that this behavior exemplified a common feeling among people who lacked digital literacy skills. In his observations, he'd seen a generation that was used to getting things done quickly through the digital technologies they used daily: smartphones, ATMs, money wiring. He noted that when these same people were seated at a desktop or laptop computer, they would peck on the keyboard, which meant it took them forever to get anything done. In his experience as an instructor, this was often how digital media and internet connection mapped onto "real life": it was discouraging.

In this storefront turned computer lab serving low-income populations in the heart of a historically African American neighborhood,

Google Fiber logos and service provision were nowhere to be found. Across both the instruction and computer lab spaces, there were no Google Fiber advertisements or promotional materials. There was no mention of Google Fiber, nor was the company's presence felt inside or in the public spaces outside the computer centers or classes. When I asked some of the instructors at the computer classes whether their learning space was connected to Google Fiber, they often said that they were not sure, that they didn't think so, and that they thought they were connected to "the free network" or "freedom network" (referring to the Kansas City Free Network provided by the Free Network Foundation).

Related to economics, access, and education levels, what became evident from attending these classes and talking to students and instructors was that media and digital literacy were key components in choosing not to adopt Google Fiber and to the issue of internet relevance more broadly. While Google, the mayor's office, and members of the Kansas City tech scene described Google Fiber services and infrastructure as transformational in terms of speed, type of connection, and augmentation of the types of services, technologies, and businesses that could be offered and built, local nonprofit organizations like Connecting for Good, the Free Network Foundation, and the W. E. B. Dubois Learning Center understood internet connection as transformational in other ways. Technology and internet connection and knowledge of how to use these digital devices were transformational because they were empowering; they enabled people to help themselves, their families, and their communities. Instead of upgrading to faster speeds, learning about and using digital infrastructure could empower a person to, as one Digital Life Skills student explained to me, "help the people you help every day."

The lack of media and digital literacy in terms of computer hardware, software, online services, and functionality hindered students' ability to embrace or engage with computers in wholly enthusiastic ways. Asking these students to rally around the imminent need for high-speed internet was so antithetical to and abstracted from their everyday experiences of digital technology that it was irrelevant. To offer someone "a different kind of Internet" that was one hundred times faster, aggregated "all your favorite content in one place," and "brings together your devices and gives you the freedom to search, record, and save shows without worry"[53] was to recognize the experience of those who already enjoyed privileged relationships to digital technology, not to mention leisure time, home media use, and economic resources.[53]

As students sat in the lobby of this social services center—situated between a church and "the place that helps with your lights" and surrounded by section 8 housing—or in a former gentleman's club turned computer lab learning what a USB port was, it was difficult to meaningfully connect the needs of these students with the capacities of Google's high-speed networks, however affordable they were. It was not that these populations were uninterested or didn't see the need for an internet connection (high speed or otherwise) within their households—quite the opposite. The recognition of their disadvantage had motivated people to sign up for these classes or to seek out broadband opportunities. Residents as well as digital inclusion activists were concerned with the "restricted production scenarios" faced by mobile-only internet users.[54] Parents without internet connections at home were worried about their kids falling behind in school. Unemployed men and women looking for jobs were frustrated by the difficulties of trying to write and upload cover letters and résumés on a cell phone. All the while, children gleefully used computer labs to play games that were blocked at school, and high school kids gathered around consoles to compose music and use recording software that they didn't have access to otherwise. However, the Google Fiber options for connectivity that were being presenting to them just didn't make sense. Kansas City community members relayed to me how Google's rhetoric around high-speed networks exacerbated feelings of being disadvantaged or "left behind" in terms of internet and computing skills, computer ownership, and network access.

These same populations had uneasy relationships with the corporations that provided technological services to households, such as electricity, cable, or telephone companies. As more companies such as Sprint, Comcast, and AT&T began to publicize their efforts to connect previously disconnected populations (such as Comcast's ten-dollar internet connection for families with children who receive free lunch in Kansas City public schools), residents mentioned their skepticism around these initiatives. Many participants expressed that they thought Comcast and Google offered these services to make their companies appear charitable, to look like they were doing "good work," but that these companies purposefully made it difficult to locate and sign up for these services. There was a shared underlying feeling that corporations existed to extract value from a household, not to provide utilities. So when these corporations or private companies seemed to "do good," their initiatives were approached dubiously and cautiously if they were known about at all.

In addition, Google Fiber, unlike nonprofit organizations such as Connecting for Good or the Kansas City Free Network, did not recognize preexisting relationships that community members had with the services (digital or otherwise) that were connected to their homes. A common practice among urban populations living at or below the poverty line was sharing digital devices and network connections.[55] Aside from preferences for pay-as-you-go services, sharing resources such as internet connections, passwords for online services, and mobile phones was common. Community organizations, digital inclusion activists, and residents voiced concerns about the fact that Google didn't allow for shared connections between households or related buildings such as series of low-income housing, community centers, and schools that were in close proximity. The sense of communalism, or the commons, around technology hardware and software was omitted in Google Fiber rules and implementation processes, which left some residents wondering what exactly Google meant by "Fiber for Communities."

Home and Household

At the beginning of Google's Fiber for Communities campaign, the iconography used to advertise Google's fiber-optic network was a series of houses linked via brightly colored underground cables. Other than the alternating color scheme, these houses were nearly identical in size and shape, each with street-facing windows, a slanted roof, a shrub outside the front door, and a network connection. The image was reminiscent of the single-family homes and lawns found in the suburbs of KCMO and in middle-class to upper-middle-class areas of KCK.

Ideologies of home and household connoted by this image resonated throughout Google's campaign and illustrated how the company imagined the users who were signing up for the service, where and how they lived, and their sense of domestic place. Imagined users resided in pri-

Figure 2.2: Google Fiber for Communities sign at an event in Kansas City. Photo credit: Sean Ludwig.

vate, single-family homes that were presumably owned, not rented, in a neighborhood with some density (but not too much), surrounded by lawns, shrubs, and individual internet connections. In addition, displays and demos of Google Fiber connection often included mock living rooms filled with giant flat-screen HDTVs, sleek modern furniture, minimalist decor, and accoutrements that evoked middle- to upper-middle-class taste cultures. These living rooms were not spaces of the imminent future but the dens of the affluent enjoying even faster connections in the comfort of their homes.

Although the participatory registration process brought separate individuals together as a quantitative mass, their numbers deemed them applicable for an *individual* high-speed internet connection rather than as a collective that shared digital resources, construction fees, or computing hardware. Images of home and household evoked individualism, implying that each household was a self-contained, self-sufficient unit. This compartmentalization was evident in Google's implementation plan as well. Google Fiber policies called for one connection per household. Any mention of communal or shared living structures and conditions, such as apartment buildings, the landlords who owned them, and the management companies in charge of their maintenance, were neglected in Google's plan and promotional campaigns. According to Google's original implementation plan, the landlord of an apartment building would not only have to preregister for Google Fiber service but would have to pay the registration and flat-rate service fee ($300) for each apartment unit. Michael Liimatta, the president of the Kansas City nonprofit Connecting for Good during this period, emphasized that the dependence of a large portion of Kansas City residents, especially poor and working-class households, on landlords meant that "literally tens of thousands of families who may have wanted to subscribe were never given the chance."[56]

The absence of apartment buildings in Google's promotional materials and implementation plans also reflected the fact that Google didn't account for diverse experiences, conditions, and connections to "home." An investment in your household did not necessarily mean an investment in the building or space you called home. Renting a place to live does not necessarily elicit the same financial and emotional investment and permanence as owning a home. Homeowners were far more likely to pay a preregistration fee and pay to install a network in a house or condominium that they would continue to live in for a number of years. Renters, however, maintained a more temporary or mobile sense of home, knowing they would vacate their living space once their lease expired. I spoke with several renters who questioned why they would sign up and pay for a service that could not move with them when they did. Some of these renters were segments of the population who had signed up for Google Fiber service but never paid for or set up installation. Other potential customers figured that a service that required a $300 installation fee and an extremely delayed installation appointment meant that they would have to stay in a home for a few years after registration to reap the benefits of the service. These differential attachments to place were neglected in the campaign. There was the assumption that prospective Google Fiber registrants had stable, static living conditions and would reside at the same address from the time of registration through the time of installation, which could take several years. Initially, Google's implementation plan did not hail renters as possible participants or recognize their temporary attachments to the many different locations that they called home over time.

Mobility

For many renters, students, and members of low-income households, their connections to the city in which they lived were shaped by patterns of mobility that provided an uncertain persistence of environmental surroundings.[57] Similar to renters' reluctance to invest in their residences, the constraints and potential for physical, economic, and social mobility could also shape personal decisions about the types of internet service provision and infrastructure to adopt. Google Fiber focused on high-speed connection *at home*. While "household" and "home" were equated in Google's campaign, Kansas City residents who resided in inner-city neighborhoods, particularly residents who had never been connected to the internet, experienced home and household in ways that didn't perfectly map onto each other. For many Kansas City residents, and urban residents more generally, where someone lived could fluctuate from year to year and several times throughout the year. Some of the lower-income parents I spoke with mentioned that it was not uncommon for their families and friends to move more than once throughout a given school year. Thomas E. Brenneman, director of technology for Kansas City Public Schools, also recognized these mobility patterns: "Our community is so darn mobile. I have students that move twice in a school year."[58]

The parents I spoke with also noted that their children, who would benefit from having a stable, accessible internet connection for schoolwork and educational purposes, did not always complete their homework at home. Members of lower-income households that maintained a mobile sense of home tended to rely on smartphones, public Wi-Fi hotspots, and institutionalized broadband connections in order to use the internet. Due to parents' work schedules, some students would go to friends' or family members' houses after school or would go to afterschool programs at community centers, libraries, or churches or to the neighborhood McDonald's mentioned earlier. Having a high-speed internet connection at home might not benefit the children or students who completed their homework at several different venues during the week. In these cases, parents and teachers recognized that a more mobile yet robust and affordable connection directly meshed with the realities and daily travel patterns of many public school students and the adults who cared for them. Their reliance on a mobile or just-in-time connection did not overlap with the mobility patterns, or lack thereof, offered in Google's broadband plan. In Google's perception of place, a high-speed internet connection was tethered to private domestic space rather than public space or a circulating body.

These patterns of mobility and this peripatetic relationship to a place called home not only influenced technology preferences, such as opting for a mobile phone with an internet connection rather than an at-home internet connection, but also influenced the places where these families and low-income populations might go to use a wired, high-speed internet connection. Digital media activists and community organizers who provided social, educational, and health services to low-income communities reiterated the fact that digital infrastructure, hardware and software, and literacy and training programs that made the internet and computing relevant to these populations needed to come to their neighborhoods, not the other way around.

As Mei-Po Kwan notes, travel outside lower-income neighborhoods generates certain psychological, social, temporal, and physical constraints.[59] For these residents, travel to locations outside their communities to take classes at distant computing centers was described as time consuming, subject to strict time constraints, psychologically and socially uncomfortable, or undesirable, and finding motivation to do so was difficult. Organizers and activists emphasized the importance of making computing classes and resources mobile and bringing unfamiliar technologies, processes, and training into the communities they were intended to serve—into spaces where populations already felt comfortable so that they realized these classes, technologies, and high-speed networks were "for them." As one low-income community member and digital inclusion supporter explained to me, low-income residents needed to interface with digital technology and internet use in spaces where they felt comfortable because they didn't realize that the same spaces that were open to everyone included them as well. If this was not the case, and she attested to how frequently this actually happened, they might not go.

The survey conducted by the mayor's office and the Google Fiber team eventually recognized these concerns and noted that "the sense of comfort (i.e., support, trust, safety, and respect) at hot spots was important to residents as a precursor to technology access and use."[60] However, in

2016 a few residents who self-identified as living in low-income, minority communities called in to a Kansas Public Radio program dedicated to celebrating the five-year anniversary of Google Fiber. These residents voiced concerns about being "left out" and felt that Google Fiber had exploited their neighborhoods to set up facilities that took advantage of low rent prices and used these spaces as headquarters to serve other communities outside their neighborhoods.[61] From the perspective of place and space, digital inclusion was not just about being and feeling included in the segment of the population that was connected to the internet but about being and feeling included in the places and spaces where digital technologies and internet connectivity were being used and taught and where conversations and decisions about digital infrastructure and what these networks meant for communities were being discussed. The ways in which Google appropriated physical space to deploy Google Fiber did not reflect these efforts.

Community

As the name Fiber for Communities suggests, the concept of community was central to Google's campaign. Sharing geographic space with people who might share common demographic affiliations and norms was perceived as defining characteristics that composed a community. Google's campaign assumed a certain type of homophily within neighborhoods, equating community with commonality, but also a sense that members of a neighborhood felt invested in one another in a way that could be transposed into individual participation in support of the collective. Google asked neighbors to influence each other by example and to encourage each other to collaborate so that some households (but not necessarily all neighbors) could benefit from a new service.

I repeatedly heard from social service workers that neighborhoods east of Troost Avenue had unique "information grounds" and "third places" where residents felt at home and where communicative exchanges took place.[62] In contrast to the events and demos for Google Fiber, which were held at marathons, college campuses, boutique bars, and coffee shops, these residents noted the importance of faith-based spaces as significant spaces of affinity and information within the urban core. Google Fiber's conception of gathering spaces were either places where certain Kansas City communities did not regularly congregate or places that they felt excluded from. These patterns worried neighborhood organizers who voiced concern that because of this conception of community, certain populations were being excluded from internet access opportunities and that the Connected Communities initiative—which offered free Google Fiber connection to community centers in fiberhoods that qualified for service—wouldn't recognize the "right" or most advantageous spaces to connect.

Community members from neighborhoods composed of minority and/or low-income populations explained that Google Fiber maintained a distinct sense of community that differed from their own and that they found to be uninviting. At several digital inclusion meetings, educators and administrators within the public school system and members of local nonprofit and social services organizations repeatedly explained that many of the people they interacted with on a daily basis regarded the term "community" to mean more than collectives formed through shared physical location or geographic proximity. Instead, lower-income and minority residents felt a sense of community based on where they lived but also through more salient markers such as shared sense of place, feelings of belonging and exclusion, and communalism and support that did not intersect with Google's campaign. Many residents I spoke with felt that Google's use of "community" actually depleted the term.

Residents who did not sign up for Google Fiber felt that their lived connections between community and communalism were neglected or misunderstood in Google's initiative. While Google's campaign urged fiberhoods to sign up for Google Fiber to support the "Kansas Citians you care about," many residents told me that they supported those they cared about by sharing time and resources. People living in lower-income neighborhoods noted that density, more than physical proximity, brought people together. The density of residences within apartment buildings and the number of people living in a single apartment were conducive to sharing resources or the cost of resources with family members, friends, partners, or neighbors. Neighbors and family members shared internet connection costs, internet signals, computers, mobile phones, data plans, satellite or cable costs, and passwords. The fact that Google offered only one connection per household was read as evidence that in areas with limited digital connection, Google wasn't really interested in digital inclusion and that the company wasn't genuinely invested in helping communities.[63] Instead, residents interpreted this policy as cultivating and prioritizing potential markets rather than investing in Kansas City; otherwise the company would support signal sharing.

The collective care and maintenance of community were other experiences that dissuaded residents from preregistering for Google's network. A common perspective articulated by residents and neighborhood organizers was that a community cared for itself. A community was self-healing and continued to grow and gain support from within. In the Cook Report on Google Fiber and the reshaping of Kansas City, the authors describe initiatives by Connecting for Good, the W. E. B. Dubois Learning Center, and the Free Network Foundation to put resources into the hands of "people who are a part of the urban inner core and who understand how access to technology can be used to provide not only physical necessities but establish a source of personal and cultural wellbeing."[64] Unlike these models of implementation, there was a discrepancy between how strongly Google evoked a sense of belonging to Kansas City in the deployment and promotion of its network and how superficial community involvement actually was in the implementation and shape of the network, which disappointed some residents.

Many families and households that did not sign up for Google Fiber were members of "small worlds" in addition to their place-based identities as residents of Kansas City as a whole. Elfreda A. Chatman defines small worlds as social spaces composed of people who are bound together by shared language, customs, collective awareness, and cues of importance that influence their "co-ownership of social reality." She observes that members of small worlds tend to perceive the larger, outside world through the filter of their shared group norms, ideologies, and information practices. For people who live in small worlds or live "life in the round," information becomes plausible when it meshes with lived experiences or is received from a trusted provider.[65] The "information-rich" Google Fiber and smart-city "insiders" articulated understandings of the city and urban infrastructure imaginaries that contradicted lived experiences of mobility and relationships to digital technologies and home for small-world members. In addition, "information-rich" actors rarely sought insight and advice from "outsiders" or members of small worlds. Ultimately, a sense of belonging to Kansas City did not map onto having a say in what gigabit technology and the future of a digitally enhanced Kansas City might look like.

There was limited, if any, mention of how Google Fiber would create opportunities for marginalized populations to have their voices and experiences heard outside their communities. For instance, after the Mayors' Bi-State Innovation Team published its Google Fiber playbook, *Playing to Win in America's Digital Crossroads*, it created a website (www.googleconnectskc.com) and invited public feedback on the ideas presented in the playbook and suggestions for how to utilize gigabit connection in Kansas City. From 2012 to 2013 a public online forum gathered and displayed input from residents alongside a voting system that allowed commenters and readers to upvote or downvote submissions with indicators like "Great Idea" or "Okay Idea." The ideas with the most likes had percentages displayed next to the titles of their posts and were categorized as "Most Popular" in the forum. The "Most Popular" posts, which reached the status of "100% of Kansas City likes this idea," included "Form Innovation Groups at Local Schools"; create "Hacker Houses," start-up districts, collaborative hacker and maker spaces in KC; create "Remote Video Production House," "A la Carte TV Service," "Distributed Workplaces," secure remote offices; and "Make KC the best place to have conferences."[66] Ideas presented by residents who did not indicate their affiliations with web or tech industries or who did not propose an idea that involved entrepreneurship, or entertainment typically did not acquire a "Most Popular" tag. For example, one resident proposed that a meter be installed in participating homes to track how utilities were consumed and how household income was spent. The poster argued that if employed in this manner, high-speed internet connection could help educate people on where, when, and how they spent money. This idea was liked by "0% of Kansas City."

Digital inclusion activists posted in the forum, urging that issues related to digital divides be kept on the agenda and visible within the forum. For example, Mike Liimata, cofounder of Connecting for Good, posted a suggestion that "75% of Kansas City liked":

Rosedale is part of KCK's urban core and is home to more [than] 14,000 residents, over 60% of whom are renters not home owners. A very significant number of the residents are children and the elderly. The average income is among the lowest in the Kansas City Metro Area. As a result, a huge percentage of people in Rosedale will never be able to afford to pay for fiber Internet in their homes. This area is crying out for a community center because it has no central gathering place for the residents. Better yet, how about an e-Community center that could be a hot spot for free wireless and set up for after school tutoring, classes for elderly residents, and even a business incubator to attract high tech entrepreneurs to the area?[67]

As Mike's comment indicates, the needs of underconnected populations do not always overlap with "innovation," entrepreneurship, or emerging technologies. Instead, small-world infrastructural imaginaries resemble ways to bring communities up to speed rather than ways to make them high speed. Instead of reaching into the small worlds of Kansas City for information about internet infrastructure and digital rights to the city, Google universalized experiences of belonging and social ties within Kansas City and re-placed the city in ways that coincided with affluent ideologies of place and digital media.

Conclusion

Infrastructure is rarely completely invisible. While the technological substrates that make infrastructure work might be buried, disguised, or otherwise concealed, the social interactions surrounding implementation and deployment, imaginations and promises, and everyday experiences of these socio-technical substrates are highly visible. How people interface with infrastructure may differ based on our technological literacies, but it is also based on our familiarity with the social imaginaries that surround digital technologies—not only legibility and access to material structures but to the decisions and imaginations around these structures.

There are several lessons to be learned about re-placeing the city based on Google Fiber's presence in Kansas City that have implications for municipal broadband projects, community networking initiatives, and grassroots organizing around digital infrastructure more broadly. Google Fiber initiatives re-placed Kansas City as an exceptional location that could be transformed and improved through digital infrastructure. The company's infrastructure deployment models were focused on a sense of belonging to place that equated signing up for fiber-optic service with showing an investment in Kansas City communities. However, Google's participatory sign-up process and discursive construction of fiber-optic connection did not account for the varied, preexisting relationships to Kansas City and the historic socioeconomic disparities that might influence geographies of technology adoption. Offering a large-scale, high-speed internet infrastructure to Kansas City communities surfaced a complex ecosystem of connection, disconnection, and potential connection coexisting in Kansas City. Discourses of urban transformation and renewal activated in Google Fiber campaigns highlighted historical geopolitical inequalities and disparate relationships to digital media that enhanced infrastructure alone could not ameliorate.

An overreliance on input from technology industry personnel and domain experts allowed privileged infrastructural imaginaries and experiences to shape possible urban futures. In many ways, Google Fiber and its advocates reiterated municipal broadband rhetoric from the early 2000s and institutionalized visions of smart cities rather than taking account of the myriad needs, desires, or understandings of digital connection, and experiences of mobility and home in Kansas City. Ideologies and models from earlier municipal broadband projects—that large-scale, high-speed internet access could foster economic development and tourism and improve the health, public safety, and efficiency of government services on the city level—proved relevant to some populations and not others. The policy of one connection per household also illustrated that Google's network was designed for a particular sense of place that was not universally shared among all Kansas Citians.

Several people I spoke with who did not have internet access at home and did not sign up for Google Fiber were eager to find other options for consistent access to a broadband connection. Some families purchased mobile hot spots from the nonprofit educational broadband service provider Mobile Beacon through the Connecting for Good organization. These parents preferred Mobile Beacon's services to Google Fiber mainly because the portable device and 4G network suited their everyday mobility patterns and allowed them to share signals with neighbors, friends, and family members. In addition, nearly all Mobile Beacon users and residents who utilized Free Network Foundation or Connecting for Good networks appreciated that the services were acquired through a local community organization that they trusted. The noncommercial status of the service provider and network affordances that more directly coincided with their place-based experiences were regarded as factors that gave users a sense of control and ownership over their internet access.

Scholars have noted the ways in which national measurement criteria and connection targets do not apply universally and that digital infrastructure advocates and implementers should consider local contexts and needs more seriously before executing implementation models, pricing, speed, and deployment plans.[68] Organizations like the Detroit Digital Justice Coalition and the Philadelphia Digital Justice Coalition have taken account of local contexts and necessities and made them central to the use of funds and network infrastructure development for their respective communities. Both coalitions employ elements of participatory design and planning as well as community feedback and information gathering tactics to plan and deploy digital infrastructure and access points within Detroit and Philadelphia.[69] Policy institutes and research teams have continually encouraged internet activists who are interested in infrastructure implementation and use to "think local first."[70] However, as this case study advocates, "thinking local" must include listening to and learning about experiences of mobility and place attachment among diverse segments of an urban population.

Digital infrastructures have politics, politics that draw us to affordances of certain artifacts.[71] In this chapter, I've argued that infrastructure politics can re-place the city and that people gravitate away from certain infrastructure models based on their sense of place. Attention to place and placemaking in infrastructural imaginaries and infrastructural affects bring a particular type of media refusal or non-use to the forefront: a form of media refusal where populations understand the relevance of digital technologies and choose not to adopt certain services and infrastructure models based on place-based realities and the biased ways in which the people who implement these technologies re-place the city.

3

The Familiar City

Navigating Space as Place

Reconciling what someone sees and knows from screens with what one experiences in one's physical environment is a routine urban experience. Even the act of walking in a city (with or without a destination), a practice long regarded by urban theorists as a quintessential urban activity, tends to incorporate digital media in some way. Having access to a device that knows where you are and using that "whereness" and "findability" to manage your mobility are so commonplace that they have become mundane and happen almost unconsciously in the background of a variety of activities. Digitally mediated information and communication are produced and consumed in transit and alter the context and purpose of movement, the knowledge of surroundings, the organization of spatial and social relations, and the sense of self within urban space.

In the 1990s GPS hardware was visible on the dashboards of automobiles. Now, bicycles, hiking equipment, even pet and child accessories are outfitted with positioning and location-tracking capabilities. Through mobile, digital media devices and services, pedestrians can navigate to popular venues, avoid getting lost in unfamiliar landscapes, and access the quickest routes between locations. GPS-equipped mobile technologies and services enable us to view and move through cities like locals without having to be one. These technologies foster a layered experience of urban place and urban knowledge by weaving together physical, social, and technological space.[1]

Today, GPS technology most commonly reaches consumers via mobile navigation devices. In 2015, Pew Internet Research found that of smartphone owners, 80 percent of young adults, 72 percent of those age thirty to forty-nine, and 50 percent of those age fifty to sixty-four use turn-by-turn navigation on their phones.[2] In fact, turn-by-turn navigation was found to be the most pervasive use of transportation- and navigation-related services by smartphone users overall. The Pew study participants reported that difficulty "getting directions or finding an address" was the most significant problem they would encounter if they didn't have use of their smartphone. Most of these digital navigation practices have become habitual and unremarkable and are probably applied without notice, but they are not meaningless. Despite their pervasiveness, researchers know relatively little about how turn-by-turn navigation and mobile maps are incorporated into everyday life, how they shape spatial relations, influence cognitive mappings of urban space, and contribute to the formation of a sense of place.

Colloquially, digital navigation has acquired a negative connotation. Navigation systems and mobile maps are often criticized on technological and ideological grounds as well as in terms of the cognitive and psychological effects they are assumed to have on mapping and orientation processes. Representations of overly reliant digital navigation technology users who blatantly make wrong turns or obliviously drive into lakes because they blindly obey their navigation devices abound in popular culture. Some researchers have argued that abstraction and disembedding occur by interfacing with the screened space of the navigation device. For example, Scott M. Freundschuh and Max J. Egenhofer have noted that psychological studies of navigation operate under the assumption that a person acquires knowledge of large-scale spaces (such as buildings, neighborhoods, and cities) through personal experience over time, and digital navigation use is often understood as subverting that process.[3] The authors associate the use of digital navigation technologies with a manner of armchair tourism, suggesting that the representations of space delivered on these systems might discourage physical mobility since the city can be "known" from the screen alone. This sort of armchair tourism can also influence patterns of street sociability. Scott McQuire notes that relying on personal navigation systems counteracts one of the most common social encounters on the street: asking strangers for directions. He warns that by relying on advice from devices rather than people, we may contribute to the decay of our abilities for conviviality and interaction with strangers.[4]

Relatedly, the representations of space on mobile mapping systems are noted to fragment the city into segments that are displayed sections at a time, which may create a "sequential form" of cognitive map rather than a totalizing view of the landscape that must be learned before the journey begins.[5] In these studies, the mobile map is not regarded as a poor representation of space; rather, the critique falls upon the users who become more "passive" in the navigation process as they are required to spend less time reading and assessing mobile maps or talking to strangers in order to gain the information needed to navigate the city.

Studies in experimental and environmental psychology have repeatedly shown that mobile map users perform worse than study participants who take more "active" roles in route planning (e.g., using paper maps or studying routes and locations before travel) when tested on spatial learning and memory, route recall, and travel distance and time measurement tasks.[6] These studies tend to construct experimental or hypothetical situations that compare a sample of digital technology users with non-users and isolate digital navigation from other contexts of space, place, and socio-spatial engagement. Researchers test study participants on route recall, learning, and memorization rather than investigate the ways in which they incorporate digital navigation into everyday travel routines.

In light of more recent scholarship on mobile media that identify the ways in which digital technologies augment a user's place-based experiences,[7] it's surprising that these negative connotations and effects persist in research. These pejorative perspectives reveal and maintain a nostalgic ideal of attentive and engaged interactions with place through previous modes of navigation and mobility. In contrast to these studies, I am less concerned with how well a technology user *learns* a space and more interested in gaining insight into how a technology user *experiences* place through navigation. Several intriguing studies have emerged in recent years that examine representations of cartographic space produced by digital and mobile maps. Nanna Verhoeff refers to these representations as hybrid spaces or screenspaces that encourage performative cartography.[8] Jason Farman and Sybille Lammes note the ways that participation and interaction with digital maps can alter the ideological status of the map and its implications for spatial understanding.[9] Other scholars have suggested that services like Google Maps and Google Earth curate and present an automatically coded and ranked "DigiPlace" that abstracts material realities and shapes the perception and cognitive mapping of physical space.[10] Relatedly, additional analyses critique navigation technologies as producers of personalized, private images, which create subjective spaces on proprietary platforms that "bring abstractions for domination" and commercial logics into public space.[11] In all these studies, digital representations of mapped space have theorized implications for the union of physical movement and the imagination of physical space with digital representation. Furthermore, when read together, these studies imply that the spatial relations and mobility of navigation technology users are unconsciously governed by algorithmic logics and corporately owned images of space and place that normalize the privatization of public space or may even encourage neoliberal attitudes about urban wayfinding. This chapter seeks to understand the connections between subjective screen spaces, physical mobility, and performative cartography by asking users about their lived, embodied experiences of navigation.

The chapter complicates the colloquial and scholarly notion that a reliance on navigation technology for urban wayfinding alienates technology users from their physical surroundings, experiences of mobility, and senses of place and space. Though some aspects of digital navigation technology outsource the acquisition and memory of spatial information and displace more traditional means of wayfinding, these technologies may also enhance users' interactions with physical environments in other important ways. This study begins where other studies end: with the fact that many users report to be reliant or overreliant on navigation technologies for wayfinding. I move beyond this endpoint to investigate the ways in which digital navigation technology use and the practices and patterns of mobility that they support assist my participants in re-placeing the city in meaningful ways.

I argue that engagement with digital, mobile navigation technologies might be read as immersive and interactive, fostering a consciousness of one's embeddedness within place that augments spatial education and re-placement rather than distraction. Building on previous chapters that focus on macro-scale projects of urban design and citywide infrastructure initiatives, chapters 3 and 4 illustrate how re-placeing occurs through individual interactions with digital media devices, platforms, and services. In this case study, re-placeing the city is enacted through the tactical use of devices that have been understood as merely producing distracted travelers with limited understandings of their journeys and the places they navigate. While previous chapters addressed re-placing in terms of strategic placemaking of urban development and renewal, chapters 3 and 4 examine individual, tactical practices of re-placing that create and express emotional connections to place and emplaced identities through habitual digital media use. In this chapter, I analyze how average pedestrians or people on the street re-place carefully programmed built environments and city street systems as *their* places through personal, handheld technologies that track their individual locations and movements.

To investigate everyday encounters with digital, mobile navigation technologies, I conducted studies of navigation technology use in two midsize American cities with comparable population sizes and similar demographics. One study was conducted in 2010, the other in 2015. Through questionnaires completed by 210 digital navigation technology users (e.g., GPS-enabled devices, digital maps, and mobile navigation systems) and interviews with ten participants, this chapter identifies the ways that users understand their own spatial relations, conditions of and tactics for mobility, and embeddedness within urban space. Ten interviews and 102 questionnaires were conducted with residents of Madison, Wisconsin, ages nineteen to thirty-three, in 2010. In the 2010 survey, seventy participants self-identified as female, thirty-one participants self-identified as male, and one participant did not respond regarding gender. The vast majority of participants self-identified as Caucasian, white, or "whiteish" while 4 percent self-identified as Asian or Asian American, and 2 percent did not state their race. Questionnaires were conducted with 108 residents of Lawrence, Kansas, ages eighteen to thirty-eight, in 2015. In the 2015 survey, fifty-five participants self-identified as female, fifty-one participants self-identified as male, one participant self-identified as gender queer, and one participant did not respond regarding gender. Of these participants, the majority self-identified as white or Caucasian, 12 percent self-identified as Asian, 6 percent self-identified as Latino or Hispanic, 3 percent self-identified as African American or black, 3 percent self-identified as multiple races, and one participant did not state their race. With more participants identifying as people of color, members of LGBTQ communities, and people who spoke English as a second or third language, the 2015 questionnaire provided an opportunity to analyze the practices and meanings of navigation technologies among minority populations. In both studies, only a few participants identified themselves as late adopters or nonadopters of digital media and mobile media, and only one interview participant from 2010 reported never using mobile maps.

The pairing of questionnaires and interviews allowed for more in-depth explanations of how participants understood the concept of a "sense of place," practices of cognitive mapping, the connections between navigation technologies and placemaking, and how personal mobility was experienced, aided, and/or altered by navigation technology use. The second round of questionnaires, conducted in 2015, allowed for a comparison of how mobile, digital navigation practices, experiences of wayfinding, and relationships with common digital navigation platforms and services may have shifted over time. Ultimately, this chapter presents an empirical analysis of the ways in which digital navigation technology use encourages pedestrians and drivers to re-place the unknown or unfamiliar space of the city as an accessible, recognizable, bounded place and how this understanding of space allows for an enriched sense of place on the part of digital media users. These findings ask us to rethink what we know about the use of navigation technologies in urban space and to reconsider how these technologies are integrated into placemaking activities to cultivate a sense of place rather than to diminish one.

Paul Dourish once quipped—in response to a reviewer's comments that his paper on technology and spatial practice (which was not a study of digital navigation) was simply about navigation —"Navigation is primarily concerned with how we might find our way; my concern here is with how, in our encounters with space, we might find *more than* our way."[12] This chapter illustrates how, by routinely using digital navigation technologies, we do both simultaneously.

Cognitive Mapping and Re-placeing the City

Since the 1960s cognitive mapping has been utilized by researchers interested in accessing images of cities that manifest through the routine travel of urban populations. Although cognitive mapping had previously been used in the field of psychology,[13] Kevin Lynch played a significant role in applying the concept to urban planning. Through extensive interviews with residents, hand-drawn maps from study participants, and fieldwork and participant observation in Boston, Jersey City, and Los Angeles, Lynch began to draw conclusions about the spatial tactics that residents utilized to move through and become familiar with the places in which they lived. Lynch argued that it was essential to have a mental image of the city, preferably an image of the city as a whole, and that being able to place oneself within an expansive urban system was a key facet in organizing urban experience. His study also regarded cognitive maps as key measurements of spatial knowledge and orientation—with an emphasis on recall and ability to articulate accurate and/or perceived relationships between points, areas, and distances, between representations and lived realities. All these findings inform practices of re-placeing urban space: they employ imagination, legibility and imageability, coherent organization of spatial information, and the construction of spatial knowledge and experience as practices in reproducing abstract or unfamiliar spaces as knowable places.

Emphasizing the necessity of having an internal, expressible image of the city in its entirety as a primary indicator of being able to place oneself in urban space is an element from Lynch's studies that resonates in subsequent scholarship on cognitive mapping. Underlying Lynch's work is the idea that in order for the city to be concretized as a mental image, it must be coherent in some way. The metropolis must be understood as a "well-knit place," a place full of structural or perhaps cultural or stylistic interconnections. While symbolic representations such as maps can provide users with one possible image of how the world coalesces and is organized, he concludes that if one's spatial reality cannot be mapped onto this symbolic diagram, then both physical and symbolic representations become disorienting. In conjunction with this, Lynch is careful to include the idea that part of one's ability to "learn" the city might also be a matter of selective viewing and retention. If pedestrians are primed or cued to look for paths rather than landmarks (or another preselected structure within the built environment), then pedestrians might begin to imagine the city from a path-centric point of view and potentially organize their actions and their images of the city around these loci.

The fact that Lynch's philosophy for measuring spatial knowledge and orientation has shaped studies on navigation and wayfinding can partially explain why the findings about digital navigation and mobile map use are typically grim. On one hand, navigation systems produce symbolic diagrams that make space legible and organize urban space in terms of selective viewing while displacing the need for retention of these images. On the other hand, a user's focused reorientation around specific loci or points of interest at the expense of images of the city as a whole are affordances designed into digital navigation systems. At a glance, the affordances and functions of mobile maps directly contradict previous methods and theories for measuring and indicating knowledge of place. However, what studies on wayfinding and orientation behavior often fail to incorporate into their analyses is the personalization of the city that occurs through processes of cognitive mapping. Navigation systems cue or signal users to focus not only on their destination but also on the relationships between themselves and specific destinations: iconically (through representations), geographically (in terms of proximity and distance), and as a framework for understanding the purpose and constraints of travel. In Lynch's method and analysis, the context and practice of cognitive mapping are inherently embodied and personal. People recognize their own movements through urban environments while simultaneously recognizing the city as a *space* composed of nodes, paths, and edges and a *place* composed of destinations, districts, landmarks, and neighborhood boundaries against which their knowledge and experiences of the city and themselves are produced and intertwined.

Studies of cognitive mapping build on other traditions and interpretations of the comparative imageability of cities as well. These studies tend to follow Stanley Milgram's suggestions that cognitive mapping allows one to measure the cognitive significance of locations within cities or understand perceptions of cities that are held by members of distinct social and cultural groups as well as how these perceptions may change throughout their lives.[14] Scholars have expanded on Milgram's ideas about imageability and legibility in relationship to cognitive mapping by interpreting *representations* of the city that shape or influence mobility patterns and urban experiences rather than the built environments directly. For example, Janet Vertesi employs cognitive mapping to analyze the significance of the London Tube map in the imageability of the city, and Frank Bentley, Henriette Cramer, Santosh Basapur, and William Hamilton expand on Milgram's 1976 study of locals' maps of "their Paris" to explore how hand-drawn maps of Chicago might dif-

fer according to demographics and technology use.[15] In Milgram's interpretation of cognitive mapping and the application of his work, the
city is socially produced not solely through the built environment but
through symbolic representations of the city. The city is represented to
and by different populations based on their constraints and access to the
city as a whole. Cognitive mapping within this tradition makes people's
experiences with the built environment—as mitigated by relationships
within social hierarchies, demographics and subjectivities, and positions
of power—more legible.

Expanding in a similar direction is Fredric Jameson's sociocultural
extension of cognitive mapping. In *Postmodernism, or the Cultural Logic
of Late Capitalism*, Jameson writes, "Disalienation in the traditional
city, then, involves the practical reconquest of a sense of place and the
construction or reconstruction of an articulated ensemble which can
be retained in memory and which the individual subject can map and
remap along the moments of mobile, alternative trajectories."[16] Jameson
suggests that people can combat the alienation caused by global capitalism by reclaiming and rearticulating their social positions within a
series of complex, seemingly unmappable, and disjointed relationships
that manifest within culture. Disalienation becomes complete when they
can represent their social positions within the world and commit these
positions to memory. The act of mentally mapping and locating one's
social as well as physical position (or understanding one's social position
as it is linked to physical position) leads to the further recognition and
understanding of the self, the "spatial fix" of the city, and culture and
society under the postmodern logics of global capitalism.

For Jameson, Lynch's cognitive map is a noteworthy example of
making visible (reproducible and accessible) "the subject's Imaginary
relationship to his or her Real conditions of existence."[17] He reads the
practice of mapping relationships within masked webs of culture, ideologies, and economic flows as an act of resistance, a resistance emanating from identifying and making sense of one's place and position
by reproducing seemingly abstract, incoherent, unfamiliar territories
and relationships as knowable and potentially visible. This interpretation of cognitive mapping has been adopted to critique the ideological
place of documentary film, topographies of resistance in Chicano/a migrant literature, the use of dynamic internet interfaces since the 1990s,

and the work that users perpetually do with computing technologies among other studies.[18] Cognitive mapping as an aide to finding "more than one's way" applies to digital navigation technology use as well. In particular, the notion of mapping as a reconquest of a sense of place to battle disalienation along shifting trajectories is integral to understanding the practices and perspectives of digital navigation users.

The most common utilization of cognitive mapping is as a method of measuring spatial knowledge and wayfinding strategies for route and distance recall, analyzing efficiency and perceptions of travel time, acquiring spatial learning, and creating accurate mental maps. As Roger M. Downs and David Stea explain, cognitive mapping has come to refer to processes that "enable people to acquire, code, store, recall, and manipulate information about the nature of their spatial environment" and is an essential aspect of the dynamic process of "spatial decision-making," which primarily includes activities such as travel planning.[19] More than any other interpretation, this focus on spatial decision making in terms of travel planning and mobility motivates the use of cognitive maps in studies of navigation, particularly in the fields of environmental psychology and behavior, where studies of navigation tend to be found.

Travel planning and spatial decision making do not necessarily exclude the alternate understandings of cognitive mapping that are evident in Milgram's and Jameson's research. Instead, I suggest that the integration of comparative imageability based on social hierarchies, alongside ideological mapping that combats socio-geographic disalienation, only strengthens understandings of travel planning and spatial decision making. Furthermore, these theoretical interpretations of cognitive mapping are evident in the everyday use of digital navigation technologies. As the studies presented in this chapter demonstrate, digital mapping and wayfinding are at once technical and ideological and are based on divergent representations of urban environments. Digital navigation as a practice of re-placeing is equally concerned with finding one's way physically as well as culturally and symbolically.

Two Studies of Digital Navigation

In 2011 I moved to a city that I had only visited once for less than two days. After conducting surveys and interviews with residents of

Madison, Wisconsin, about how they used navigation technologies to move through unfamiliar places, I found myself relying on these same technologies to find my way. The process of driving from Madison, Wisconsin, to Lawrence, Kansas, and exploring this new place with the help of Google Maps offered intimate insights into the participant responses I had collected a few months before. Over the next few years I noticed significant changes to GPS services; not only were mobile mapping tools updated with new features that re-rerouted travelers past traffic jams or that sent alerts about ongoing construction and detours, many smartphone users also began to sign up for crowdsourced navigation services that provided directions based on tracking the speed and location of other users. Finding myself among a similar population in 2011, I decided to conduct additional surveys to garner further understandings of emerging relationships with navigation technologies.

The responses that appear in this chapter are drawn from 210 questionnaires and ten interviews conducted with participants in Madison, Wisconsin, in 2010 and Lawrence, Kansas, in 2015. My own participant observation of digital navigation technologies and mobile maps informs this study as well. In addition to these interviews and questionnaires, I also collected blog posts that describe and analyze the personal experience of using GPS applications and navigation technologies in a variety of large and midsize cities. I chose my sample based on the population that was most likely to use digital navigation technologies and mobile maps on a regular basis and was most likely to consist of early adopters of other geo-coded or emerging navigation applications.

In 2010 Pew Internet Research published findings from a study on cell phone and smartphone use in the United States. Its national survey found that traditional-college-age students were most inclined to incorporate digital technology into their daily lives and were cited as most likely to use locative media technologies and applications.[20] Over the course of 2010, I recruited university students and residents in Madison, Wisconsin, to voluntarily participate in a long-form questionnaire and interviews pertaining to their everyday mobility patterns, practices and experiences of navigation, and use of digital navigation technologies and mobile maps. In 2015 I recruited participants for a similar study in Lawrence, Kansas.

Of primary concern in these studies were the ways in which technology users understood their spatial relations, mobility and navigation practices, and sense of place through digital screens and positioning systems. Some of the questions asked of participants dealt with their frequency and perceived dependence on networked navigation technologies, their definition of a "sense of place" and the characteristics that cultivated it, the influence of navigation technologies on patterns of mobility, feelings about travel, and experiences of place while navigating. Most of the stories and scenarios that emerged from questionnaires and interviews described experiences of driving or walking alone with the aid of mobile navigation technology. While a few participants mentioned navigating while on road trips with friends or family, use of navigation technologies was generally considered an individual experience.

Spatial Information and Spatial Knowledge

In both 2010 and 2015 navigation technology users distinguished between what I refer to as "spatial information" and "spatial knowledge." Information is regarded as a pattern of energy or matter that can be extracted, stored, and used by sensing beings and may be subjectively interpreted.[21] These patterns of organization precede knowledge and wisdom once they are assigned meaning. As Marcia J. Bates explains, knowledge is built on the interpretation and integration of information "with other contents of understanding."[22] As employed in this study, "spatial information" describes the type of geo-coded information that is typically provided through GPS-enabled navigation systems like mobile maps: route guidance, directions, representation of a city's streets and how they intersect, a traveler's location on the map, cardinal directions, etc. One participant noted that such spatial information provides "a general consciousness of our surroundings," such as familiarity with spatial structure or how paths and nodes connect. Spatial information is often the type of information tested in environmental psychology studies on wayfinding: Can you recall your route? Which streets did you take to travel here? Which direction did you travel to get from point A to point B? Spatial information was not regarded as personal, particular, or unique by my participants and could be acquired in different ways (by asking directions, reading static or digital maps, or using a compass). Spatial information was understood as somehow universal or standardized: "raw" data about place and space.

Participants recognized that digital navigation devices readily provided spatial *information* but did not report spatial *knowledge*. In contrast, spatial knowledge is composed of elements more closely related to a sense of place: information about the character, culture, or history of a place; landmarks; a sense of the social environment; neighborhood boundaries and characteristics; safety concerns; etc. Spatial knowledge was typically noted as situated knowledge acquired over time through embodied experience and repeated patterns of mobility by traveling to and exploring new or unfamiliar places or living in a place for a series of months or years. Spatial knowledge was viewed as a more robust way of knowing place and was more difficult to acquire.

As will be discussed in depth, the majority of participants did not necessarily rely on their digital navigation systems to provide them with both spatial information *and* spatial knowledge. Instead, they used these systems to enable their acquisition of spatial knowledge once they had access to spatial information. Information about urban space, and their place within it, obtained from digital navigation technologies (particularly mobile maps), was viewed as a foundation for other enriched experiences of the city. Participants readily offloaded or shared the acquisition and effort of remembering spatial information (not spatial knowledge) with their navigation devices. The outsourcing, management, and accessibility of spatial information were ways in which digital navigation technologies could aid participants in organizing and understanding spatial relations and thus contributed to other social interactions and placemaking processes.

By differentiating spatial information from spatial knowledge, the position of mobile, digital navigation technologies as an informational tool within an ecosystem of everyday wayfinding tactics becomes evident. The next sections will highlight some of the practices cultivated around the acquisition and use of digital, dynamic spatial information and the manner in which these practices endow users with the confidence needed to explore and experience urban places more incisively and expansively and without anxiety. These tools, and the perspectives on mobility and spatial relations they provide, encourage users to move through and re-place the city in ways that cultivate place attachment. In addition, participants' comments regarding managing spatial information and knowledge, cultivating information practices, and relying on constant access to mobile maps revealed the ways in which participants experienced a combination of cognitive mapping theories in practice.

Managing Spatial Information

Imagining the City as a Whole

Digital navigation technologies such as Google Maps or Open Street Map are able to relay an image of the city as a whole. By zooming in or out and panning left or right, users are provided with an aerial view of the city in its iconic entirety as it exists within recognized borders. However, digital navigation technologies also portray the city as discrete, sequential segments that represent the city as a space that exists within a ten-meter radius while the rest of the urban environment lies in darkness somewhere off screen. According to study participants, these devices and applications were used to see the image of the city both in parts and as an expansive whole. Above all, digital navigation technologies helped organize the image of the city as readable and recognizable. For example, one participant noted, "Sometimes, I have a hard time maintaining my bearings and coordinating where I am in real life with an overhead map-view image in my head. Technology helps with that."

In both 2010 and 2015 the majority of study participants noted that it was important to know how streets connected to one another, as well as the existence and layout of paths, nodes, and edges, aside from the way participants used these routes in their routine travels. Acquiring such information was regarded as a sign that a person "really knows" a city, that a person had lived somewhere for a "considerable" or "decent" amount of time, and that the person was "a local." In some cases, navigation technology users equated knowledge of path structure with a "historical or practical" knowledge of place, a way of understanding urban design that signaled people were invested in or curious about a location beyond their own pedestrian mobility. Participants in the 2015 study understood familiarity with the city in its entirety as knowledge acquired by residing in a place over time and that having a mental map of the city as a whole makes the city feel more like home.

Related to Milgram's interpretation of cognitive mapping, participants noted that cultivating an image of the city as a whole was an asset in that the image could be used to organize the social layout of the city (characteristics of certain residential neighborhoods, where stores and bars are located, etc.). Participants discussed the ways in which they used digital navigation technologies to this end to feel more connected to cities: "If I am reading a newspaper article and it mentions a business, I am able to Google it and see exactly what it looks like and exactly where it is." Relatedly, several participants explained that the combination of access to the segmented and aerial maps of the city provided them with an image or model to fill in to help organize social or cultural information. Many users reported searching for the specific names of restaurants, bars, cultural institutions, universities, and businesses in Google Maps and Google Street View to visualize cities in terms of districts and neighborhoods and to begin to imagine what the culture and character of these neighborhoods might be like.

In a more practical sense, participants in 2015 noted that having a mental image of the city as a whole made travel more efficient and augmented personal safety. In terms of efficiency, participants thought that having a mental map contributed to knowledge of alternate routes and was helpful in creating a general understanding and awareness of one's physical location. Mental maps had value for personal safety in terms of prevention from either getting lost or "wandering into the wrong neighborhood." For these reasons, an image of the city as a whole was regarded as information that a person should know, especially "if your phone dies."

Although participants from both studies thought that having an understanding of the city as a whole was important, participants also admitted that they lacked proficiency in aspects of orientation and legibility that are traditionally associated with Lynch's interpretation of cognitive mapping (e.g., knowledge of how and where streets intersect, cardinal directions, distance between locations, or city boundaries). Instead, participants reported a dependence on their mobile, digital navigation technologies for this type of information. One participant brazenly remarked, "My friends are still shocked that I don't have a grasp on where I am even in downtown Madison. And I'm a senior!" Digital media users readily critiqued their own wayfinding abilities, noting that they had "terrible," "horrible," or "embarrassingly bad" senses of direction or the "inability to understand directions." Several participants noted that an advantage of using mobile maps and digital navigation devices was that these devices and applications helped alleviate personal shortcomings in terms of navigation skill and enabled travel despite inadequate abilities. For example, "They [mobile maps] show you where to go when you have no idea," and these devices "get me to places I may not have been able to get by myself."

However, participants' lack of spatial information proficiency was not regarded as a detriment. In 2010 participants reiterated that an extensive grasp of spatial information was not necessary for everyday travel and presence within a city; in other words, "just getting to the destination is fine." Or, more extremely stated by one participant, "The only place that really matters to me is my destination. How I get there is pretty irrelevant. I think it helps [to know how streets connect to one another], but it's not completely necessary. As long as you know the general direction streets are going in, it is easy to figure out where they will end up." The majority of users answered similarly, that an image of the city as a whole was important but not necessary. Many participants reported that receiving a "play-by-play" set of directions was "enough."

The belief that *mental* maps or knowledge of the city as a whole were nonessential was more frequently and emphatically emphasized in 2015. Participants noted that an image of the city as a whole was practically insignificant and that they weren't concerned with trying to develop one right away: it took time and happened through travel, exploration, and experience. If an image of the city was cultivated over years, a lifetime, or not at all, that was "fine" as long as some sort of image of the city was accessible. A minority of participants stated the irrelevance of having a mental image of the city at all, noting, "I'd like to say yes [that I have a mental image or mental map of the city], but with all the communication to help us navigate places, it almost doesn't matter anymore." More frequently, participants noted that an image of the city didn't have to be entirely cognitive or internal; having access to an image of the city through GPS or mobile maps was just as helpful if not more beneficial than mental or static maps alone. The majority of participants unabashedly indicated that they readily offloaded their sense of direction or shared a joint responsibility for wayfinding with mobile, digital navigation technologies in order to focus on and experience aspects of place beyond the perceived affordances of digital navigation systems. In other words, by offloading spatial *information* to navigation systems, participants were able to acquire a richer sense of place.

Offloading

Underlying participants' evaluations of their own technology use was a sense of excitement and anxiety that the city as a whole was too complex to comprehend and control; therefore they needed to segment the city on a screen in order to make it legible. Even in midsize and smaller cities, residents recognized that urban environments were sometimes difficult to navigate or were cumbersome spaces to "find one's place" within. These same participants noted that the practice of locating oneself within the city was incredibly important. Cognitive mapping, though read as desirable by most participants, was also understood as something worthy of technological assistance. However, participants articulated mixed feelings about their reliance on digital navigation and mobile mapping.

Certain comments about cognitive mapping and route recall resonated with findings from previous studies on digital navigation. Some participants recognized that their use of navigation technology negatively affected their ability to remember directions and routes. For example, one participant noted, "I really rely on GPS service now. I don't need to remember the directions to find the new place." Another noted, "It makes it so I don't remember how to get places by not making me have to remember. I can just look it up whenever I need to get there."

Although some people expressed regret over their reliance on digital navigation technologies for directions and route recall, many indicated that this was because they felt like they "should" or "ought to" be able to orient themselves without the use of navigation technologies. A few participants from 2010 mentioned that dynamic or mobile maps disrupted their mental map of the city. For example, one participant stated, "I feel like using GPS or MapQuest limits my imagination of what the city is like. Meaning I see the city only through the sample of directions I've been given." In 2010 several navigation technology users supported this claim by suggesting that spatial information provision (like directions and route guidance) through navigation technologies encouraged laziness about gathering spatial information on their own. One user's comment in particular is representative of a viewpoint expressed by several participants: "Just like spell check lets us all get away with not knowing how to spell a word, directions from MapQuest or verbal directions from your GPS take away your sense of direction (if you had any to begin with). . . . Just like the calculator makes us lazy with math, navigation systems make us lazy in our understanding of space." As this quote reflects, many participants in the 2010 study understood their use of navigation technology as a crutch. A subset of these participants viewed the comprehensive, "spoon-fed" instructions as a temporary support that could one day, hopefully, be abandoned as they learned urban patterns and routes. Participants also recognized this crutch as part of a didactic system. For example, mobile maps as learning devices was a theme echoed by many participants: "After a while, I don't have to use the technologies anymore, and it's as if the app taught me how to get there."

The majority of participants reported that technologies such as smartphone applications, mobile GPS systems, and Google Street View in particular allowed them to gain familiarity with, "preview," or "imagine" a given location or route either before they arrived or while they were there. As one user commented, "I enjoy Google Maps because it has the Street View feature, which helps me *literally* visualize where I'm going, and what is near my destination. It helps me imagine what the city is like overall, because I can see what landmarks are near where I am going."[23]

Using digital navigation systems to identify landmarks was a common practice: "I recognize other buildings and businesses around the place I am going to use as landmarks during travel." The identification and use of landmarks as a navigation practice further emphasizes the type of embeddedness and immersion provided by navigation technologies. Instead of being absorbed in the images behind the screen, users routinely matched screened spatial information within their physical environments in order to cultivate hybrid navigation tactics and imagine themselves within the built environment. Unlike previous studies that reported users' dissociation from physical environments, digital navigation users whom I questioned explained that they felt "more connected" and knowledgeable about physical space because of the omniscience and interactivity that the technology provided access to "because I can see whatever I want at the click of a button" and "it allows the viewer many options and tools that help bring the viewer as close to the real space as you can get." Participants also repeatedly described how digital navigation technologies rendered the city more familiar and recognizable: "If I only have an address for a place and then I look at the map or Street View and I realize the place is somewhere I've been before or know the area, I feel like it's familiar even if I haven't been there yet. It's like I might not know anything about the inside of the place I'm going, but I know what to expect of the place's surroundings making it seem less foreign."

Some participants even noted that navigation technologies helped them learn and remember street names and figure out "how cities work." One user articulated that learning street names and internalizing routes was unavoidable through navigation technology use, which was a common sentiment among participants: "You are looking [at] and listening to the navigation and saying and hearing the names of streets and landmarks. Because of this, it can help you remember places better." Several participants observed that navigation technology use helped them understand "how to use highways." Participants mentioned that they started driving on highways because of the ability to preview the city through a screen: "I don't worry so much about freeways, interchanges, and turnpikes as much as before [I started using digital maps] because I can now mostly see their quirks before being there."

By 2015 the trope of digital navigation as a crutch had shifted. The sense of a crutch was replaced with a regard for digital navigation technologies and mobile maps as a partner or prosthesis, sharing the burden of route guidance and spatial information with the user, not disrupting or supporting comprehension of spatial information but outsourcing it. In terms of navigation, people referred to their phones equipped with mobile maps as "the other half of my brain" and said, "I trust my instincts and my iPhone." This discursive shift highlights the process of "technogenesis," or the "adaptation, the fit between organisms and their environments, recognizing that both sides of the engagement (humans and technologies) are undergoing coordinated transformations" in regard to navigation technologies.[24] Participants recognized their practice of thinking "through, with, and alongside media" to navigate space.[25] This rhetorical construction of digital navigation technologies as partners, collaborators, and aides (rather than crutches) in sharing or offloading spatial information such as directions, route guidance, distance, and time traveled not only alleviated some of the resentment or guilt around the use of these devices but shifted their views into a more positive light. Participants' experience of technogenesis as a perceived partnership between themselves and digital navigation devices resulted in comments that reified collaboration and the offloading of spatial information to a device as advantageous for all parties involved. Ultimately, the benefits that participants described directly related to cultivating a sense of place for themselves (as will be discussed in subsequent sections). While there was evidence of this in 2010, participants more closely related their use of digital navigation technologies with placemaking five years later.

Participants recounted various experiences that legitimized their constant use of navigation technology and confirmed that they should not take wayfinding into their own hands when traveling to new places. Digital navigation users noted that they would rather rely on devices and mobile maps for directions than other people. Participants perceived their reliance on digital navigation devices as a means of being self-sufficient, and in some cases the navigation technology was thought to save participants from themselves. For example, one participant recounted a time when he was driving to get a haircut in an unfamiliar neighborhood in Wichita, Kansas. The participant turned off his navigation system on the way home and instead followed what he presumed to be the main road back. Instead, the participant drove in the opposite direction of his destination and ended up in the next town. Relatedly, another participant remarked, "I am horrible at it [navigating] and should not be left alone to do it."

The paradox of self-sufficiency through technological dependence has been understood in terms of "flexible alignment." Troels Fibæk Bertel discusses how, beyond microcoordination, "flexible alignment"—the ability to look up spatial information through mobile connections and adapt to this information while on the go—fosters feelings of autonomy among smartphone users.[26] Mobile phone users develop perceived autonomy due to the fact that information can be accessed individually rather than through mediated interpersonal communication. As one participant summed up, "I'm more likely to go places on my own now, which is nice because it means I don't have to depend on my friends to show me around or have to embarrass myself by stopping random people all the time." Or, as another participant noted, "I have become more independent (in terms of people) and more confident that I can travel on my own. I also know if I didn't have the technology, I wouldn't be able to get around a whole lot."

As illustrated by these perspectives, flexible alignment might not only aid in coordination and wayfinding but also encourages perceived independence in terms of navigation abilities and travel habits. The emphasis on autonomy and independence was often coupled with comments about travel as an individual pursuit. Participants noted that since acquiring their navigation devices, they traveled alone more eagerly and frequently. In addition to statements indicating that participants felt more independent and autonomous traveling with mobile maps and digital navigation devices, participants also indicated increased self-efficacy and confidence in terms of navigation. Clare L. Twigger-Ross and David L. Uzzell find self-efficacy to be a major aspect of place attachment and place identity.[27] If a person has feelings of self-efficacy—that they can accomplish tasks and goals within a place—the person is inclined to feel more strongly attached to or identify with that place. Participants noted that they not only felt more "confident" or "brave" while traveling but also felt more confident in their abilities to complete navigation tasks and goals and solve wayfinding problems with, and eventually without, the help of their digital navigation devices.

Participants in my studies framed their lack of recall differently from findings in experimental environmental psychology. Forgetting and not memorizing routes were not viewed as detrimental. Instead, participants regarded remembering directions as a behavior that they didn't have to spend, or "waste," time and effort engaging in. They had devices that would store and represent this information for them. Their time and effort could be spent *accessing* these directions, an activity they understood as convenient, efficient, time saving, and less stressful than acquiring and memorizing directions themselves. These perspectives support Jordan Frith's suggestion that digital, mobile navigation technologies function as part of "transactive memory networks" for wayfinding rather than primarily detracting from or impeding spatial knowledge and learning skills.[28] In transactive memory networks, members or actors within a given network are responsible for storing or maintaining certain types of specialized information or knowledge. In this case, digital navigation technology users held their devices responsible for providing spatial information to the rest of the network. Travel experiences, such as the trip described by the participant who lost his way in Wichita, indicate a process of learning one's place or role and the place of the device within transactive navigation networks. Since participants perceived the device as being better equipped to handle spatial information, participants' roles were to access and assess spatial information and to build on this information to produce spatial knowledge.

The digital navigation aides were not the only actors within the transactive network that could provide spatial information. A participant's network might also comprise friends, people on the street, paper maps, street signs, or other spatial information aids, but digital navigation devices were emphatically noted as the most advantageous and reliable sources for spatial information. In contrast to previous studies, several participants noted that routine and repeated use of navigation technologies within transactive memory networks, more so than other nodes in the network, served as spatial learning aids in terms of legibility of the city and of their place within it. Participants who shared this view noted that over time or with frequent travel to certain locations, the device would play a less significant role in their transactive memory networks and that they might offload less or different types of information to their device. While participants voiced tempered concern that their navigation devices gained prominence within their transactive memory networks, users also noted a general satisfaction or perceived improvement in their own wayfinding abilities and route recall because of the incorporation of these technologies into their navigation tactics.

Managing Spatial Information Overload

While digital navigation devices assisted participants in accessing and retaining spatial information, digital devices were also employed to organize and curate this information. Digital navigation technologies rendered the city familiar and manageable to participants by making information about the city manageable. As Milgram argues, "City life, as we experience it, constitutes a continuous set of encounters with overload, and of resultant adaptations."[29] Although Milgram, like Georg Simmel, is referring to overload in terms of social interactions with strangers and excessive stimulation on city streets, the concept of over-load is applicable here as well.[30] Overload in systems analysis indicates a system's inability to process or handle an overabundance of inputs. Participants expressed urban overload in terms of their inability to cope with a seemingly incomprehensible overabundance of new information about an unfamiliar city or section of a city. In response, they eagerly allocated the task of wading through what was perceived to be immense amounts of spatial information to their digital devices. The segmented, sequential image of the city that was critiqued in previous studies became a useful affordance for managing spatial information overload. Navigation systems were coping mechanisms to sort information about unknown or unfamiliar places, thus providing guided entry points from which to access the city. Digital navigation technologies helped users understand possibilities for urban mobility and allowed participants to better process inputs of urban experience.

Participants expressed feelings of agency and control once they realized that spatial information about the city could be managed and manipulated. This type of cognitive mapping served as a platform for other experiences and means of re-placeing the city. Participants in my studies identified navigation technologies as providing spatial information that reproduced abstract, unfamiliar space as manageable, smaller, more understandable, and familiar. They recognized and appreciated the way mobile maps and GPS devices put the city literally "in the palm of their hand," "at my fingertips," or "in my pocket" and "provided all the knowledge" about place, which allowed them to feel more confident in relation to spatial information and urban programming as they could call up personalized information about their embodied location at any time. As one participant summarized, "The technology shrinks the space that I live in. The more I know about the area around me, the closer everything seems."

The desire for the city to become a bounded, organized place was reiterated when describing the influence of navigation technology use on creating a sense of place. Freundschuh and Egenhofer have noted that one of the affordances that geographic information systems (GIS) allow is the ability of users to interact with large-scale spaces (like buildings, neighborhoods, cities, etc.) as if they were small-scale or manipulable spaces.[31] Gary H. Winkel notes that "creating a manageable environment" enables people to not only engage with location but also evaluate whether a particular setting or location supports their social, emotional, or psychological needs.[32] Many of my participants recognized this connection in terms of social and emotional needs as well as utilizing urban resources: "I can make better use of the city's resources if I'm comfortable with the environment. It [technology] helps with that." By re-placeing the city as a manageable environment through the use of navigation technologies, participants were not only more equipped to manage information overload but by doing so were more equipped to assess and make sense of the places in which they were embedded and how they were physically, symbolically, and socially inscribed in these places.

My participants' responses illustrate that navigation technologies assist in ordering and organizing unknown or unfamiliar environments and that technology use does not entirely eclipse the opportunity or desire to explore an environment more fully. A common perception among participants was that digital, mobile navigation technologies "took care of" finding and processing spatial information and orientation so that people could travel more reliably and with less anxiety and effort. One participant summarized this perspective by saying, "I love that it [digital navigation technology] makes it easier for me to travel and makes finding directions less of a priority." The next section analyzes what the statement "makes it easier for me to travel" means and what it looks like in practice.

Curating Patterns of Mobility

Digital navigation technology use fostered an imagination of the city as a spatial and social system that could be ordered through technological management. For participants in 2010 and 2015 this imagination provided feelings of freedom, confidence, and security that enabled them to explore cities in various ways and to travel to new or unfamiliar places more frequently and more readily. Overall, participants noted that they felt liberated through their use of mobile GPS devices: "I spend less time worrying about getting directions because I know I don't have to go print them out or stick to a route I decide upon before I leave. I have more freedom to change my route quickly, and I can look up directions once I'm in my car." The sense of liberation reported by participants was generally rooted in freedom from preparations preceding travel, freedom from worry about being late, freedom from concern about getting lost, freedom from a reliance on other people for directions, freedom to improvise, and freedom from travel anxiety. A majority of participants noted that the use of navigation technology actually alleviated some of the perceived "stress," "intimidation," and "fear" of individual travel and navigation. Mobile map users in particular reported that they felt more willing, comfortable, and confident when traveling to new locations or unfamiliar parts of town. In response to a question about whether owning or using navigation technologies changed their travel habits, one participant recounted,

> Yes, actually! For example, there was a time recently where I had to go to Topeka to get some necessary appointments done. Once I was finished, I remembered this video store that I heard about that I had wanted to go to. Also considering that I had a plethora of mobile data left, I looked up the store on my phone's internet, plugged in the address to the Google Maps app, and then drove there. It made my otherwise busy day a lot better.

As indicated in this story about adding a leg to a planned route, participants noted that their navigation technologies enabled them to "explore" and "wander" without the anxiety associated with getting lost. Participants noted that they were grateful for the opportunity to explore and that they wouldn't or couldn't have done so without mobile or digital navigation devices on hand. A participant in 2015 summed up what these feelings of freedom and liberation meant for patterns of mobility: "I have more freedom because I know my phone will show me where to go, so I can wander wherever!" As another participant noted, "I definitely wouldn't have been able to explore or navigate some of my favorite places around the world without technology."

Supported wandering was often mentioned alongside the desire for seamless, frictionless, and spontaneous travel. For example, "I never get lost and I can get virtually anywhere I want, no matter how far or unfamiliar the place is. I got to Florida driving this summer solely relying on my GPS. Didn't get lost once." This participant continued to describe a shift in his routine travel habits from well-planned endeavors to impulsive journeys and spontaneous trips, a pattern of mobility that was echoed in other questionnaires and interviews. The emphasis on travel to unfamiliar, distant places; travel as a spontaneous activity; and the perception of navigation as a convenient, technology-aided endeavor evokes the image of an adventurer or explorer (which adheres to marketing iconography, language, and narratives around these devices).[33] However, participants in this study rarely recognized their own mobility or style of travel as "adventurous." While semblances of curiosity about place and playfulness in regard to navigation were evident in participant responses, the experiences of travel described were void of uncertainty or trial and error. The desire to travel to new, unknown places was common among navigation technology users, but their travel patterns were focused on getting to target locations in timely manners and streamlined or efficient processes of arriving at given destinations or areas even if the journey itself was spontaneous or impulsive. The "adventure" of being adventurous was dulled or nonexistent in participants' recollections. The absence of hazardous, risk-taking, or daring travel (or other tropes associated with adventure and exploration) were desired outcomes of traveling with GPS. A participant in 2015 noted, "I feel like I am more willing to travel places by myself with the help of [Google] Maps, although it doesn't feel like as much of an adventure." Removing the chaos and the unknown from adventurous journeys was implied as a reason to acquire navigation technology. Ironically, several participants noted that they took more "risks" when they traveled, which they generally interpreted as traveling to unfamiliar places on a whim.

Exploration through physical mobility and personal experience was most frequently noted as the practice that rendered the city familiar: seeking out and traveling to new places and neighborhoods, going to unfamiliar parts of town, and "getting out more." The exploration of the city that participants described in their own travel routines was similar to the intentional wanderings of immigrants in New York City who were interviewed by Jessa Lingel in 2011. The author highlights several "information tactics" used by recent immigrants to navigate and negotiate social and physical "lostness" in New York City.[34] A tactic commonly used by immigrants is "the deliberate use of wandering" around the city to become familiar with their new environment. My participants understood mobile navigation systems as tools for intentional wandering and their use of these technologies as an "information tactic" to negotiate lostness. According to my participants, a significant motivation for using GPS and mobile mapping technologies was that these applications alleviate anxieties associated with getting lost or losing one's way. As one participant stated, "I'm more willing to go to new places and explore because I know that if I get lost, I can at least use GPS to get back on track."

Metaphors of digital navigation systems as insurance or safety nets was exceedingly prevalent in participant responses but emerged in distinct ways from various participants based on demographics and social status. Alleviating fear, feeling safe, and managing risk were especially noted by participants from minority and marginalized demographics. As one African American female participant noted, "Technology just makes sure I get there safe." Participants who self-identified as female, queer, African American, Asian, Hispanic, mixed race, nonnative English speakers, and recent US residents articulated a more intense and detailed discomfort around "getting lost." For example, as one African American female student indicated, "I hate being lost in settings that I am unfamiliar with because you never know what type of people are out there." This was a common sentiment echoed by other women of color, as one Asian female participant explained, "It's stressful being by yourself and getting lost. I don't like being in unfamiliar areas and not knowing how to get out."[35] Minority participants noted that mobile navigation use helped to alleviate these sentiments by providing safety through constant surveillance and tracking, allowing participants to view locations and become familiar with street names as premarkers before travel.

While the tracking and surveillance aspects of navigation technologies have been noted as a contemporary mechanism for the governance of bodies and/in space,[36] several participants recast the affordances of tracking personal movement as an aspect that supported exploration, discovery, confidence, and security within urban spaces. Participants who were recent immigrants or spoke English as a second language felt more poised and autonomous while traveling with digital technologies since they didn't have to navigate language and cultural barriers by stopping to ask for directions. These users noted that they frequently traveled alone, which emphasized the importance in cultivating a personal sense of the place and an image of the city.

Overall, but in the case of minority groups in particular, there was an intense desire, practice, and perception of using digital navigation technologies to negotiate social and physical "strangeness" as well as "lostness." Participants eagerly understood their use of navigation technologies as making the city feel familiar, but they also made *themselves* appear familiar. To visibly perform an assured sense of direction and act as if one knew how to navigate urban space was to show that one belonged. This type of performance can be read as the navigational derivation of Gayatri Chakravorty Spivak's suggestion that in order to negotiate or disrupt the demand of certain people to be marginal, "the only strategic thing to do is to absolutely present oneself at the center."[37] Among my participants, there was an intense desire not to feel or be recognized as a stranger. In 2010 negotiating strangeness was articulated as a desire to be, feel, or travel like a local. However, in 2015 participants voiced concerns about and negative consequences of being unknown or of not knowing the city. Some of these were safety concerns, but there were also concerns and preoccupations about being able to find one's place or feel a sense of belonging in the city.

The interaction of software and spatiality demands our reassessment of boundaries and belonging, of being situated within and out of place, which seems at first glance paradoxical; we turn to digital media to negotiate these feelings. My participants' responses indicate the ways in which they use digital navigation technologies to create safe zones within cities. Polson observes how expat professionals collectively utilized digital media to create "social safe-zones" to negotiate a mobile sense of place and to feel like a local within foreign socio-spatial geographies.[38] While transnational expatriates who desired to feel more "local" constituted safe zones through mailing lists and meet-ups in lively bars in foreign cities, students who internalized the risks of being perceived as strangers in midsize college towns turned to digital navigation technologies to re-place the city and find their place within it.

Digital navigation technology users expressed a lived, perceived, conceived triptych of geospatial empowerment. Geospatial empowerment was expressed in terms of propensities toward exploration and traveling to unfamiliar or new places (lived) and less anxiety and stress about travel (conceived) due to the legibility of urban space provided by digital navigation technologies (perceived). Ultimately, these spatial moments led to a focus on "being there" rather than "getting there" among my participants. As one participant noted, "At first I think that navigation technologies hinder my sense of place, but once I get the directions down and travel the area more, I get familiarized with it more." As the next section will elucidate, digital navigation use plays a major role in the acquisition of spatial knowledge of a city. Through the acquisition of spatial knowledge, I argue that the patterns of mobility, travel choices, and attitudes associated with geospatial empowerment derived from mobile maps allow users to experience the city in ways that deepen their sense of place.

Acquiring Spatial Knowledge

When asked what it means to have "a sense of place," my participants offered a variety of interrelated definitions. While some participants regarded a sense of place as being associated with geographic location and navigation—for example, understanding where you are in relationship to other places, geographic scales, or being keenly familiar with your surroundings, including knowing how to navigate a space—most participants associated a sense of place with possessing particular emotional or psychological attachments to a given location.

The majority of participants in this study regarded a sense of place as a feeling of being at "home," having a sense of "belonging" or "comfort," being part of a "community," having an emotional attachment to and familiarity with the social and cultural uniqueness of a place, and understanding its value. The behaviors and attitudes on this list involve juxtaposing spatial information with social experience. These participants also identified several characteristics and behaviors that cultivated this sense of place within the cities they lived and traveled in. Participants mentioned patterns of mobility such as frequent and/or repeated travel to certain places, exploration of different areas and routes, frequenting local businesses and events, exploring new places, and diverging from one's routine as activities that contributed to their sense of place. Being able to recognize places on any sort of map; being able to recognize people, streets, stores, neighborhoods, scenery, noises, landmarks, etc.; and learning about site-specific culture and history while moving through a city augmented a sense of familiarity. Social encounters and instances of resourcefulness such as meeting people and making friends, sharing experiences in a place or exploring with others, knowing how to access resources, having a sense of purpose, or figuring out how you "fit in" all created emotional attachment and feelings of belonging in place.

Participants who regarded a sense of place as cultural, social, or emotional tended to note that spatial information such as knowing routes, directions, and the layout of a city were elements that digital navigation technologies could provide but that did not directly contribute to their sense of place. Spatial information was something that was necessary and important to cognitive mapping, wayfinding, and gaining familiarity with the built environment, but directions and orientation provided by mobile navigation technologies were seen as the platform or foundation required to access spatial *knowledge*. Participants explained how mobile, digital navigation technologies played significant roles as inanimate collaborators in re-placing the city by allowing them to focus on characteristics and activities (such as exploring without anxiety, traveling to unfamiliar places, and concentrating on social encounters) that reproduced the city as a rich and meaningful place in ways that were important to them. For example, one participant articulated a sentiment that was shared by many other participants in this study: "If you know a place well enough, you aren't preoccupied with directions. You always know where you are in relation to your home, and so you can't get lost. Once that is out of the way, you can spend more time on other aspects of it: the diners, the architecture, the murals, the parks." Navigation technologies were seen as mechanisms for obtaining directions and orientation that were to be gotten "out of the way" so that participants could focus on destinations and social experiences that made them feel at home.

In fact, a preoccupation with directions and navigation was seen as a distraction or detriment in creating a sense of place. Participants took pleasure in the fact that their digital and mobile navigation devices would take care of wayfinding so that they could focus on aspects that made places meaningful to them. These technologies allowed participants to cultivate a sense of place "quicker" and "easier" and more comfortably, securely, and confidently than if they relied on analog forms of navigation. Because navigation technologies streamlined travel to places that would make users feel comfortable or at home in the city, they began to perceive their navigation technologies as devices that would contribute to or help them find their sense of place. Mobile maps set the foundation for and hastened the process toward placemaking and cognitive mapping practices that participants regarded as more significant than navigation.

Participants noted that although they felt as if navigation technologies emphasized their destination, it was often their destination that created place attachment. As one participant explained, "[With mobile navigation technologies] I have more of a connection to the place [I'm traveling to] rather than the way there, which is also important." Their destinations were described as where their friends or family were located, somewhere they had researched and wanted to go, a place that would provide a needed good or service, or a destination that would contribute to their sense of purpose or belonging in the city. Navigation technologies allowed them to enjoy their journeys to these locations, which made them want to travel and explore more frequently and to discover new areas of the city.

Although mobile maps and digital navigation services like Google Maps, Bing, Apple Maps, and various vehicle navigation systems included expanded offerings such as points of interest and the ability to type in a venue category such as "restaurant" or "1980s music night club," participants didn't mention the use of these affordances. Instead, they stated that they read or heard about a place they wanted to visit and typed the specific name or address of the destination into the search function on their map. Participants used their navigation systems to search for specific locations and destinations—utilizing mobile maps to chart routes, not as recommendation systems. Digital navigation technology users in these studies repeatedly described how they carefully researched exactly where they wanted to go before typing an address into a navigation device.

Navigation and Re-placing the City

The participants in this study expressed a desire for legibility and imageability of the city—even if the image constructed wasn't entirely one's own. McQuire warns of the risks involved in "outsourcing the management of social encounter to software," particularly commercial software such as Google Maps.[39] While every digital media user should be aware of the contexts in which their personal information and location are shared and their rights regarding that information, it is also necessary to recognize why and under what conditions people *choose* to outsource spatial information and place-based experiences to machines. In this case, people chose to offload spatial information to navigation devices to enrich their sense of place.

Throughout interviews and questionnaires, participants offered explicit links between digital navigation technology use, mobility patterns, and placemaking. Participants worked to re-place the city through the eager incorporation of coded representations of space and GPS tracking to guide physical movement and to produce an enriched experience of being in place. Previous studies have argued that digital, mobile cartography algorithmically filters and controls what users see and know about cities and warn that people should be wary of ceding spatial decisions to these platforms.[40] However, when asked about how they interfaced with these platforms, users noted a willingness to cede certain types of spatial decisions and outsource prescribed forms of spatial information to algorithmic maps and navigation technologies. Digital navigation users identified sets of tactics and perspectives that allowed them to utilize ranked, curated "DigiPlace" in the service of creating meaningful, personal place.[41] Mobile GPS software provided a sense of control over spatial information, which resulted in feelings of autonomy and confidence to explore and familiarize oneself with urban space more readily. By altering patterns and sentiments about mobility and navigation behaviors, participants discovered that unfamiliar and expansive urban spaces began to feel more like places, that the city was manageable and familiar, and that participants were better equipped to access destinations and resources that would encourage a sense of belonging to the city or encourage a sense of the city as "their place." Participants noted that navigation systems were often the starting point for journeys that led to discovery, an augmented sense of the culture and character of the city through personal travel, and feelings of belonging. Digital technologies were understood as apparatuses in the poiesis of place as well as the re-placeing of one's self within the city. The use of these devices was made meaningful alongside other transactive spatial information networks and everyday interactions with urban environments, populations, and social hierarchies.

Participants articulated differences in how they used digital navigation technologies to re-place the city between 2010 and 2015. In 2010 participants used digital navigation aides to place themselves within the city in an effort to re-place the city as familiar and lived in. My participants considered GPS and mobile maps as tools to "help me get an image of where I am in relation to the city around me." The symbolic spatial representations these tools provided assisted users in mentally mapping *themselves* or their embodied "place" within the city. The desired mental map was not of the city as a whole but of the users' position within the city as a whole or within the neighborhood or district in which they were currently located. As one user noted, dynamic maps such as Street View or mobile GPS helped her to "see the spatial relationship of buildings, streets, and other landmarks. By seeing the streets in relationship to one another, I can usually visualize myself in that area if I have been there before and map out where I am headed beforehand." This expectation that maps or mental maps would help to orient an individual for travel within urban space was not a novel development. However, the ways in which navigation technology users expressed their interest and need to know *their location* or *their place* within the city was inherently linked to "locatability" and "whereness" in regard to urban structure.[42] Articulated in myriad ways by my participants was the perception that navigation technology allowed users to "move through space with a better sense of where I am." For these participants, navigation technologies helped them imagine their place within the city. Their location was the central locus, and the image of the city was forged around this point.

In 2015 these feelings were reiterated by participants with distinct descriptions and affect. Although some participants noted that with mobile maps and digital navigation devices, "I rarely wonder where I am," this was read as more valuable in terms of "not getting lost," being able to "know where I am going," or tracking their mobility rather than creating a mental image of the city or their place within it. One participant noted, "You never really feel lost as long as it's [mobile maps or GPS] there and working." Another referred to mobile maps as a "safety net." Several participants noted that they liked having the "big red 'you are here' dot" and "the arrow" and "the dot moving on the screen" and said, "I like that it follows along with me." Relatedly, participants' language regarding locatability shifted between the two studies. In 2010 participants explained, "*I always know where I am*" because of navigation technology use. In 2015 participants expressed a more ambient positionality based on mobile tracking: "*It always knows where I am*." The sense of "it," the device, being able to locate their place within the city at any moment helped forge the peripatetic safety net that would encourage them to wander, explore, search out experiences, and visit destinations that contributed to their sense of the city as place and their embeddedness within it. For participants in 2015, placing themselves within the city had more to do with personalized surveillance and consistent access to a device that was tracking their movement through an avatar on screen. In these statements the desire to construct a mental map of the city as a whole in relationship to their location was displaced in favor of negotiating a sense of strangeness or lostness.

Participants' reliance on digital, mobile navigation technologies for route guidance and orientation in 2015 was understood as a means toward developing a mobile sense of place through embodied mobilities, personal rhythms, and collections of destinations, stories, and experiences to call their own. Lefebvre understands "rhythms" as repetitions composed through space, time, and the expenditure of energy that compose everyday life.[43] Digital navigation played a significant role in these studies for curating, learning, and internalizing routes for personal, quotidian urban rhythms. Participants who shared anecdotes about moving to a new city or a new residence within a city or visiting a location that would eventually be incorporated into their everyday routine noted the importance of having digital navigation devices to help them find the supermarket, post office, neighborhood bar, or laundromat for the first time. The shift in understanding the incorporation of navigation technologies as tracking personal rhythms and re-placing the city by visualizing and tracking one's mobility emphasizes a customization and sense of control over the city. Instead of legibly relaying their position within a complex metropolis, digital navigation technologies helped participants imagine the city as a place to be discovered and understood through their movements, rhythms, and beats. In this way, navigation technologies allowed them to imagine the city not only as *a place* but as *their place*.

Getting "Inside" Place

Although Edward Relph understands all manners of media and infrastructures of mobility as creating "placelessness," his concept of "insideness" helps to summarize participants' practices of everyday use of digital navigation technologies. "Insideness" refers to feelings of attachment, involvement, or concern for particular places based on feelings of inclusion or embeddedness and feeling at ease, safe, and at home within a given environment. In both 2010 and 2015 participants re-placed the city by employing digital navigation technologies to get "inside" place and negotiate various sorts of "outsideness" or perceived incongruences between themselves and the world in which they lived and traveled. Through the process of ordering and managing images of the city, navigation technologies encouraged users to explore, experience, and locate themselves "inside" of places to cultivate more profound connections to the social and physical environments around them. The striking discomfort or displeasure with strangeness and lostness and the anxiety about unaided travel that radiated throughout questionnaires and conversations with participants gesture toward what is at stake in getting inside place or working toward embeddedness. Participants used digital navigation technologies to re-place the city and themselves as "local," recognizable, and inclusive (or included) and to assuage concerns about the city and themselves as unknowable or unfamiliar. Farman theorizes that space and our sense of embodiment are continually coconstructed and that mobile technologies, including mobile mapping applications and GPS, reconfigure how people experience and embody space.[44] In practice, navigation technology users utilize mobile maps to manage differential mobilities and to produce place-based identities that combat feelings of alienation by creating places of dwelling while in motion.

To see the city as organized through a graphical user interface such as a map or computer interface in the service of disalienation is to see the city through an organizing structure related to Jameson's cognitive map. As Wendy Chun notes, *"instead of a situation in which the production of cognitive maps is impossible, we are locked in a situation in which we produce them—or at the very least approximations of them—all the time, in which the founding gesture of ideology critique is simulated by something that also pleasurably mimics ideology.*"[45] Chun suggests that through pervasive computing opportunities, members of the public potentially can (and often do) map and remap societal structures through the situated, individual cartographic and categorical ordering of information. However, instead of cognitive mapping as an end point to disalienation (as Jameson indicates) or as a mechanism for reinstating ideological structures of sovereign power (as Chun suggests), participants utilized cognitive mapping as one act in a larger performative process of making, and making sense of, place.

The cognitive map—forged through technogenesis and tactics for offloading spatial information in order to acquire spatial knowledge— gains salience as a tool for navigating the built environment through curated personal mobilities based on users' understanding of themselves within urban power-geometries. While digital navigation technology users gained a sense of control through the standardization, choreography, and legibility of spatial information provided by their navigation devices, they interacted with this information in subjective ways based on diverse desires and needs for feeling included or "inside" urban space. Although digital media users strictly adhered to the directions provided by their navigation systems,[46] these stringent directions were utilized in customized, context-dependent ways in the service of feeling "at home" in a space. By employing digital navigation systems as collaborators in re-placing the city, participants enacted a form of geospatial empowerment. With the help of digital devices and software, participants maintained agency in organizing spatial relations and mobility and appeared confident under the gaze of companions or passersby by tactically maneuvering through urban environments and interactions that might render them immobile (because of travel anxiety, the perception of being a tourist or outsider, fear of getting lost, or misunderstanding "how a city works").

When the affordances and practices around digital navigation technologies are contextualized in terms of re-placing the city, the potential for aspects of mobile, digital navigation technologies in regard to communities' "right to the city" open up.[47] Although participants didn't directly articulate navigation practices with analyses or deconstructions of power relations and social struggles, they did understand digital navigation to play a role in reclaiming equity and agency in terms of urban embodiment, security, and access to the city. By making cities legible as places, participants were afforded opportunities to recognize and re-inscribe the ways that social, political, and economic power operates in cities—by locating and navigating the interconnectedness of or divisions between neighborhoods, the design of built environments, and the oscillating cartographies of the city as both bounded and unknown. As this study indicates, the more people visualize how routes connect and districts intersect, how highways work, and how they can arrive at their given destinations the more they desire to move through space in ways that exert agency in placemaking. Digital navigation devices make spatial organization readable and manageable by providing opportunities to imagine and manipulate urban space around who a person is and what they need the city to be.

Conclusion

As noted by participants, particularly those from minority populations, there is a link between geospatial empowerment, navigating social relations, and placemaking. As suggested in this chapter, the legibility of urban place through mobile maps illuminates the spatial tactics people use to navigate and move through a city: how networked urban subjects organize space as place; how this organization coincides with, disrupts, or excludes previous understandings of urban navigation; and how screened realities and standardized images of the city actually help people make sense of unique physical and social realities. These findings augment more theoretical examinations of mapping and representations of space by focusing on routine experiences of digital wayfinding and propose a trajectory for navigation studies that veers away from demonizing digital navigation systems and toward assessing the meaning of these systems within urban life. Studies of spatial cognition could consider the role of digital and mobile wayfinding aides as a foundation for spatial knowledge and the social production of place rather than as a means for comparatively testing recall of spatial information. Rob Kitchin and Scott Freundschuh recognize that designers of GPS and other consumer navigation systems rarely incorporate or consider findings from cognitive research on navigation and spatial recognition into their devices.[48] However, as the outsourcing of navigation and mobility continues in the form of self-driving cars, automated public transportation systems, and the Internet of Things, technology designers should consider studies that focus less on experimental cognitive research and more on quotidian incorporations of machines into wayfinding practices.

Aside from analyzing practices of re-placeing the city through digital navigation technologies, this study highlights differences in practiced understandings of cognitive mapping. The desire for legibility and imageability in urban spaces and the construction of an image of the city are still valuable but have been noticeably transformed through the use of navigation technologies. While participants found cognitive maps of the city advantageous in terms of traveling efficiently and signaling insider status, they did not find it necessary to have these maps be mental or memorized. Instead, the purposes and processes of cognitive mapping through the use of digital and mobile navigation technologies were understood as *accessing* representations that helped people make sense of and cultivate social meaning within a space.

When we consider Milgram's and Jameson's cognitive mapping alongside the environmental psychology and geographic interpretations of Lynch's work, navigation technologies aid in negotiating disalienation in terms of orientation, gaining access points, acting on structured opportunities to interact with the city, and placeing oneself in a way that not only makes sense logistically but also provides a platform for constructing a sense of belonging and comfort within abstract space. Through the use of navigation technologies such as mobile maps and GPS services, urban residents and travelers found their social and physical "place" within the city and constructed a platform that allowed them to imagine the city as a manageable space to be known, cared for, and dwelled within. Even without additional exploration and wandering, navigation technologies allowed users to appreciate aspects of the city that created place attachment rather than focus on directions and orientation.

Based on the findings from the studies presented here, future research could analyze the ways in which navigation technologies create a negative sense of place or highlight moments when people realize that they are "out of place"—when users attempt to get "inside" place with navigation technologies and instead reinforce feelings that they don't belong. Future directions for this type of research could also include studies of non-use of navigation technologies and how motivations and behaviors of non-use affect sense of place and re-placeing. While my research identifies ways that people use digital navigation technologies to support exploration and discovery, these findings could inform questions about how and when people feel encouraged to deviate from chosen routes and explore the city in unintended and/or orchestrated ways.

As urban navigation continues to encompass more digital activities and services, users of online navigation systems explicitly become producers and performers of spatial images and spatial meanings. For example, through the collection and display of automated geo-located information through services like Waze or the production of geo-coded documentation of place through applications like Foursquare, Yelp or other social media sites, participants tend to be hailed as contributors that influence the meaning of place and the mobility of others. This study of personal uses of mobile navigation technologies highlights spatial practices and understandings that precede, or occur instead of, more specialized mobile media and navigational services. The next chapter further explores the power and prevalence of individual placemaking practices by focusing on re-placeing activities in social and locative media that produce collective social constructions of place, place attachment, and place identity.

4

The Social City

Belonging, Social Media, and the Spatial Self

While GPS-enabled phones became an essential part of everyday travel (as discussed in the previous chapter), the development and adoption of location-based systems throughout the early 2000s emphasized social interactions with geo-coded information and encouraged reflections on the meaning and relationships ascribed to presence within places. By 2007 technology pundits and scholars alike were commenting on the "explosion" of locative media applications that were suddenly available on mobile phones. As cell phone and smartphone ownership increased, so did the fact that millions of people were carrying mobile, GPS-equipped devices that were capable of locating themselves and those around them while on the go. In general, the terms "locative media" or "location-based media" are used to refer to mobile media that primarily rely on information about location in order to function and provide the user with an augmented sense of space and place. Some locative media projects enable searching, filtering, and cataloging places while other projects allow users to tag or annotate maps or photographs of places to share stories or experiences in specific locations. Mobile applications and platforms categorized as locative media provide self-surveillance and social surveillance for communicative, playful, and commercial interactions. All these projects reallocate the power to share and curate the meaning of space, reconceptualize spatial relations, and re-place the city into the hands of the public.

Where someone is from, where they've been, and where they choose to spend their time have always been utilized as social signals, ways of shaping and articulating identity and reaching out to bond with others. Predigital examples of people archiving and exhibiting their personal mobility and place-based experiences abound. Diaries of urban flaneurs maintained as early as the Victorian era not only archive individual physical movement through urban environments but also document social and cultural change and serve as a window into relationships between social class, gender dynamics, and public and private spaces and the city.[1] Curated photo albums, slideshows, or home-video footage detailing family vacations that can be displayed or shown to friends and family members are expressions of where someone was located both socially and spatially.[2] Store-bought and "real photo" postcards with photographs of distant locales or familiar places annotated by the sender articulate something social and spatial about presence at particular moments in time.[3] As Humphreys argues, all these efforts are forms of "media accounting," or ways that we utilize media to document traces of our presence and activities in place that can be shared with others.[4] However, the affordances of locative and location-based social media projects encourage sharing this information in new ways. Historical mediated practices of archiving presence in place are combined with real-time tracking, computer-mediated communication, and the possibility of continuous, habitual location announcement.

Through the use of locative or location-based media, people are able to express and share embodied, polysemic, social imaginaries of place on a wider scale. Locative media projects such as Yellow Arrow, Urban Tapestries, Uncle Roy All Around, BrightKite, and later Foursquare, Instagram, and wearable self-quantification devices not only answer the navigational questions of "Where am I?" and "Where am I in relationship to everything or everyone else?" but allow people to imagine and live in a world composed of cartographic networks of connected, personalized places.[5] Instead of merely knowing where you are, platforms can now recommend places to visit based on your location and past mobility patterns. As analyzed in the previous chapter, digital media users exhibit a general appreciation for navigation software and the ability of the device to know where they are and track their mobility. Locative-media projects introduce new affordances that shift the meaning of "locatability" from verifying longitude and latitude for route guidance to algorithmically curating and suggesting socio-spatial experiences. The interest in visualizing mobility and tracking one's location documented in chapter 3 is combined with a desire to document and share experiences of emplacement or "being there," which is the focus of this chapter. Expressed via locative media is a representation of the world as a series of places with you in it, a place where you are or could exist—because you traveled there, you documented your experience, you viewed others' experiences in relation to your own, or you were emplaced through virtual reality, augmented reality, or simulation. When the world is presented as an expansively locatable series of places where a person can perpetually belong, does this alter individual or collective agency to intervene in the social production of place? Or the style and tactics through which these interventions take place?

The representation of location through locative and social media emphasizes the mobile, social production of place through the announcement and archiving of personal, physical experiences. Underlying all the aforementioned platforms is the understanding that people produce place: reading and writing place into being, composing and circulating the identity of specific places over time through their situated thoughts and embodied actions. Much like digital affordances shape networked publics, creating new possibilities for interaction,[6] new situations emerge through the use of mobile social media that shape the dynamics of participation and engagement with placemaking. While digital media users contribute to the meaning of place by presenting geo-coded photographs and videos, texts and status updates, experiences and recommendations, they are also harnessing location and a sense of place to present themselves. Mobile placemaking, or the social production of place through mobile and location-aware technologies, involves two simultaneous and overlapping processes: the presentation of location and the assemblage and presentation of the spatial self—making place as information sharing and making place as identity performance.

Digging deeper into the placemaking practices of individual digital media users, this chapter illustrates the ways in which re-placeing the city coincides with self-expression and self-presentation. Edward Casey forthrightly claims, "There is *no place without self and no self without place*."[7] Building on this idea of the "geographic self," or what Jason Farman calls the "sensory-inscribed body," this chapter focuses on the performance of place through self-presentation and information sharing as an expression of personal and social imaginaries of the meaning of place and presence as they intersect with digital media use. While Casey and scholars of place attachment and place identity have focused on the way place is harnessed in the production of the self, the examples in this chapter are employed to investigate how digital productions of the spatial self are indicative of the ways people understand the symbolic value of place and their place in the world.

Similar to chapter 3, the examples in this chapter evidence personal practices of re-placeing the city by urban residents or travelers at the scale of the street. In this case, expressions of place meaning, place attachment and place-based identities are produced through user-generated, publicly circulated texts, posts, and personal cartographies. While the rise of the particular and the personal are evident in the expression of place-based identities online, there are networks constructed around configuring jointed commonalities between these intensely personal experiences of place. Urban identities that are simultaneously specific and rooted yet relatable are routinely expressed publicly and shared, mimicked, aggregated, or remixed by other users. The mediated traces of physical presence that are recorded via locative and social media evidence creative practices of re-placeing the city and the social and symbolic value that accumulates through the conscious production and purposeful circulation of vernacular expressions of place. In the sections that follow I analyze how the spatial self is leveraged to re-place the city through social media. As some of the examples in this chapter illustrate, the meanings produced by suturing urban subjects to urban place sometimes contradict or reconsider official imaginations of urban locations and parody dominant placemaking practices. The examples in this chapter also evidence how digital traces produced through GPS and geo-location technologies can be read as performative rather than precise.

Social Media and Re-placeing

In *The Rise of the Network Society*, Manuel Castells argues that in a constantly changing world of flows and under the structuring and destructuring forces of advanced capitalism, identity gains a monopoly as the key "source of meaning." Castells continues to describe a split between abstraction and particularism, between instrumental and historically rooted identities. Under this calculation, Castells suggests that the abstraction and selective deletion of identity that occur over "the Net" is in binary opposition to the specificity of self that is encouraged through social fragmentation as well as the historical rootedness of the "space of places." He contends that as identities become more specific and are instrumentally demarcated and interpellated through networked services and platforms, they also become increasingly difficult to share. The "choose one option" menus, templates, or preset algorithmic linkages that construct profiles of someone's race, ethnicity, gender, search history, and friend groups for marketing or database-building purposes represent a strategic desire for specificity, but they also reveal challenges in articulating and sharing identities over these systems.[8] Although these strategic mechanisms for constructing identity are often inadequate, digital media users have access to a variety of "expressive equipment" and have worked within these systems to cultivate tactics for potentially "more controlled and more imaginative performances of identity online."[9]

Accompanying the increased social fragmentation that Castells identifies is the notion that fragmentation encourages the proliferation of identities and positions from which to read the world. The scale, reach, networked architecture, and sheer quantity of users on social networking sites create "situational geographies"[10] where the perspectives of these various imagined and unimagined audiences are circulated within shared environments. Within these situational geographies, we can also observe the ways that place attachment, place identity, and personal mobility patterns are harnessed and performed in search of social interaction and self-expression.

Digital placemaking, or the social production of place through digital media, has been understood as related to the "presentation of place" and the "presentation of location" or "the potential to develop and access dynamic aspects of a location via location-aware technologies" that influence physical mobility patterns and social decisions around where or how one travels.[11] Heidi Rae Cooley describes this combination of affordances as "findability," or the union of identifying the existence of a place and patterns of mobility so that movement can be tracked and anticipated through user-generated data or the automatic generation of data.[12] Eric Gordon and Adriana de Souza e Silva offer the term "net locality" to describe recent shifts toward location and location awareness as the central logics that organize networked interactions.[13] The primacy of "whereness" in locative and social media is reinforced as GPS-enabled devices implicitly and continually collect location data in the background of everyday activities as well as through conscious actions of mobile and social media users. Cooley has argued that the myriad ways that digital media users are tracked by their networked devices are often not visible to users, but de Souza e Silva and Frith have noted that the capacity to filter, preview, and produce information about locations and the people who have visited these locations fosters a sense of control, customization, and comfort for digital media users.

In this vein, scholars have connected the production of place identity, place attachment, and place memory to locative and mobile social media practices as well as physical environments, noting the ways that a sense of place and sense of self are cocreated virtually and physically.[14] For example, Didem Ozkul and Lee Humphreys explain how location-based media users share geo-tagged texts and photos to create digital archives that preserve nostalgic places and representations of past selves.[15] The desire to share performances of place identity through digital media emphasizes Tim Cresswell's suggestion that place is the "raw material for the creative production of identity" and can also serve as an impetus for communicative, bonding, or social interactions across networks.

As Raz Schwartz and I elaborate elsewhere, expressions of place via digital media are examples of the "spatial self": instances where individuals document, archive, and display their experience and/or mobility within space and place to represent or perform aspects of their identity to others. Digital expressions of the spatial self are a particular type of "networked self," one that primarily relies on the curation of representations of physical place and mobility to perform identity online. Expressions of the spatial self are not always precise in terms of calculating actual mobility or physical presence, but they are precisely calculated, choreographed articulations of space and the self based on identity production and self-expression. The spatial self presents a highly curated depiction of an individual or group mobility that is shaped by the polysemic character and meaning of a physical place and the ways users associate themselves with particular locations.[16] Ultimately, digital traces of the spatial self can be read as emerging forms and practices of inscribing the body within digital and physical sociocultural environments, revealing fragments of larger ontological stories about space, place, and embodied mobility through unique instances as well as aggregated representations.

Digital expressions of the spatial self are becoming increasingly indicative of our spatial practices and social productions of space. As millions of people use social media platforms, websites, digital tracking devices, mobile phones, and sensor-based projects to annotate their physical locations and instantly share them with various social groups or archive them for later reflection and self-assessment, the spatial self gains prominence in daily life. Although linked to physical mobility and presence, the work of the spatial self takes place on screen. Digital articulations of the spatial self rely on the act of engaging with the screen and the affordances of "screen-ness" in body-technology-place relations.[17] The images, texts, utterances, and geospatial data produced as part of the spatial self can be thought of as similar to Sarah Pink's emplaced visuality,[18] as articulations created in movement and about movement, harnessing an imagined, shifting sense of place alongside an imagined, shifting sense of self.

The relationship between embodiment, screens, and sense of place has been critiqued by geographers and media scholars to illustrate the ways in which place is both made and undone through screened somatic experiences. Casey, who has established theory on place identity, adheres to the idea that screens compose a *lability of place* that flattens its uniqueness and integrity and caters to "a fickle self who seeks to be entertained" or an "aesthetic self" that is only interested in the gratification of the present.[19] However, re-placeing the city counters the lability of place by linking imagination with social practice. The spatial self is the performance of one's flexible, mutable, curated imagination of a person's place in the world. These performances of identity that harness individual and shared meanings of place are more than a superficial or aesthetic map of one's own, they are acts of re-placeing space through the articulation of social position and the significance of social networks in conjunction with a sense of place.

Social media sites that host online traces of personal mobility provide unique opportunities to observe performances of place that have persisted for centuries (e.g., place naming, mapping, sharing stories, and photographing places) and newer actions (e.g., data visualization and real-time location announcement) as they're circulated in order to archive presence and connect with others. The fragility and symbolic value of place need maintenance, just as physical structures need upkeep. Performing place through the spatial self is an iterative, continuous social and cultural production where the meanings, tools, and audiences for performances are continually updated as well—a process where place is continually "narrated back into existence."[20]

Understood in this way, the expressions of the spatial self that are used to re-place the city are employed in the service of the "qualified self" rather than the "quantified self." As Humphreys explains, while the qualified self is a self-tracking process, it uses media representations or mediation rather than datafication to create subjectivity and to present qualifications for what we do and who we claim to be.[21] Representations of the spatial self on social and locative media qualify or characterize us through the meanings we ascribe to the places we choose to represent on screen and the ways that we choose to connect ourselves to these meanings. The following sections investigate the ways in which individuals use social and locative media projects in their daily lives to reproduce the city as a polysemic place of identity formation. I analyze three trends in social and locative media use as placemaking activities: playful exploration and memory, location announcement, and self-quantification.

Playful Exploration and Remembering as Re-placeing

Playful Exploration

Digital projects that populated cell phone screens in the early 2000s were structured around playful engagement with physical space through an overlay of game space and virtual objectives. Reminiscent of analog activities such as letterboxing or "I Spy," where players visually and physically survey spaces in search of objects that advance game play, early locative media projects sought to creatively reproduce urban space as a playful place. Several projects created by artists, game developers, researchers, and start-ups in the 1990s and early 2000s—such as Yellow Arrow (USA), Murmur (Canada), Urban Tapestries (UK), Social Light (USA), Mogi (Japan), Pac-Manhattan (USA), and projects by the UK collective Blast Theory—incorporated game mechanics or took the form of puzzles or scavenger hunts that re-placed the city street as a platform for digital interaction. Physical mobility and different forms of presence and urban experience were documented through templates for annotating, commenting on, and captioning places. In other cases, participants in these projects moved through urban space with a digital overlay of game mechanics and avatars indicating the locations of other players or walked through the city in search of physical markers that allowed users to interact with or upload virtual information or rewards.

The playfulness within these systems re-placed the city as a polysemic archive of interactions by leaving visual, textual, or oral traces of presence for others to explore. Larissa Hjorth and Ingrid Richardson refer to this mode of placemaking as "ludic placemaking," which encourages participants to rethink what it means to be present in public space.[22] In addition to game spaces, Marc Tuters and Kazys Varnelis have recognized the playfulness in "annotative" projects, or digital platforms that allow users to tag and filter information linked to physical locations. Unlike traditional tours, user-generated, networked annotations linked personal narratives and vernacular experiences and guided participants through spaces based on the placemaking practices of residents and travelers. Exploration and unexpected encounters with other spatial stories, bodies, situated knowledges, and personal pasts opened up the meaning of cities in layered and contradictory ways.

Interviews with creators of locative media projects that encouraged playful exploration, as well as the projects' mission statements and press releases, promoted a common idea: distinct ways of seeing the city, and seeing *in* the city, might influence ways of living within the city. Urban Tapestries' mission statement declared that the goal of the project was to promote the practice of "annotation and story-sharing" through mobile devices as "an integral part of urban living." Yellow Arrow creators encouraged users to focus on specificity and detail, "enabling every place to become an attraction," creating a "deep map" of the city.[23] Murmur attempted to "build an entire, opposite, one-of-a-kind, popular mythology of a city at a citizen level" through locative media.[24] Annotative or "urban markup" projects created new settings for Le Courbusier's "spontaneous theaters," where people could "act out their own dramas . . . erupting out of the collisions and contact that might occur between different events and groups."[25] The traces and texts that were produced as part of these projects expressed as much about the participants uploading them as they expressed about the places exhibited. Mobile media affordances such as information retrieval in situ and proprioceptive connection coupled with the familiarity of the device created an intimacy of being present within the spaces narrated by digital texts. Participants in these projects were able to touch the objects that were described in captioned images and audio files, which offered a distinct type of urban possession or somatic sense of the city that was literally within one's grasp.

Remembering as Re-placeing

Distinct in design and use, the activities supported by early locative media projects could be categorized as creative coexploration of both the street and the self in the company of friends and strangers. As the practices that populated these projects indicate, the meaning of place to the networked passerby is sometimes experienced via the representation of loss and longing, which in these activities took the form of stores that no longer existed, the stumps of favorite trees that had been cut down, childhood bedrooms that had become bodegas, recollections of engagements on hilltops, and subway stops at which relationships had gone sour. While this sort of understanding of urban space was nothing new, the personal layering of past and present that could be accessed publicly and used to tour the city rendered these images not only artistic but also tactical.

Represented in Yellow Arrow photographs and Murmur sound recordings were the processes of going back to or *returning* to urban places by the people who produced the stories or images. These projects, and the cultural productions they exhibited, encouraged the documentation and celebration of the city as a place that had once been completely different. For generations people have revisited or journeyed to places to document what the places once were but also what *they* themselves once were. These journeys somehow attempt to archive a memory even if the location in its present incarnation is nothing like the traveler remembers. This sort of practice—of saying "here I am" or "there it is, but it's nothing like what I have known, thus it is deserving of documentation"—manifests itself in literature, photography, journalism, and film as well as a plethora of other art forms. However, this juxtaposition of temporality and spatial relations was regarded as both useful and jarring by locative media participants whom I interviewed and in participants' written accounts of their use.

Circa 2004 I began to critically observe and document participant engagement with locative media projects. Through interviews, questionnaires, participant observation, and textual analysis, I investigated the ways in which early adopters of Yellow Arrow and Murmur chose to engage with annotative projects to represent their relationships with urban space. The most common practice I encountered within these projects was the utility of memory and remembering in re-placeing the city. Digital media texts and practices produced through these projects tended to represent and rescue the practice of "passing by" and particular ontologies or ways of being in the city at a particular time. The stories and annotations that were created and consumed with digital media and mobile technologies often included a personal or collective past and/or future in a version of the present: instances of remembering or nostalgia, knowledge of how certain places or people "used to be," or memorials of personal or collective events. In 2011 a chapter of my dissertation focused on these practices and the ways participants re-placed cities around the world through their engagement with Yellow Arrow and Murmur.[26] Inviting "thick descriptions" of lived experiences within cities and aggregating these disparate and often-conflicting stories onto a single map emphasized the polyvocality of place alongside the contributions and agency of individuals and communities in the process of placemaking.

Mike Crang and Stephen Graham suggest that a symbolic or artistic representation of memory, or the "haunting of place with absent others," destabilizes the meaning of place. The authors propose that coding multiple knowledges and memories onto particular locations defers the meaning of place indefinitely, that the "narratives and information carried in digital networks may actually serve to disperse our notion of both person and place" instead of enriching these perspectives.[27] However, my reading of these practices is similar to Michel de Certeau's and John Fiske's consideration and creation of "tactics" within a spatial realm. Instead of deferring and destabilizing meaning, the exhibition of memory within these digital narratives added to a vernacular historicity or genealogy of place. What occurred within these projects was a reproduction and restabilizing of place through the sharing of memory and layered situated knowledges of the city. I suggest that remembering as a tactic or spatial strategy can be understood as re-placeing the city. In re-placeing the city, locative media participants identified spaces that already had iconic or symbolic value and reproduced these places in accordance with individual memories, DIY participation, and urban subjectivities. What occurred through these projects was a grassroots tactic of reclaiming, retelling, and re-writing place or reproducing place through the representation of poly-vocal memories over digital networks. Articulating memories became an act of dwelling or temporary stability in that place, allowing the poster and the reader to linger a little longer.

In early annotative locative media projects, participants displayed and appropriated the locational capital of experiencing "the before." The concept of locational capital has circulated in economics and business disciplines to indicate how behaviors may take on augmented value if they occur in places with positive affective or industrial connotations.[28] In regard to re-placeing, locational capital means that a person gains ad-ditive value from the placement of themselves within certain locations at certain times. For example, claiming that someone used to live in a neighborhood before it was gentrified or emplacing oneself at a location at the time when a historic event occurred might enable a place or per-son to accrue certain types of locational capital depending on the audi-ence for the performance of place and the affective and aesthetic style of association. Contributors to these projects described and illustrated to those who could never access "the before" what it was like to be in that place at that moment. Participants narrated the value of place back into being through a time before the creative economy took over, before that building was torn down, or as one Yellow Arrow participant noted, "before the white people moved in." Participants attached themselves to an image of the city and staged the production of authenticity of certain places. It was not solely *their* place but a place they employed to com-pose their spatial selves and perform locational capital publicly.

The ownership or possession of place that is conferred through the exhibition of memory in these projects is related to Marianne Hirsch's concept of "the before" and the simultaneous inclusion and exclusion embedded within "postmemory."[29] As Hirsch notes, "the before" is for-ever inaccessible, especially to those who were never "there" or never directly privy to it. Massey elaborates on a similar concept, arguing that you can never simply "go back" to a place because "when you get 'there,' the place will have moved on just as you yourself will have changed."[30] In regard to the urban quotidian, "the before" can refer to the experience of irrevocable loss that triggers nostalgia so that a person might desire to memorialize a space or place that no longer exists. However, the urban "before" could more commonly represent a move away from memorializing trauma toward remembering and archiving the occurrences linked to urban place in the most mundane ways—remembering the places that have made us who we are in everyday life and not necessarily at a moment of crisis. They are places that we know will change regardless of our presence in them.

Reveling in "the before" as an embodied performance of place is an exclusive practice. It excludes those who were not or could never be emplaced in the ways described by participants in an effort to mark themselves as insiders. However, it also bears the potential for collaboration and community formation for the same reasons. A shared knowledge or understanding of "the before" can be recognized and reified by other members of a networked public or social network, while a dissonance of interpretations and experiences on these networks often draws attention to the social hierarchies at play in the production of place.

While Farman analyzes urban markup and mobile media platforms as "interfaces of re-membering," or means to create and disseminate embodied individual and community histories of place, he also talks about the stories told as representations of the potential loss of community histories amid a constantly changing urban environment.[31] The performance of locational capital in these early and subsequent locative media projects not only documented the types of changes occurring in physical environments but also called attention to the performances and knowledges that marked someone as a member of a particular community of people with a shared sense of place, as "insiders" or "locals" of a given epoch. Subsequent locative and social media projects monopolized on this practice of sharing hyperlocal and insider information about place through recommendation systems and travel tips, which made it more complicated to distinguish tourists from residents. Instead of showing up at a neighborhood haunt, where one's presence alone would have marked someone as a local, a person's presence might actually indicate digital literacy or the ability to access information about place rather than lived experience.

Location Announcement and Selfies as Re-placeing

Emblematic of the "second wave" of locative media projects were more exclusively mobile phone–based announcement and recommendation services like Dodgeball, BrightKite, Foursquare, Loopt, Gowalla, and Yelp. Via mobile phones, app users could alert a select social network about their journeys through urban environments and the places they stopped along the way. While the first wave of locative media projects was organized around the logic of a cartographic gallery and thick description of place, later projects were organized around the logic of real-time location announcement, enabling users to track movement and collect points, rankings, and virtual loot with visits to particular locations. The annotations of place that occurred through these platforms were reconceptualized as tips and recommendations about venues rather than stories about locales. Whereas early locative media design and use focused on pedestrian voices and emplaced memories, subsequent projects focused on location disclosure and datafication for social and commercial engagement.

New modalities such as the check-in or the geo-coded status update or tweet, which were quicker to produce on the go, exemplified forms of "emplaced visuality" or "visuality mapped by geospatial sociality" that emerged and dominated locative media markets.[32] Projects and platforms that focus primarily on location announcement and social media platforms that have integrated location announcement (e.g., Places API or Google Latitude on Twitter and Facebook) have garnered millions of users worldwide. Although the cataloging and archiving of physical mobility, place attachment, and place identity are evident on these platforms, location announcement services emphasize connection with social networks and the venues represented on these systems through conspicuous mobility and the commodification of location. In these applications, urban experiences are reconceptualized as accumulative transactions and recurrent, voluntary location disclosures that create curated narratives of who people are based on where and how they travel.[33]

The registrational interactivity of writing oneself into place was usurped by the ability to disclose locational presence as the main performance of place. Instead of deep representations of personal histories of place or spatial stories, scholars have noted the ways in which location announcement promotes distinct feelings of presence and prox-imity. Locative media projects are understood to re-place the city as intimate, creating a parochial sense of place where a perceived familiar-ity with curated locations fosters a sense of ownership, territoriality, or exploration of seemingly expansive or unknown places.[34] Re-placeing the city as inhabited and as a place where one could potentially belong can be reinforced through repeated images of locations posted within social networks or through observations of others' documented travels through urban space. For example, de Souza e Silva and Frith suggest that viewing others' mobility patterns on location-based social media systems might foster a sense of comfort and familiarity with unknown places by allowing users to preview photos, descriptions, and comments about the places they visit from people they perceive to be somewhat similar to them.[35]

Studies have shown diverse motivations and contexts for location announcement over social networks. Scholars identify myriad socially driven motivations for cataloging and expressing personal mobility and presence through location announcement platforms: intimate bonding with friends, bragging or "showing off," self-promotion, inside jokes, or receiving points or rewards for particular habits or actions.[36] The game mechanics integrated into location-based services like Foursquare and Gowalla have been understood to render sociality and place into a net-worked game or "turning life into a game" by encouraging participants to alter mobility patterns because of game-based rewards.[37] Henriette Cramer, Mattias Rost, and Lars Erik Holmquist provide evidence for lo-cation announcement as ludic placemaking in their study of Foursquare and the common practice of creating "imaginary" places and fictitious or creative names for locations or events.[38] Relatedly, Mimi Sheller notes that several mobile media artists and activists have attempted to over-ride the commercial and surveillance aspects of mobile and location dis-closure technologies to create "disruptive spaces of resistance, of sharing, and of convivial publics" and "serendipitous play."[39] However, unlike the playful exploration of earlier locative media projects, location announce-ment is commonly framed by participants as additive value or context for other information and interactions expressed over social networks. Location-based social media users often understand their location an-nouncement as augmenting or reinforcing other online profiles or forms of digital self-presentation. As Louise Barkhuus, Barry Brown, Marek Bell, and Scott Sherwood observe, expressing "where you are" over a social network informs others of your location while signaling a mood, a lifestyle, or life events and maintaining or supporting more intimate social relationships.[40] Participants in all these locative media studies have noted that the personal narratives and individual representations of physical mobility disclosed on social media are not representative of all the places they travel to, nor are these traces of mobility necessarily accurate. Check-ins and tips omit certain locations, emphasize others, and reveal traces of mobility, which, like practices of self-presentation on other digital platforms, are calculated but imprecise.

Locative media projects celebrate the activity of embodied and embedded mobility within the city, undoing the "procedures of forgetting" that de Certeau associates with the making legible of the individual's traversing of space on a map. He argues that with the practice of cartography comes a finite and fixed visibility of paths and arteries that erases the process or act of travel, transforming action and movement into legibility and causing "a way of being in the world to be forgotten."[41] Platforms centered around the creation, exhibition, and sharing of geo-coded photographic images and video highlight the camera as the primary tool needed in order to record embodied presence and remember and share ways of being in the world. And these platforms continue to grow in popularity. For example, launched in October 2010, the photographic location-based social media service Instagram reported a user base of one billion international subscribers in 2018.[42] One of the most noteworthy and infamous practices on Instagram and other photographic social media sites is the selfie.

Analysis of the selfie primarily relates to representations of the body and embodiment. Typically, the selfie has been connected to the display of the body or as a means for inviting acknowledgement and attention from others. Theresa M. Senft and Nancy K. Baym remark on the overreliance on psychological analyses of selfies as narcissistic and as showcasing emotional or mental instability, body dysmorphia, and low self-esteem in lieu of more sociologically and culturally nuanced examinations.[43] Upon further interpretation, the selfie takes on salience to producers and audiences as a practice in the construction of identity performance or as a political expression of one's place in the world. For example, Jon M. Wargo concludes that in the everyday life of LGBTQ teens, the selfie is part of a curated suite of life-streaming practices and serves as a "sedimentary identity text" where audiences for and viewers of the selfie can construct a "'story-ed' assessment of a subject."[44] The composition of the image, the mise en scene, the choice of clothing, and the setting, situation, and place where the photo is taken all indicate aesthetic and ontological choices that reveal the values, social positions, and identity performance of the person taking the selfie.[45] The selfie can be read as a tactic for reembodiment within digital media forms that are construed as disembodying. As Katrin Tiidenberg explains, selfies allow us to exert control over how we are seen and to construct our identity through the people, places, and activities that we imbue with value.[46]

Furthering the discussion of the selfie as productive form of agency and identity, David Nemer and Guo Freeman regard the utilization of the selfie in Brazilian favelas as a tool for "(re)claiming control over one's embodied self" and expressing "true selves" or genuine feelings and thoughts in the face of adversity and socioeconomic and/or cultural constraints.[47] Similarly, in his ethnographic research, Wargo notes that selfies are "connective identity texts" in that they suture divides of space and place and allow people to find and make place for themselves in digital environments that feel more accessible or safe.[48] For the youths interviewed in both studies, the selfie served as a modality for strategic self-expression and self-reflection that was inseparable from lived experience of place. In terms of place, participants in these studies used selfies to convey personal safety and critiques and experiences of being embedded in poor, crime-ridden, and surveilled environments but also as ways to celebrate perseverance and life in these places. They used selfies as a mode to communicate feelings about place and express place identity and attachment but also to reshape the meaning of living in the favela or in their hometown for themselves and others. Building on Tiidenberg's assertion that selfies allow us to control how we want to be seen, they also allow us to take control of how we want the places we inhabit and value to be seen as well.

Traces of placemaking practices in the production of selfies can be found in the practices of selfie producers, but it is only in the margins of scholarly analysis about selfies. As Aaron Hess notes, in order to understand the intersection of power and authenticity in selfies, we must also pay attention to the physical spaces in which selfies are produced, read, and circulated.[49] In the following section I will examine the work of the selfie in re-placeing the city and how thinking about selfies as placemaking practices informs the productive, potentially empowering, and contested nature of this photographic practice.

Selfies as Placemaking

Selfies are generally understood as producing a sense of "being there" or emplacement for the participant(s): "I was there," "I witnessed this event," or "I am here at this moment." Hess identifies this as a unique type of "place expression," where the selfie visualizes users as specifically embedded and present in physical space as well as within their social networks.[50] The author argues that the selfie reframes the body and materiality through a "new language of space, place, and presence." While the visual rhetoric of the selfie is uniquely recognizable, framing a person as both photographer and subject, as are the apparatuses that aid in this rhetoric such as outstretched arms and selfie sticks, the type of emplacement that the selfie produces deserves further attention. What cultural and spatial work do selfies do? How do selfies re-place and circulate meanings of place through the material presence and emplacement of bodies?

Larissa Hjorth and Sarah Pink observe that people who participate in photographic practices on location-based social media are not just emplaced within digital social networks but also express "situatedness in ecologies of place."[51] The authors argue that these ecologies of place are forged through movement—that the act of moving, sharing, and documenting mobility aids in the configuration of place and the self. Relatedly, Henri Lefebvre notes that "the body serves both as point of departure and as destination," upholding the idea that the social production of space is dependent in part on relationships between the body's movement through place and its return "home."[52] Bodies travel to other places and return to their starting points, marked by traces of the places they've been.

The selfie is a digital expression of how bodies hold on to the presence of places, make these traces recognizable to others, and share "the persistence of place in body" through location-based social media.[53]

Whereas Casey and others have argued that habitual (as in Pierre Bourdieu's habitus) threads that weave place and self together are attenuated through mediated, postmodern conditions, I argue the opposite. Location-based social media artifacts, including the infamous selfie, can be read as coherent practices of suturing the self, place, and positionality together. Similar to our experiences of other creative and artistic practices and texts, the production and viewing of embodied images of the emplaced self through mobile social media can create a shared sense of place and augment feelings of place attachment. In his discussion of performance and place, Rob Sullivan observes how songs, gossip, restaurant reviews, and place naming, as well as other artistic and affective cultural productions, can create a shared sense of place.[54] Through one's presence in a place and the recounting of the experience of being in that place, Sullivan focuses not only on the construction of authenticity of that place but also its "reputation," or circulated and consensual connotations and expectations. Because stories create layers of meaning and significance, sharing stories about place or performances of place tend to narrate place (back) into existence.

Selfies can be read as part of these vernacular and creative placemaking performances, one in which the body and its spatial habitus within society and social networks are prominently read and inscribed as part of the narrative. Although the selfie emerges as a mobile media practice during an era of location announcement, it can be read as more akin to the creative annotation, playful exploration, and thick descriptions of place identified in early locative media projects. More explicitly than other forms of the spatial self, the performance of place in the selfie is staged in the production and curation of the body, its social and physical positionality within hierarchies of power, and the visual culture and aesthetics that shape its interpretation and connotation. Selfies re-place the city twofold in that they rely on digital representations of place for meaning but also add meaning to the places and situations in which they are embedded and digitally displayed.

The selfie performs ownership of the body in that it constructs location as a place where a body does not necessarily "belong" but which it owns in the moment. Bourdieu notes the ways in which individual bodies carry the marks and memories of social position and social distance, and Cresswell suggests the ways in which these classed, gendered, racialized, and sexualized bodies are constructed as "out of place." The selfie is a tactic to exert temporary but visible territoriality over place by visualizing and circulating the marks of one's social position as "in place." When people recognize a body in place, the reciprocity of other participants legitimizes visible bodies and presence. The iterative aggregation of a selfie in multiple news feeds and the performative placemaking of the selfie as a means of control can encourage a sense of polysemic, distributed "ownership" of place and the agency of diverse populations as placemakers within a given location. However, through the same visibility and systems of reciprocity, the selfie may also reinforce place as being available for certain social networks and not others. Although millions of people around the world produce selfies daily, the public visibility and circulation of these images is tempered by access to digital networks, the algorithms that promote select images over others, and the recognition of particular forms of social and locational capital. It is more likely that people view images of place that reify their own and their friends' territoriality and belonging in place or a public persona's or celebrity's re-placeing practices rather than conflicting interpretations of place or images of place as inclusive of all.

However, services like the Instagram Photo Map or the ability to filter geo-coded images, posts, and updates based on location or hashtag rather than social network increase the possibility for unexpected encounters and differential territorial claims within place. For example, the ability to click on the name of a place in mobile social media services like Foursquare and Instagram and open a stream of images taken at that location increases exposure to contradictory claims over the meaning of place and forms of placemaking beyond one's social network. This distributed practice of performative placemaking leads to both recognition and potential clashes over the performances of place that are practiced through selfies. While social media users may form an image and expectations of locations based on their perception of people who have been there,[55] social media users often monitor and critique others' selfies as inappropriate or inaccurate. Websites, institutions or organizations, and public commentary police collective meanings of place through attempts to delegitimize or discredit selfies as placemaking practices. Parody Instagram accounts like Socality Barbie and Tumblr sites like Selfies at Serious Places or Selfies at Funerals not only satirize visual cultures of selfies as a digital media practice but also critique or police location-based social media users' production of place and spatial self.

Socality Barbie, an Instagram account created by Darby Cisneros, a wedding photographer in Portland, Oregon, highlights the curated, gendered, raced, and classed construction of place evident on the social media service. Upon closing the account in fall 2015, the author posted a caption explaining to her 1.3 million followers that she had started the account "to poke fun at all the Instagram trends that I thought were ridiculous." Socality Barbie's parody reveals two key aspects of re-placeing practices on social media. The account critiques the repeated stylistic and generic conventions in the performativity of place where certain places were photographed repeatedly and with intentionally similar framing and composition. This conspicuous consumption of place moves beyond location announcement to construct the value of these representations as commodities that other social media users desired for themselves. Second, the ritual of identifying the self in congruence with location (mapping one's place within society and situational geographies) is not an instrument for microcoordination but a social cue that signals status and social or locational capital to a wider audience through highly visible, branded performances.

Although most commentary understands Socality Barbie's critique of "hipsterdom" in terms of the "inherent phoniness of self-presentation" by "privileged millennials" as well as all Instagram users more broadly,[56] most of the "ridiculousness" represented on the account revolves around similar, stylized performances of the spatial self on Instagram. While other Instagram parody accounts have drawn attention to selfie trends that reify colonialist and exploitative relationships between white, affluent Westerners in developing countries,[57] Socality Barbie satirizes intentional constructions and appropriations of locational capital, the conspicuous consumption of luxury products, and conspicuous mobility in the performance of place through selfies. Many of her photos include a sartorially en vogue Barbie lounging on beaches or perfectly made beds, standing in luxury boots on forest floors or in front of waterfalls, or "relaxing in my hammock in the most absurd places." These photos include hashtags that mimic popular branding and influencer tags such as #exploreeverything, #neverstopexploring, #lifeofadventure, #wildernessculture, and #letsgosomewhere.

Figure 4.1: Instagram post from Socality Barbie account (2015).

Although most of Socality Barbie's posts place her somewhere in the Pacific Northwest, articles in the international popular press remark on the fashion in which she captures "East London life" or Instagram photos of life in other cities.[58] Finding similarities between Instagram productions of place across geographic locations was one intention of the project. When interviewed about her impetus for the account, Cisneros explained, "People were all taking the same pictures in the same places and using the same captions. I couldn't tell any of their pictures apart so I thought: 'What better way to make my point than with a mass-produced doll?'"[59] Cisneros takes issue with the fact that, from her perspective, the performance of the spatial self and claims to "authentic" emplacement have become overly staged and standardized. The commodification of locational capital and the stylization of marking oneself as visible and present in place, although experienced through different spatial habitus and contexts, celebrates universality and strives toward homogenous styles of expression. This parody of placemaking on Instagram highlights the generic and stylistic conventions of re-placeing the city through photographic social media and exposes the ways in which these images have become replicable and commodified.

The Instagram selfie presents new opportunities to express spatial habitus and locational capital to potentially global audiences, but as this parody account reveals, it also mimics strategies of place branding and place promotion used to sell places as competitive locales for attracting labor, affluent residents, and creative communities with disposable income. The genre of selfies parodied by Cisneros is, ironically, reminiscent of the idealized moments produced by wedding photographers like herself in that they are carefully edited and curated to capture picturesque instances of being embodied in place and time. However, the images that she parodies also call attention to the ways in which Instagram users internalize strategies of place branding and place promotion that are traditionally used by marketing companies to sell cities as attractive and desirable places to inhabit. Alice Marwick notes the ways in which social media users internalize and employ neoliberal branding practices in their own status updates, reputation management, and self-presentation strategies online.[60] In this case, social media users brand themselves through their embeddedness in certain places and consume and reproduce marketed connotations of places, but they also contribute to the brand or reputation, feelings and associations, and expectations of that place. Strategies of professional place branding consultants, such as fostering an emotional relationship between place and consumer and connecting aspirational lifestyles and values to particular locations,[61] are definitive qualities within this genre of selfies as well as what Socality Barbie aims to critique.

Websites such as Selfies at Serious Places, Selfies at Funerals, or Grindr Remembers have launched critiques of other placemaking practices on Instagram and mobile social media. These projects identify specific social media photos that showcase a presumed dissonance between the frivolity and self-centered aesthetic of the selfie and the desire to place oneself in a location where crisis, tragedy, or death has occurred. These websites aggregate and display Instagram, Twitter, and Grindr photos at places such as Chernobyl or Auschwitz or at funerals of friends and family members, where the choice of the selfie as a placemaking practice feels inappropriate or is taken and circulated at inappropriate locations. Although James Meese, Martin Gibbs, Marcus Carter, Michael Arnold, Bjorn Nansen, and Tamara Kohn as well as Lee Humphreys interpret selfies at funerals to be evidence of reckoning and coping with loss and documenting presence in social situations or rituals around death, most interpretations of these practices revolve around the meaning of place. As Hess suggests, sites like Selfies at Serious Places reveal the tensions between the meaning of the selfie and the "decorum" associated with certain places.[62]

In terms of place, the palpable tension should not be understood as existing solely between these "serious places" and the genre of selfies but within the affective performativity displayed in the selfie and its power as a placemaking practice. Journalists and technology blogs have connoted this emerging genre of selfies as "cringe worthy" while shaming and reprimanding the social media users who appear on these sites.[63] They take issue with the emotional incoherence between the perceived purpose of the selfie and the consensus about the meaning of certain places. More recently, administrators of physical spaces that serve as PokéStops in the locative media game *Pokémon Go* such as the US Holocaust Museum in Washington, DC, have raised concern about the perceived mismatch between the meaning of place and the practice of digital, ludic placemaking.[64] The Holocaust Museum has issued cease and desist announcements and pleas to the company to omit the site from the game as a location where players can visit to advance their game play. The jest and nonchalance depicted in the faces, bodies, and captions at sites such as Pearl Harbor, Holocaust memorials, and toxic spills are in direct opposition to a dominant, official, or "common sense" sense of place and the stories that the creators of the websites think ought to be acted out on such premises.

These sites collectively critique the ways that the body maps affect onto the ownership of place through the selfie. As Sara Ahmed notes, emotion aligns bodies as insiders or outsiders.[65] The affective performance of place assigns a particular positionality to these selfie producers and marks their status as outsiders who actively or unwittingly resist or disrupt dominant structures of feeling or reputations of place. Their stories resonate as part of a potential affective counterpublic in the way that they provide recognizable cacophony and counterdiscourses within preexisting "bonds of sentiment" that shape place and contextualize behavior.[66] While some journalists and aghast social media users perceive these productions as an affront to "selfie etiquette," the images are more accurately understood as ruptures in consensus around the hegemonic meaning and social productions of certain places. The reactions to these selfies and parody accounts reveal cultural agreements about the meanings of certain places and invite the policing of performances of place that discredit the role of certain people as placemakers and the alternative meanings they construct. In addition to delegitimizing the sense of place produced through these dissonant photos and captions, the websites also discipline selfie creators as participants in "soft structures of storytelling" around emotionally sensitive and affectively controversial locations.[67]

In her discussion of mobile imaging practices among young migrant women in China, Cara Wallis argues that practices such as taking and sharing selfies "are about self making and actively deploying the imagination . . . as a form of negotiation between sites of individual agency and globally defined fields of possibility."[68] Selfies construct the world as a place to be pictured, to be framed and expressed through one's imagination and creative productions. While selfies can be read as a form of empowerment in place because of the role of imagination—allowing participants to express and control the meaning of a place and working to create a sense of belonging or emplacement through habitus and identity performance—the agency of the selfie can be read as relegating placemaking to the networked individual as well as the collective. The dominant practice and cultural influence of repeatedly harnessing preexisting meanings and connotations of place for self-presentation and identity performance obscure alternate or emergent readings of place in the selfie and create the illusion of a collective, coherent sense of place for particular locations. When the affordances of "screenness" and social media help to profile the imagination of a single producer front and center, especially one that disrupts the imagined consensus around the meaning of place, the results are jarring. Websites like Selfies at Serious Places and Grindr Remembers work to emphasize (and ostracize) the singularity of these expressions, constructing these disruptions as aberrant meaning making by careless individuals rather than as coherent, and potentially shared, alternative interpretations of the meaning of place.

Self-Quantification and "Datafication" as Re-placing

"Datafication," or the "process of rendering aspects of the world not previously quantified" into data points,[69] constructs place as an entity made more knowable through data. Researchers, municipal governments, public utility companies and commercial enterprises as well as members of the public have become concerned with how the world can be known through "data-driven urbanism" and the coding of place as data.[70] Open-city data and city-sponsored hackathons devoted to uncovering patterns in urban systems and urban life have proliferated. Working with open, accessible datasets about water supplies, air pollution, retail and restaurant locations, budgets, bus schedules, census tracks, or 311 calls, programmers build apps that propose to improve access to resources, help people make informed decisions about urban systems, and augment the quality of urban life. The datafication of everyday social, physical, and economic practices is compiled from and plays out on the individual bodies of urban residents. Smartphones, networked devices that we carry close to our bodies every day, have increasingly been imagined and utilized as sensors or tracking devices that record mood, heart rate, sleep patterns, steps taken, purchases made, or weight gained or lost, all with date and time stamps as well as geospatial coordinates. These categories of personal data about individual bodies are not (yet) universally collected on the municipal level but are recorded and archived by the people who are producing the data.

Datafication of the self has come to be known as self-tracking, self-quantification, or "self knowledge through numbers." Consumer markets worldwide have seen a surge in devices and software that measure and produce data about everyday life. An established subgenre of self-quantification apps is entirely dedicated to collecting and visualizing information about an individual's movement and presence in place. Applications like NikeFuel or Nike+, Map My Run, Garmin Connect, Paces, and FitBit track and record exercise-based physical activity. LocationSwap, Trackr, and Mappen allow users to monitor their location in relation to and in addition to their friends. My Ways, Last Night's Check-Ins, Where Do You Go, MapMe.at, Geoloqi, TrackMe, and Moves allow users to track, record, and share logs of their movements through space. Getupp and I Move You keep track of the places where users commit to being present (e.g., at the gym, at home for dinner, etc.) or allow participants to challenge their friends to go for a walk or go shopping together and reward or shame participants accordingly. In addition, several applications allow users to map social media and self-generated data that is downloaded from self-quantification devices and programs (e.g., WebTrack, Fluxtream, Zenobase, Resvan Maps, MMapper, Move-O-Scope).[71] All these apps, APIs, and websites promise knowledge through numbers and the accurate pinpointing of individual locations over time. Descriptions and promotional materials for these projects offer insight into individual patterns and habits as well as insight into presence and experiences of place as well.

The affordances of smartphones as individual, almost always on, tracking, recording, and reporting devices—as well as the self-quantification apps and software that they support—echo smart-city sensors and intelligent monitoring paradigms in purpose and in promise. The screen of the smartphone is not a frame or window but a sentient object that demands user attention (but not directed focus) and allows people to make decisions about their place in the world through access to information about themselves in their environments. Self-quantification through mobile devices evokes the "promise of agency through mediated self-knowledge"[72] and makes us and our activities and the spaces we inhabit more knowable and ordered.

Self-quantification devices and apps promise to make our environments more manageable and create situations in which our bodies are more responsive. Knowing oneself and one's surroundings, as well as the way the two interact, is meant to produce more informed choices about the self and space, adjusting routines and habits to be more interesting, efficient, healthy, or safe. In both self-quantification apps and smart-city projects, data conveys knowledge and insight, allowing people to quantify systems and exchanges that previously seemed uncertain or indeterminate and to qualify decisions about them. Through these processes, the gathering and analyzing of data fuels social imaginaries of place.

In getting to know ourselves through data, we become emplaced in new ways. You know more precisely that at 9:36 a.m. on Friday, July 31, you were running along Sixteenth Street with a heart rate of two hundred beats per minute and were taking more steps than you normally do during the week. It is possible to know at what time on what day you went shopping at a specific store or to a museum, or where your friends are and the location of the closest restaurant at any given moment. If users desire, they can view maps, charts, or logs of this data; share them with friends; see friends' maps or archives; and in some cases view personal mobility and activity in relationship to a network of familiar or unknown others. This combination of datafication and location awareness produces place as a series of locations where visible, observable, quantifiable activities happen. Additionally, it is the individual user who drives these activities and an individual presence that beckons these places into being.

What narratives and relationships with place are produced through data-driven urbanism? How do we re-place the city through our engagement with devices and apps that track, analyze, and map our movements and presence in space? The datafication of place-based experience and presence leads to predictive and prescriptive practices of re-placeing. The datafication of location and emplacement can expand one's "field of awareness" of the activities that occur in and compose the meaning of a particular place and our embodied proprioception.[73] This field of awareness can also be interpreted as a particular genre of mindfulness that develops through the use of self-quantification apps. Tamar Sharon and Dorien Zandbergen have found that people who regularly track their behavior through self-quantification apps cultivate an active, conscious attention to habits that they previously took for granted or that went unnoticed.[74] In a similar manner, locative media projects that offer tracking and monitoring of movement and presence help cultivate focused attention to place in a way that allows "quantifying selves" to think more consciously and strategically about where they go and don't go. As Helen Kennedy, Thomas Poell, and José van Dijck note, providing data about the self and embedded environments to participants enables them to intentionally "orient themselves in the world."[75] In relation to place, attention to one's own movement and the movement of others can restructure geospatial agency, self-reflection, and decision-making processes about past and future travel.

Tracking and aggregating an individual's movement through urban space is utilized as not only informative but predictive of future movements, actions, and meanings of place. The incorporation of locative media data in urban studies has been interpreted as the "'preemptive' imagining of unknown future cities,"[76] where the traces left by locative media users can be used to extrapolate what might happen next. Researchers have visualized and mapped social media check-ins, geo-coded tweets, posts, photographs, and self-quantified data to assess mobility decisions among friend groups or mobility patterns of individual users on a given day as well as place attachment based on mapped social media photographs.[77] For example, Raz Schwartz and Nadav Hochman have overlaid Instagram images on New York City park maps to reveal density and social congestion patterns, record activities in certain locations over time, and access visitors' affective and personal experiences of place.[78] Justin Cranshaw, Raz Schwartz, Jason Hong, and Norman Sadeh have aggregated check-ins and geo-coded tweets to compile a sense of place based on the digital media traces of people who visit and move between specific neighborhoods.[79] In both studies, geo-coded, user-generated data left by digital media participants is used to evaluate the character of a given location as well as predict who might travel there in the future and for what purpose.

Geo-coded self-quantification data is prescriptive as well as predictive. Matthew Wilson suggests that location-based services render mobilities into data objects that represent existing and speculative mobilities, the "potentiality of action."[80] The information provided is meant to be responded to and to effect a change or repetition of mobility patterns based on augmented awareness of spatial relations over time. However, this awareness and potential for responsive action is based on spatial routines and the places that people tend to travel to. Drawing from recorded, habitual patterns of active mobility or perceived sedentariness, location-based self-quantification programs encourage users to move through space based on data gathered about past experiences, preferences, and exchanges, which may result in exploration but may also filter locations and prescribe mobilities that value familiar or algorithmically similar places over others. As Farman suggests, difference and otherness become flattened in these representations. Locative media projects tend to reiterate to the user the places and people they're already aware of.[81] Instead of exhibiting places that users have yet to explore, tracking and self-surveillance projects tend to mirror perspectives and experiences of place back to us and even recommend more places that are algorithmically perceived as similar to the places we've been—re-placing the city as a locational "filter bubble."

Based on past travel patterns, these services offer suggestions for where you belong. Although people's spatial perspective and possibilities change as they move, as different places become within or out of reach, the profiles and positionalities of users remain the same wherever they go. As this profile or "new algorithmic identity" becomes linked to place, the possibility of experiencing strangeness in terms of the places one visits, of being a stranger in the city, or of feeling out of place in a recommended location decreases. Feeling and moving like a local, qualities that many services promise to fulfill, shift from knowing where you are or "the best places" to go to being perpetually embedded in places as an insider among people with similar profiles and preferences. Instead of employing navigation systems and meet-ups to find places you belong, more recent locative media services promise to find these places for you. Tracking and monitoring physical movement and mapping place as data undermine the strangeness of the city by ensuring that places are slightly different from where you've been but also that they are never completely other or for others.

Studies that draw conclusions about the meaning of place based on geo-coded social media and self-quantification data alone can be paired with other methodologies and information sources to ascertain a more holistic perspective about the character and experience of place: combinations of ethnography, offline observation, events calendars, restaurant or bar or tour reviews and guides, and/or newspaper coverage. However, the reliance on social media, GPS, self-quantification, and automatic tracking paired with the visualization of this data produces information about place that feels organic and contextualized as well as precise. The lure of this data lies in the illusion of quantification of social practices that are often difficult to observe en masse or in a laboratory. However, the attractiveness of these visualizations risks indicating that the places shown on screens are where activities are happening, where publics are gathering, and where the social life of a city takes place. The visualizations produced by location-based social media and geo-coded self-quantification programs are often visually interesting and offer discernable complexity in the form of points that can be dissected, filtered, layered, and analyzed such that the enticement of knowable cities positions researchers and participants on the precipice of forgetting that the data being viewed and analyzed is only a very partial, privileged view of what the city is and who uses it.

Scholars have critiqued the type of knowledge produced through "big data" and the datafication of social and cultural aspects of everyday life as well as location-based data specifically. Kate Crawford and danah boyd note that although big data is shrouded in the mythology that large datasets produce higher forms of intelligence and knowledge, taking data out of context depletes or obscures its meaning.[82] Often, location *is* context in big-data analysis. Although location is typically perceived as the variable that adds context to "big" or quantified data, in the case of location-based social media and self-quantification data, it is location that needs further contextualization. In the datafication of location, paradoxically, a sense of place is often the context that is both lost and sought through data collection and analysis.

Researchers have begun to critique the types of knowledge and insight produced through the datafication of location. Rob Kitchin suggests that although data-driven urbanism processes a Foucauldian *dispositif* that is the city, the data visualizations and assemblages that are produced present themselves as objective and politically neutral.[83] The same can be said for the social media and self-tracking data that are used to make claims about where and why people gather and travel and what these places collectively mean. As Schwartz and I have previously argued, the fact that an image, text, or artifact is geo-coded does not mean that it is a representation of objective reality or a precise location. Instead, because these digital traces are geo-coded representations of particular ways of being and representing the world, they are performative and flexible and require cultural interpretation in order to be unpacked and analyzed. Added to these conversations about context and epistemologies of datafication, there should also be a recognition that sensed or volunteered information about "where people are" is never apolitical, and the sense of place constructed through these representations reveals economic and social inequities and privileges as much as they suggest where to go next.

Re-placeing in Social and Locative Media

The manner by which people relate to and understand the places they encounter within urban environments has remained the same over several decades in many ways. Examining premarkers and connotations of

place preceding travel, documenting presence in place, and photographing or archiving place-based experiences as souvenirs still structure
social rituals and practices around mobility and tourism. However,
re-placeing the city through locative and social media enables intimate access to curated presentations of the multiaxiality of place and
constructions of place identity and place attachment by known and
unknown digital media users. The ways in which situated individual and
collective knowledges about urban places are expressed and exhibited
have been expanded to include placemaking practices relayed through
creative forms of media accounting and datafication that rely on digital
affordances and personal devices for their production and exhibition.

Disparate temporal relations are expressed, archived, and juxtaposed
through new genres and styles of production, distribution, and consumption as well as expressions of overlapping and sometimes conflicting mobilities and experiences. Data scientists and big-data researchers
rely on the traces left by location-based social media users to make arguments about the meanings, activities, and patterns of mobility that
compose certain places. However, upon closer examination of the traces
themselves and the interactions around these traces, a far less coherent
data set emerges, and the meaning of location-based social media norms
and texts become polyvalent, contextual, and contentious. By viewing
location-based social media traces such as selfies, check-ins, and other
publicly shared mobility patterns as re-placeing the city through performative placemaking, we can better understand what these traces signify
within the everyday lives of their producers and as bids for the cultural
meanings of place.

The networked projects discussed in this chapter employ cartography, photography, status updates, and sensing technologies in order to
document place in an artistic and symbolic manner, track and archive
embodied mobilities, and publicly express the "representational spaces"
of urban inhabitants as tactics of urban mobility and presence. The narratives produced by urban residents and visitors are displayed as interactive but also as interacting with each other. The style in which these
stories are told, what participants choose to tell, the mechanisms and
situations for mobile reception, and the digital structures for exhibition
all orchestrate the meanings of these stories for a larger audience. The
imagination of the city as a "place of encounters" remains intact, yet the

types of urban encounters that extend into digital spaces are shaped by networked technologies and networked publics.

Lefebvre celebrated the city as a "place of encounters" and as a "place of the unexpected," which scholars like David Harvey have linked to urban imagination.[84] As Harvey notes, experience is mediated by imagination, and at times, encounters and experiences (invited or unanticipated) will alter urban imagination or the preconceived notions derived from pre-markers of place. The projects and practices discussed in this chapter can be understood as augmenting Lefebvre's place of encounters, creating and enabling numerous, layered interactions with urban place. However, the encounters constructed through re-placeing the city are often contested. Unlike previous metaphors of unexpected encounters in public spaces and street sociability as ballet, or drama that can be shared by passersby, locative media placemaking practices emphasize the polysemy of place, hierarchical agency around placemaking practices, and the critique of social norms around digital placemaking in public spaces. For example, selfies as efforts to re-place the city might foster a sense of embeddedness and ownership over certain spaces while also calling attention to distinct ideologies about the meaning, decorum, and use of place. Self-quantification and predictive systems of locational presence might augment a user's intimate relationship with and consciousness of their own mobility patterns, but they can create locational filter bubbles that re-place the city as more of the same. In these cases, re-placeing the city through locative media has created friction not just between different connotations or interpretations of place identity but between different styles and practices of placemaking.

If we consider, as Lefebvre does, that power is concealed beneath and within the organization of space, then the projects examined in this chapter tend to illustrate new ways in which power and difference are being reinscribed in space. While critics of digital media within public space directly link the "etherealization of geography" to communication technologies and warn of a perceived decomposition and eradication of a sense of place,[85] I have suggested that the projects analyzed in this chapter evidence a contradictory trend. Instead of dispelling understandings and allegiances to place, urban locative and social media projects are employed by networked urban subjects to re-place the city and offer tools through which to curate a sense of place and locational capital. These re-placeing practices illustrate that in light of rapidly changing physical and social environments and expanding digital opportunities for geo-coded self-presentation, people embrace the practices of marking and being marked by place and desire to trace personal histories against the patterns of activity and differential mobility of others. As this chapter also illustrates, these placemaking practices not only re-place the city but produce social and technological situations that should encourage us to reflect on the types of places we create through digital media use.

5

The Creative City

Digital Media in Creative Placemaking

One day, while lounging in a chair at the public library, I was approached by a man with a high-end camera. I was revising a chapter for this book and had paused to send an email on my mobile phone. The cameraperson asked whether he could take a photo of me reading. The image was to be included in a promotional film about Massachusetts Street, the main street in downtown Lawrence, Kansas. It would be shown only once to a group of investors and public officials in Houston, Texas, to highlight the amenities and activities of downtown Lawrence. The cameraperson explained that he had already taken exterior shots of people shopping, eating, and strolling and that the photo of me reading a stack of papers would round out the sequence and would be used to illustrate "relaxing." He assured me that the photo wouldn't take up too much of my time. All I had to do was lean back and resume reading. I could sip my coffee maybe. But first, I had to put away my mobile phone.

The idea that using my mobile phone in a public space could mark me as doing the opposite of relaxing or indicate that I was socially withdrawn or didn't appreciate the surroundings that the photograph was meant to promote permeates public consciousness. The popular press often warns of digital-media-addicted youth who can hardly carry on a conversation with companions while dining out or are absorbed entirely by the light of their screens while strolling down the sidewalk. Indeed, streets and public spaces sometimes feel and look this way: people with their heads down, consumed by the exchanges occurring behind individual screens. The cameraperson's request was not uncommon. Promotional materials for cities, real estate developments, and public spaces rarely show images of people using mobile phones or laptops except to indicate spaces of productivity, innovation, or entrepreneurship like office buildings in business districts, lecture halls on college campuses, and coffee shops or Wi-Fi-enabled parks and plazas catering to the freelance creative class. However, when the cameraperson asked me to conceal my phone, I was surprised. I wasn't a distracted, zombielike social recluse trying to ignore the place I was in or the people around me. Instead, I had gone to the library to take to heart Cresswell's claim that "place provides the conditions of possibility for creative social practice,"[1] to sit by the large windows in the company of other people who were reading and writing, to try to write a book in a space where I felt inspired and comfortable and where I enjoyed visiting. Ironically, at that moment, I was every bit enjoying and relaxing in place.

The aim of this chapter is not to convince the reader that every time people sit at the library on their mobile phones they feel at home or are productively carving out a place for themselves (although in some cases, this might be true). Instead, I want to suggest that placemaking practices that foster creative production and digital media use in public spaces are not mutually exclusive. As the previous chapters have illustrated, people make place tactically and strategically through digital media. However, institutions that support creative production of urban space often perceive digital media as antithetical to their mission. In this chapter, I will explore the phenomenon of "creative placemaking"—a term coined by the National Endowment for the Arts (NEA) and promoted by arts-based organizations in the United States—and argue that much like the cell phone–free image of the library that the photographer chose to present, the imagination and integration of digital media within creative placemaking initiatives and funding opportunities has been misplaced and misunderstood.

In 2010 the National Endowment for the Arts presented a series of white papers explaining how municipal efforts to increase the accumulation of talent, resources, and global attention for specific urban centers could be achieved through the cultivation of arts and culture institutions and activities, an effort the NEA described as "creative placemaking." According to the authors of these papers, creative placemaking is a process where "partners from public, private, non-profit, and community sectors strategically shape the physical and social character of a neighborhood, town, city, or region around arts and cultural activities."[2] At present, grants, academic degrees and certification programs, the popular and industry press, and municipal planners and architects have incorporated this term and concept into their programs and initiatives. However, it is rare that digital media technologies and practices are mentioned in conjunction with creative placemaking. Often, digital media, particularly mobile media such as cell phones and smartphones, are held up as culprits that impede the promise of placemaking through the arts and humanities.

In this chapter, practices related to re-placeing the city are investigated from the perspective of those who professionally plan, program, and fund creative placemaking activities. The examples in this chapter combine the strategic placemaking practices of urban development discussed in chapters 1 and 2 with the tactical practices of street-level community and artistic intervention analyzed in chapters 3 and 4. Unlike previous examples of re-placeing the city, where placemaking was mundane or habitual, the cultural institutions and communities examined in this chapter consciously and officially act as designated placemakers and even publicly label their activities as placemaking. In regard to re-placeing the city, a case study of creative placemaking reveals the ways in which institutions and artists who are charged with (through funding and/or mission statements) remaking place are incorporating digital media into their vision and work. Through participant observation and textual analysis of creative placemaking projects, content analysis of funding practices and funded projects, and discourse analysis of published interviews with municipal officials, urban planners, and grassroots or community organizations who have undertaken creative placemaking projects, I evaluate the ways in which digital technologies and practices are imagined and implemented in order to "animate public and private spaces, rejuvenate structures and streetscapes, improve local business and public safety, and bring diverse people together to celebrate and inspire."[3] In addition, I analyze why digital technologies and practices are largely *not* being associated with and incorporated into prominent creative placemaking endeavors.

Creative Placemaking

Although projects, initiatives, and ideas that resemble creative placemaking have circulated for decades, particularly at the municipal and community levels, Ann Markusen and Anne Gadwa Nicodemus coined the term in a white paper commissioned by the NEA and the Mayors' Institute on City Design in 2010. Six years later "creative placemaking" has come to be associated with the idea that the arts, writ large, can improve the meaning, significance, and quality of a place—that cities and communities can embrace the arts to drive innovation and economic development, spark urban renewal, attract talent, and reproduce a sense of place for visitors and residents.[4] Practitioners and journalistic accounts of creative placemaking tend to disseminate the idea that spaces in need of creative placemaking are typically underused, abandoned, or vacant and thus in need of renewal.[5] Simultaneously, grant applications and calls for applicants often focus on places with deep histories and rooted populations. In these latter projects, embracing and implementing creative placemaking does not entail building something where nothing exists but celebrating the engrained, yet potentially forgotten or fragmented, uniqueness of a place.[6]

Creative placemaking is constructed in Markusen and Gadwa Nicodemus's definitive text as a solution to a problem that plagues cities, suburbs, and rural towns across the United States. "The problem" as Markusen and Gadwa Nicodemus envision it is that "American cities, suburbs, and small towns confront structural changes and residential uprooting" that can be ameliorated through "creative initiatives that animate places and spark economic development."[7] "The solution" echoes the desired outcomes and goals of creative placemaking endeavors: to generate jobs and income for residents, augment diversity and livability, increase tourism, and foster innovation by creating products and services within culture industries. In offering creative placemaking solutions, practitioners and funders have tried to develop strategies that not only attempt to meet these goals but also speak to the collaborative and coordinated spirit of the original description: to bring together various stakeholders invested in serving and developing a particular locale and offer orchestrated arts-based strategies and projects. Unlike tactical urbanism, which creates ephemeral, rapidly implemented, guerilla-style arts projects to alter understandings and experiences of public space, creative placemaking is intended to create strategically orchestrated projects with measurable outcomes that are maintained over time.[8]

As housing, transportation, public safety, utility provision, and economic development are recognized as integral in building and sustaining thriving communities, creative placemaking organizations strive to be seen as part of this collaborative consortium.[9] To this end, creative placemaking efforts are structured around conversations and collaborations between various municipal and community actors with the intention to partner diverse stakeholders and interest groups around arts-driven urban revitalization. Throughout creative placemaking campaigns and initiatives, theories of placemaking draw on definitions by urban theorists such as Jane Jacobs and William Whyte: "community planning and development that is human-centric, comprehensive, and locally informed."[10]

According to several NEA documents and presentations, fostering conversations among community members and between community and funding organizations is a foundational step toward these goals. Public input, forums, data gathering, participatory planning sessions, and ongoing opportunities to identify and discuss community needs, desires, crises, or challenges jumpstart creative placemaking processes. These conversations are followed by further discussions, sessions, or events that focus on how artists and arts organizations might tend to community concerns. Subsequent to the original NEA report, there have been various interpretations of creative placemaking and the role of "the community" in cultivating or restructuring sense of place. Arts nonprofits with some longevity tend to emphasize that local communities are placemakers and that community interests are served by creative placemaking efforts (e.g., Artspace and Artscape in Minneapolis), while newly established organizations tend to focus on creating artistic communities that are forged through creative placemaking as an approach to planning, designing, and managing public spaces (e.g., Connecticut Office of the Arts).

The goals of creative placemaking projects are simultaneously concrete and vague. As practitioners expressed during a summit on creative placemaking practices in 2014, the NEA's vision of creative placemaking frames "transformation" as a core tenet, promise, and outcome: "transformation of the audience; transformation of content; transformation of space; transformation of institution; transformation of the community's access to artistic expression; transformation of the artist."[11] As in smart-city discourse, transformation tends to be an amorphous term that is applied to a general "upgrade" of place but is ultimately difficult to measure. Reports and proposals for creative placemaking projects tend to emphasize terms such as "quality of life" and "vibrancy" alongside economic development and attracting investment in a given location.

The polyvocality of these terms is evident in organizations' attempts to define them. For example, ArtPlace defines "vibrancy" as "places with an unusual scale and intensity of specific kinds of human interaction." Vibrancy is often explained in terms of its effects rather than its characteristics, but overall, it's framed as an essential quality of place. In addition to attracting and retaining talent, vibrancy is also meant to "change the trajectory of the community" and to "make a difference" in the rural, suburban, and urban locations where creative placemaking occurs.[12] Creative placemaking is meant to "animate," "rejuvenate," and "improve" spaces and "celebrate" and "inspire" people.[13] The emphasis on activating and animating spaces and people through creative placemaking implies a sedentary or dull lassitude that precedes these initiatives and obstructs the means by which this vibrancy can be produced. Although Markusen and Gadwa Nicodemus insist in several articles that "fuzzy concepts" are intentional and essential to the success of placemaking initiatives, they also recognized that vibrancy, livability, and rejuvenation are contentious and difficult to measure.[14] However, as indicators and attempts to quantify creative placemaking outcomes are developed, concepts like vibrancy have been defined as population density, employment rates, creative industry clusters, independent businesses, walkable neighborhoods, and concentrations of restaurants, bars, and nightlife.[15]

Shortly after the NEA white paper's release, grants and funding agencies gained a stronghold: Our Town grants (NEA), ArtPlace America (a consortium of granting organizations composed of thirteen foundations and six banks),[16] Kresge Foundation creative placemaking grants, creative placemaking workshops funded by the Citizens' Institute on Rural Design,[17] state departments of economic development (e.g., Connecticut shifted all arts funding toward creative placemaking around 2012),[18] and funding for projects that incorporated plastic and performing arts, murals, installations and exhibitions, music and cultural events, arts incubators, and workshops into social and economic development. Cities that have been awarded Our Town, ArtPlace, and Kresge Foundation creative placemaking grants have used these funds to support or incubate local art scenes, foster art appreciation, or curate performing arts, film and media arts, installations, exhibits, and events to promote economic and social improvement through artistic practice. Many grant-funded projects involved building new studios, workshops, or arts-driven innovation spaces; staging events and performances; and renovating abandoned buildings or public spaces, all in the name of cultivating community efficacy, pride, and arts awareness. Anne Gadwa Nicodemus notes that US Department of Housing and Urban Development programs for neighborhood development have altered funding guidelines to include strategies that incorporate the arts.[19] By 2013 the NEA and ArtPlace alone had awarded 232 grants across the United States, totaling $41.6 million.[20] Unlike other US or European arts initiatives, which are gradually adopted by funding institutions and practitioners, creative placemaking has received attention extraordinarily quickly.

As Jamie Bennett, executive director of ArtPlace, explained in 2015, ArtPlace, Our Town, and other NEA-affiliated organizations and proponents of creative placemaking work to undo common misconceptions and negative associations with the term. Bennett notes that some people associate "creative" with Richard Florida's ideas around competitively attracting a "creative class" that would homogenize and gentrify neighborhoods and "leave Starbucks, bicycles, and gay couples in their wake."[21] He indicates other common (mis)conceptions that understand "placemaking" as a process of discovery and colonization whereby place "makers" disregard or ignore preexisting histories, people, and ways of life as they make way for an exclusive future. In response, creative placemaking organizations have promoted the idea that their efforts alter a shared sense of place from bearing a negative or troublesome connotation into a more positive or enhanced image that increases visits to underused public spaces. Instead of turning storefronts into Starbucks, Bennett's vision of creative placemaking turns traffic congestion and busy construction sites into destinations rather than obstructions or turns empty lots into places brimming with creative activity.

Critiques of Creative Placemaking

At a summit in 2014 creative placemaking professionals were asked to explain what "creative placemaking" meant to them in practice. They collectively noted that "creative engagement" was a term more generally used by their organizations to describe their efforts and that it was also a way to move beyond the idea that placemaking is about physical space. Many creative placemaking projects adopt the framework of urban revitalization and urban renewal in rhetoric and purpose. Often these renewal solutions involve building or revitalizing a physical or tangible structure or somehow altering the preexisting physical environment. Critics have noted that although "placemaking" is associated with Jacobs and Whyte's conception of community-centered, collaborative design, the notion of "place" in creative placemaking projects is heavily directed toward the built environment and an "if you build it, they will come" mentality.[22] A review of creative placemaking projects has found that permanent or temporary designs and installations for public spaces are the most frequently funded type of project.[23] An overview of project descriptions funded by Our Town grants shows that a substantial majority of projects engage the public through development, redevelopment, or conservation and reinvention of abandoned or new buildings, parks, schools, streetscapes, and pedestrian corridors with an emphasis on public art installations (as well as classes, workshops, and events occurring in these spaces). Perhaps due to the required criteria for measured outcomes, emphasis is often placed on tangible artwork or visible changes to the built environment such as artists' studios, designated districts or public spaces, or choreographed and structured events at a specific location and time.

Practitioners' comments and key ideas that emerged from the summit implied that the way "placemaking" was initially framed by the NEA excluded forms of community engagement that were not linked to physical space. In addition, one of the central inspirations for creative placemaking—to bring diverse stakeholders together under the umbrella of the arts as an impetus for economic and social development—encouraged organizations to pursue partnerships that might secure funding but were not always beneficial to the communities they aimed to serve. Instead of attempting to shoehorn current or future artistic practices into the framework of development or urban improvement efforts, summit attendees suggested that creative placemakers listen more carefully to the communities they serve and alter creative placemaking strategies to mesh with the goals and intentions of the projects that were already being created locally.[24]

Several creative-placemaking-funded cities and organizations encountered resistance or public criticism of their efforts. For example, I am writing this chapter in a city that was awarded a $500,000 ArtPlace America grant for a creative placemaking project in 2013.[25] The grant was approved for the redevelopment of a seven-block section of an arterial street that connects downtown to an eastern warehouse turned arts district. The street is currently lined with vintage stores, an elementary school, boutique restaurants and cocktail bars, artists' studios, a maker space, new luxury apartment condominiums, and commercial spaces as well as folk art sculptures and historic houses. While the grant-funded project didn't explicitly request funds to demolish or repurpose preexisting buildings or to create art installations, it did propose to embed new lighting and sound installations along the street and create a large rock sculpture, a bike path, and collections of native prairie plants.[26] The project was slated to be led by urban design, engineering, and landscape architecture firms.

Community members, particularly people who for years have lived on or near what will be called the Ninth Street Corridor have voiced mixed feelings about the project. In particular, they insist that the area around Ninth Street is already a creative place and is in no need of rebranding. Aside from the threat that redevelopment might undermine or significantly redirect the character of this place, several residents are also concerned about being priced out of their neighborhood as the branded redevelopment progresses, especially since some residents regard their collective interests as existing at odds with the advisory board that is meant to represent them at City Hall.

In opposition to creative placemaking endeavors, community members directly affected by the changes to the Ninth Street Corridor have established a coalition called the East 9th Street Placekeepers and created a website dedicated to compiling "critiques of placemaking," which displays a copy of the creative placemaking grant application and budget, excerpts of letters from concerned citizens, and "visual responses" that include DIY banners, posters, and stickers.[27] The stickers and posters equate the placemaking grant to a Trojan horse and warn of the clandestine agenda to destroy the neighborhood as it currently stands. Instead of claiming ownership of their neighborhood, celebrating the artistic expression of community members, or creating new spaces for people to congregate in order to foster a sense of place or discuss issues facing their local community, these residents read creative placemaking as a way of bringing outsiders in, possibly at the expense of the place and people already embedded there.

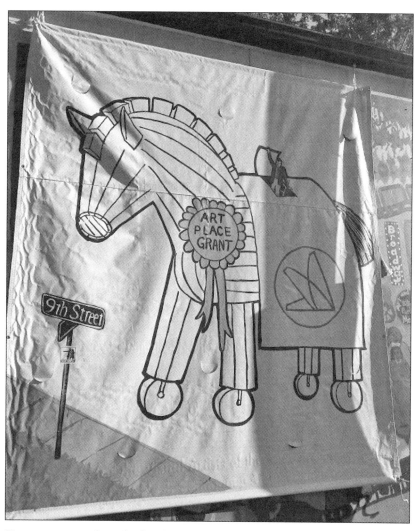

Figures 5.1, 5.2, 5.3: Signs displayed to protest creative placemaking efforts in Lawrence, Kansas. Photo credit: East 9th Street Placekeepers.

Stephen Pritchard has called these protest tactics "place guarding," or activities developed to protest the potential gentrification initiatives and displacement of people from their place.[28] Similar concerns and complaints about NEA-funded creative placemaking projects have been launched in cities across the United States. The artists and community members involved in Transported + Renewed—a series of events and public art displays celebrating urban renewal in Houston's East End, partially funded by the Our Town grant program—highlighted several qualms about the administration and ethics of the project. These concerns included limited community input, the influence of a powerful oligopoly in determining how creative placemaking worked in practice, lack of response to misgivings about the inequitable inclusion of Latino artists, and lack of transparency, inclusion, and accountability to the people who lived in the locations marked for redevelopment through the arts.[29]

Local blogs and groups voicing community concern in various cities including Milwaukee (Wisconsin), Portland (Maine), Detroit (Michigan), and Brooklyn (New York) have been launched in reaction to creative placemaking grants and funded art projects. Most complaints mention the lack of representation and social equity and discontent over the process of discerning the meaning of place, the future of place, and the artistic and creative projects that might help communities achieve directed goals. One of the key lessons learned by a collective of creative placemaking grantees (as expressed directly to NEA representatives) is that creative placemaking should celebrate the community and unite community members in order to identify and work through shared issues and concerns. According to creative placemaking grantees, any dialogue around placemaking should be inclusive and representative and should not import people from outside the community to solve community problems or identify goals.[30]

In these cases, economic development or revitalization seemed to be the desired outcome of the projects. In her review of grant applications, Gadwa Nicodemus also noted the prominence of funded projects that proposed economic development and tourism as desired results of creative placemaking proposals.[31] Economic development and tourism indicate an outward-looking focus in terms of placemaking: the place is being made for people who reside outside the neighborhoods. For these reasons, creative placemaking as outlined by Markusen and Gadwa Nicodemus and the plethora of funding institutions and arts and urban planning organizations that have adopted their definition have been critiqued as neoliberal cooptations of the connection between community and the arts.

Roberto Bedoya, executive director of the Tucson Pima Arts Council and creative placemaking grantee, published an article that circulated among arts organizations and ultimately appeared in an influential journal for grantors and policy makers in the arts. His article addresses how social justice and equality issues are not adequately represented in creative placemaking projects. He reifies concerned citizens' remarks by compelling other communities to research and address the politics of belonging and disbelonging within placemaking practices and to incorporate "an aesthetic of belonging" into their projects.[32] The Project for Public Spaces (PPS) critiques creative placemaking in a similar vein. The organization calls attention to the fact that in creative placemaking projects, experts are identified or brought in to manufacture place, which is antithetical to the collaborative spirit of placemaking. These experts, such as artists, designers, architects, and planners, are invited to work alongside community members but are criticized for silencing or obscuring the desires, needs, and input from diverse communities and not helping to cultivate the "community as expert."[33] This critique implies that rather than listening to communities, outside experts instruct select community members to produce a sense of place that can be shaped by artists. Instead, PPS, Bedoya, and others have suggested that creative placemaking should emphasize an inclusive process that promotes feelings of efficacy, investment, strength, and belonging through a completed work or arts-based event. Critics and community leaders engaged in and affected by placemaking efforts have noted that community arts engagement is employed as a rhetorical device rather than as a practical investment.[34] After the NEA's placemaking programming had been instituted for a number of years, practitioners and grant awardees worried that creative placemakers might be internalizing a disingenuous or tainted sense of community engagement and artistic practice in order to fit within perceived parameters of creative placemaking initiatives.[35]

Similar concerns over inclusion and citizen engagement within processes of placemaking have circulated within urban planning networks. The rise of participatory planning as a common practice in urban renewal and development projects has been coupled with the pervasiveness of internet connection. Urban planners and researchers have observed the potential of digital media tools and applications to foster community participation in urban and neighborhood planning projects as well as the use of social media for neighborhood mobilization in opposition to development projects.[36] Online forums and discussion boards as well as social media such as Facebook, YouTube, and Twitter have been regarded as useful tools in bringing local populations into conversations about placemaking endeavors or changes to built environments. Although the lack of inclusion, community input, and equitable community engagement have been substantial issues within creative placemaking efforts, digital tools that have been shown to foster social capital, deliberation, and collaboration among place-based communities have been largely ignored by creative placemakers. In addition, while scholars and artists have noted the ways in which digital media can foster a sense of play with/in place, the playful and exploratory qualities of digital placemaking have been underutilized or buried under rhetoric that implicates media use as a perpetrator in the disintegration of physical interactions in cities. The following section examines the discursive construction and actual use of digital media within creative placemaking projects. An assessment of grant applications, project outcomes, statements and public presentations from artists, community members, and grantors reveals that digital media tend to be circumscribed as promotional rather than as placemaking tools within NEA- and creative-placemaking-funded efforts.

Digital Media in Creative Placemaking

Dominant Trends and Interpretations

A content analysis of creative placemaking grants awarded by the NEA, ArtPlace, OurTown, and the Kresge Foundation indicates a lack of integration between digital media and arts-based work. Although the Kresge Foundation has funded digital-media-related projects, such as New Detroit and the Allied Media Project (Detroit) and Street-Level Youth Media (Chicago) as well as twenty-two creative placemaking projects since 2009, these grant categories tend to be mutually exclusive. According to the publicly accessible database of Kresge Foundation grants, there are no creative placemaking projects that incorporate digital media directly. Between ArtPlace and Our Town awards, more than six hundred projects have been generously funded under creative placemaking initiatives. Only thirty-six of these projects explicitly incorporate digital media technologies, workshops, or experiences into their proposals. Of the seventy-one finalists for ArtPlace's 2016 creative placemaking grants, only two proposals—one for the inclusion of digital street art as part of the People's Emergency Center CDC in Philadelphia and another for a website by the University of Oklahoma that is set to host an interactive, bilingual resource center—propose to include digital media arts in their work.[37] In a year when, despite profound digital divides, 89 percent of Americans use the internet at least occasionally and 72 percent of Americans own a smartphone,[38] it is surprising to see only two applications proposing the use of digital media for creative community engagement in public spaces. However, the near absence of digital media technologies and practices within NEA-sponsored or related placemaking projects echo the imagination written into documents where creative placemaking is introduced and discursively maintained.

In Markusen and Gadwa Nicodemus's initial white paper, they recognize "digital media" as one of the "creative sector" industries at which American companies excel economically. Although the authors recognize that technology companies and talent are driving forces in the US economy, the white paper rarely mentions digital media technologies and practices as influential tools within creative placemaking processes. In fact, in their sixty-nine-page paper, the authors mention (but do not describe) only one digital public art project: Jennifer Steinkamp's *Hollywood and Vine* (2009), which consisted of eight digital animation panels on the Wall of Fame in Los Angeles. The piece was sponsored by W Hotel's Gatehouse Capital and Legacy Partners. The authors also devote two pages to a case study of ZERO1's biennial festival and placemaking efforts in San Jose. The authors and interviewees quoted in the case studies and examples of digital media and placemaking emphasize that San Jose and Los Angeles need to be remade or improved through the union of "technology prowess" and "artistic talent."

The ZERO1 biennial and related events sponsored by the city of San Jose and the Office of Cultural Affairs united art and technology to transform the sense of place within Silicon Valley.[39] In the report, ZERO1's executive director insinuates that Silicon Valley maintained a lackluster public image and that the union of art, technology, and digital culture could revamp that image. In a section of Markusen and Gadwa Nicodemus's report called "Out of the Garage and Into the World," they highlight the main event at the 2010 ZERO1 biennial where artists led workshops showcased Silicon Valley's creativity and innovative entrepreneurship.[40] The public art displays, presentations and workshops, gatherings, and performances aimed to brand the digital start-up environment as more "vibrant" (to use a descriptor circulated in creative placemaking calls for applications). The following year Silicon Valley Inside/Out received Our Town funding, and its proposal explains that although San Jose and Silicon Valley are extremely creative places, "its population tends to be very focused on technology, spending long hours in offices working on specific digital programs and applications. The city wanted to apply that same creative approach to its urban fabric, transforming the downtown area from a place to work into a vibrant community, where art installations would encourage technology workers and residents to intermingle."[41]

The examples of ZERO1 and Silicon Valley Inside/Out are unique in that they re-place and rebrand digital media capitals through arts-driven events and exhibitions. These projects link digital media use with work, particularly the work of Silicon Valley–based technology industry entrepreneurs, which they portray as economically attractive and intrinsically creative but problematic in terms of arts-based place branding and creative placemaking goals. Contentious relationships between technology industry personnel and preexisting California communities have been liberally documented in popular press that frames industry employees and their use of digital media as exclusive and even detrimental to the social life of neighborhoods in which they reside.[42] Instead of remaining uncomfortable bedfellows, these creative placemaking projects attempted to intertwine digital media labor sectors and activities with other forms of local creativity and community.

Aside from the Hubbard Street Dance company's project, Dance as Learning Platform (ArtPlace 2012), which introduces dance as a learning platform for digital technology entrepreneurs, most creative placemaking proposals do not partner with or address technology industry image and personnel. Instead, the most common ways in which digital media is incorporated into Our Town or ArtPlace applications is through proposals for website development, publicly accessible databases, or online cultural asset maps and resources for residents and tourists. Funds were most frequently requested for website-based projects that hosted directories and resources about local artistic and cultural activities.

The most commonly recognized and celebrated digital media affordances were the reach and scale of the internet as a global distribution network. In several grant applications, reports from the field, interviews with creative placemakers, and blog posts about projects funded by ArtPlace, OurTown, and the Kresge Foundation, the internet is viewed as an important way to gain national and international reach for arts-based organizations, publicize and showcase their efforts, and distribute and exhibit artwork. Two organizations were granted funds to host digital exhibitions of creative work: the Northern Initiative in Anchorage, Alaska (ArtPlace 2012), and Tinta Digital (Our Town 2014). The Northern Initiative applied for funds to host a simultaneous digital and physical exhibition of performance, print, installation, and new media artists that explore themes related to "the North." The exhibition intended to engage artists and invite interaction from participants and visitors in Alaska and beyond. Tinta Digital proposed a series of digital publications composed of work compiled from writing workshops for adults, seniors, teens, and tweens conducted in San Antonio, Texas. The publications would jumpstart a Tinta Digital Community Literature Collection at the all-digital county library, BiblioTech. In a similar vein, the Watts House Project (ArtPlace 2011) in Los Angeles requested funds to create an online 3-D model of alterations to abandoned houses that were slated for redevelopment as an art studio, office, and exhibition space. The virtual representation would be deployed for participatory planning—to allow the public to view and comment on changes to the online model in real time.

Information distribution in the form of interactive websites, online classes, and cultural asset maps is mentioned in a number of proposals. Proposals note the use of social media to publicize their projects, maintain momentum and interest after events, and invite feedback from community members and visitors. One project, NEWaukee, tried to unite physical and virtual space by installing a giant mailbox in a Milwaukee,

Wisconsin, park where people could send letters to the city. The social media hashtag #LettersToMilwaukee could be used to disseminate the letters online so that people could connect to place through a virtual platform as well as in person.[43] At the Soul of Brooklyn Festival, organizers set up a photo booth where participants were invited to take candid photos that were tagged, distributed, and shared via Facebook.

Documentation from the Creative Placemaking Summit in 2013 supports this mode of social media use. Reports highlight the use of social media to create a narrative or "buzz" around placemaking projects and outline "key takeaways" in response to two questions: "How can creative placemakers work with local partners, journalists, and audiences to get meaningful buzz, attention, and coverage for projects? How can buzz help a project achieve its goals?" Suggestions for social media use provide instructions for utilizing services such as Instagram, Twitter, and Facebook that echo strategic communication and public relations paradigms and best practices: create a "social media voice" or comprehensive identity online; use a wide range of pictures, videos, sounds, and dialogue to gain followers; forge a connection with followers so that your organization can "earn media" by encouraging others to cover the event. However, this report as well as many other documents from creative placemaking summits and information sessions explicitly privileges face-to-face conversations with volunteers and community members as a preferable means toward meaningful investment in events and initiatives.

A few organizations requested funds to transfer their organizational and informational content online. These organizations claimed that moving content online would more consistently and reliably inform the public of their activities and allow registered users to provide feedback and receive information about upcoming arts-related events and exhibitions. Organizations such as Artspace Hawaii (ArtPlace 2011), Art of the Rural in Winona, Minnesota (Our Town 2015 and 2016), and Chamber Music of America (Our Town 2016 for Louisiana regions) all received ArtPlace and Our Town funding to experiment with online learning technologies and/or to create online classes.

Maps that visualize information and locations of "cultural assets" such as addresses of artists' studios and exhibition spaces, public art displays, workshops and classes, and arts foundations were awarded funding more frequently than any other digital-media-related requests. For example, CultureBlocks (ArtPlace 2011) in Philadelphia, Pennsylvania, was one of the earliest projects to request funding for a cultural assets map. In their proposal they state that one of the goals of the site is to create an online space for local artists to share resources and information, to upload data about cultural events, and to "generate custom reports on communities of interest and share their findings with friends and colleagues." Cultural asset maps resemble open-data and smart-city initiatives where community members can use data sets to influence decision making:

> Performing artists might use the tool to expand marketing to new audiences. A nonprofit after-school arts program, for instance, might use the tool to determine the neighborhoods in which they could expand their programs. Or a start-up creative business might use the site selector tool to identify where to locate their office or warehouse. More broadly, City agencies will use the tool to identify emerging clusters of creative activity.[44]

Project Willowbrook in Los Angeles; Warehouse Arts District in Tucson, Arizona; Nuestro Lugar: Engaging, Creating, and Activating Community Folklore in Los Angeles; Block by Block in Savannah, Georgia; and a cultural mapping project in Baltimore, Maryland, all requested funding for similar creative asset mapping projects from 2011 to 2016. Some of these projects, such as the C4 Mapping Tool in New Orleans, Louisiana (Our Town 2011), created an online platform that mapped and sorted direct input from community members about cultural and economic activities into a database for planners and municipal officials.

At least four projects intended to build or outfit labs or studio spaces with digital technologies or to create events that would incorporate digital media opportunities and experiences. Proposals and updates to labs and maker spaces were where Markusen and Gadwa Nicodemus's original interpretation of the value of digital media lay: breeding technology companies and talent that drive the US economy. For example, FabLab, a maker space in Detroit, specified that it would install a digital media lab as well as fabrication equipment and small business and start-up mentorship. Projects that requested funds to start digital media labs often intended to use the grants for digital media training and literacy programs as well. Many of these labs and instructional spaces offered workshops led by digital media entrepreneurs or local digital media start-up personnel in order to teach community members about the value and "how to" of digital media for economic gain. Innovation spaces, like OPEN MiKE in Milwaukee frequently invited local entrepreneurs to discuss strategies for honing a proclivity for digital media use into a for-profit company.

Digital Storytelling and Interactive Art

In my review of three major funding organizations for creative placemaking, the Kresge Foundation, ArtPlace, and NEA's Our Town, I found only three projects that specifically requested funds for digital storytelling or interactive art projects.[45] All the digital art projects represented were innovative in how they combined community engagement through the merging of physical and digital space. The three projects discussed in this section are examples of "site-specific storytelling" or "sited narratives" that aim to suture community narratives or create communal experiences of specific locations to reshape the character and meaning of place.[46]

A team of artists in residence at Chinatown North Social Practice Lab, Anula Shetty and Michael Kuetemeyer, proposed a public art and online project including digital media workshops that would "culminate in a series of interactive, 360-degree oral history panoramas of specific streets and locations in the neighborhood." Time Lens, as the project was ultimately titled, documented the lives of past and present residents on four blocks of Pearl Street in an area known as Chinatown North in Philadelphia, Pennsylvania. Oral histories, videos, archival photographs, and recorded memories and dreams of housed and homeless residents were displayed on the street in a solar-powered kiosk and through a smartphone app. Reviews and experiences of Time Lens fondly note how the smartphone app allowed participants to uncover "the stories hidden within the pavement."

OhHeckYeah in Denver also received significant mainstream media coverage and critical praise for its inventiveness in transforming Denver's Theater District into an open-air arcade. The project's initiator, Brian Corrigan, notes that the video games incorporated into the outdoor arcade were all designed around the same thematic question: "How can we build technology to connect people in the psychical world?" OhHeckYeah spanned two city blocks and was built around the central idea of exploring the identity and fabric of place through communal, immersive video game play in public space. These publicly accessible games incorporated haptic and physical movement as well as social interaction and coordination among friends and strangers and aimed to change the way urban residents interacted.[47] As one participant exclaimed on her Instagram account (a sentiment that was echoed by many others in downtown Denver), "#ohheckyeah is truly the most inclusive event that actually brings together all types of people in the name of connection and play. We need more of that. So proud to be part of it!"

Similar to the orchestrated relationships between place and people that Time Lens and OhHeckYeah offer, Scott Snibbe, an Our Town–funded artist and member of the Iron Triangle Interactive Art project in Richmond, California, described one of the outcomes he hoped to accomplish with his digital pieces: "Every type of art is some kind of interaction, but interactive art actually requires you to move, breathe, speak or interact with other people in order for it to really come alive."[48] Snibbe installed four interactive LCD screens in the storefront windows of a renovated performing arts center. Three of the screens displayed performances by faculty and students in the East Bay Center for Performing Arts. As passersby approached the fourth screen, their bodies and movements were scanned and incorporated into the performances displayed on the three adjacent screens.

All three projects received attention for the "newness" of or novel approach to the experiences of place and sociality they created. Participants in OhHeckYeah, Time Lens, and Iron Triangle Interactive Art who are represented in videos, photographs, blogs, and social media posts about the projects are shown expressing affective attachments to the places in which they were standing through engagement with the digital art projects.[49] People posting and being interviewed about these experiences explain how the projects allowed them to encounter the places they passed through every day in an entirely different manner, to reimagine their neighborhoods and public spaces, to think about their connection to place-based communities and fellow residents in more profound and attentive ways.

Contradictions and Conflicting Imaginations

The few digital-media-oriented projects funded by the innovators of creative placemaking seemed to engage and reorient sense of place within the communities they collaborated with and impacted. However, creative placemaking rhetoric is not only characterized by limited imaginations of digital media technologies and practices but also by disparaging comments about the depleting effects of digital media in public and private spaces. In fact, creative placemaking applications frame their proposals as responses to the negative effects of digital media in everyday life. For example, on the ArtPlace blog entry for the WaterFire Learning Lab (funded in 2012) in Providence, Rhode Island, executive artist director Barnaby Evans explains:

> There is another challenge to the civic vitality of our streets and cities—there is so much competition for our time and our attention and our presence indoors and on-line, shopping, talking, playing games, catching up with the world, that this virtual world is beginning to impoverish our real lives out on the city square. More and more of us are listening to recorded music instead of attending live concerts, watching film and dance and theatre in our home going without the essential audience interaction, shopping in virtual stores, leaving the street front bookstores empty. WaterFire works to restore vibrancy by embracing the cityscape and wrapping it in an ever-changing arts and urban environment that is designed to engage all of our senses.[50]

The juxtaposition of virtual space and physical space summons early imaginations of digital media that are commonly refuted: that digital media abates engagement and resources in physical space. In Evans's description of everyday life, people are being forced to choose between online and physical activities, are distracted from potentially rewarding physical interactions in the city streets and plazas, and are instead being lured into isolated, antisocial spaces of digital exchange.

Disadvantages of digital media use is also positioned in more direct economic terms. In several instances, creative placemakers justify their efforts as methods to undo the economic losses suffered by small businesses at the hands of e-commerce and online marketplaces. According to these arguments, consumer attention shifts toward online shopping at stores in distant locations at the expense of neighborhood small businesses. Several placemaking efforts attempted to remedy this outflow by installing public art or arts-based events in neighborhoods with abandoned storefronts or suffering local enterprise.

Evans and other creative placemakers often express a perspective that being outdoors or in shared public space is antithetical to using digital media. Paradoxically, funding agencies support two distinct types of projects and perspectives. On one hand, creative placemaking grantors recognize that digital media use in public parks, plazas, and sidewalks can animate public space and encourage people to cultivate a unique sense of place and community as shown in OhHeckYeah, Time Lens, and Iron Triangle. In contrast, creative placemakers also understand digital media use as an impetus for social withdrawal and lack of engagement within public space. In this latter conception, creative placemaking projects work to counteract these trends by eschewing digital media technologies and interactions in favor of physical art installations, art spaces and events, or improved built environments.

Another dichotomy exists within the discursive construction and funding practices for creative placemaking projects. Digital media use is imagined as both necessary within contemporary society and positioned in opposition to active learning and immersive experiences. The perception that digital media promote superficial or distanced engagement with place is often articulated in terms of the manner in which the body interfaces with physical space. The interaction of the body, hands, or sense of touch is regarded as enriching and profound when it is linked to material objects and physical presence. For example, Art @ the Feed and Grain, a project in Colorado, focuses on the construction of large public installation pieces. The focal point of its report to ArtPlace regarding the use of funds and initial outcomes of the project are quotations from a conversation between two participating artists posted on the project's Facebook page. In celebrating the success of the project, the artists describe the type of learning that occurs through haptic engagement with art installations:

> The mind cannot forget what the hands have learned [this is a quote attributed to Jon Zahourek]. . . . I had a delightful conversation this morn-

ing with another artist about the train of thought an installation artist follows, a virtual catalog of textures, techniques, materials, reactions, spatial relations and the language of physical interaction with the materiality of a space. . . . It's refreshing to be creating with my hands in an actual space instead of in my head. Some of my spatial, textural, material "vocabulary" had gotten a little rusty.[51]

These installation artists speak about creating in physical space versus virtual or mental catalogs of images and blueprints. However, the idea that their collective "spatial, textural, material 'vocabulary' had gotten a little rusty" tends to be evoked in reference to the proliferation of digital media, which create spaces where ideas and experiences are often immaterial and therefore less profound.

One of the projects that actively incorporated digital media into its proposal, the Northern Initiative, noted that building community outreach and engagement with its programming would be difficult due to competing information sources and sites. The chief curator of the project notes that getting people engaged in a vibrant and aspirational way "is a challenge in a time when information is abundant and rapid and much happens on the internet rather than in physical spaces."[52] The perceived profundity of the material or tangible echoes the prioritization of the built environment in creative placemaking documents and presents an oppositional perspective on re-placeing. Digital media re-place the priority and purpose of physical space with virtual spaces that encourage superficial interactions and knowledge.

Creative placemaking practitioners and grantors reiterate the idea that physical space exists at odds with digital space and also consider internet and digital media technologies such as gaming consoles and mobile phones to exist in competition with physical environments for public and individual attention. Digital technology start-ups that benefitted from creative placemaking funding and initiatives mention the idea of distraction as a challenge for their business endeavors. One digital entrepreneur who led a workshop at a Milwaukee innovation lab challenged participants to "find ways to enjoy new media without distraction. We're all distracted—when we watch TV we have internet on, text and more. We're a media company that wants your full attention. What do we need to do to capture your full attention and get you to turn everything else off?"[53] The media lab organizers responded to this statement with a comment on the persistence of media in everyday life. They wholeheartedly agreed with the entrepreneur, but significantly altered his observations: "Schools and offices are filled with people who have never known a world without videogames, cell phones and the internet. And because of that, people habitually divide their attention among several things at once. Competition for the fractured attentions of students and employees is tougher than it's ever been. We see it every day ourselves—when's the last time you sat through a staff meeting without at least one (if not all) of your co-workers checking their email?"[54] Instead of expanding on the speaker's idea that a successful digital media company creates an immersive product that uniquely channels user attention and investment, the creative placemaking practitioners evoke an image of a world saturated with digital media opportunities and suggest that these opportunities are inherently distracting from more productive or valuable interactions such as a class or business meeting.

As evidenced throughout this section, contradictory arguments about digital media and placemaking punctuate creative placemaking documents and commentary. In most documentation, digital media technologies and practices are to blame for diminished interactions with physical space, dearth of rewarding local social interactions, and decreased economic prosperity for neighborhood and small businesses— the enemy of place to be combatted or stalled through creative placemaking. Simultaneously, the commercialization of digital media is read as a catalyst for economic development through creative industries and innovation, albeit a vehicle in need of "animation" and "vibrancy" through an infusion of arts and culture. Digital media projects are also regarded as immersive, playful, and creative impetus to be out in public: as entry points into untold oral histories and endangered stories about place, expanding exhibition spaces, and creating effective tools for publicity, sharing resources and information, and outreach. What do these contrasting imaginations and limited inclusions of digital media as placemaking tools illustrate about visions of re-placeing the city in creative placemaking? In the following sections I offer an interpretation of these discursive constructions and examine creative placemaking imaginations and practices through the lens of digital media.

Creative Placemaking and Re-placeing the City

The National Science Foundation's CreativeIT program and universities nationwide have taken an interest in the overlap between arts, innovation, and information technologies goals and discourses about creativity. Interdisciplinarity between the arts and technology-centered fields has been both critiqued as an intellectual trend and considered a hopeful outlook for the future of research and problem solving. Jill Fantauzzacoffin, Joanna Berzowska, Ernest A. Edmonds, and Ken Goldberg advocated for exchanges between human-computer interaction (HCI) and the arts as well as innovation policy and arts discourse and practice as efforts to better understand human imagination and identity, to discover and solve problems, and to develop novel, interdependent interfaces and artistic practices.[55] Digital media's inclusion in creative placemaking policy, initiatives, and discourse is related to perceptions of STEAM (science, technology, engineering, arts, and mathematics) as a productive approach to understanding everyday life, arts, and technology. However, the issue of digital media's absence and blinkered construction within creative placemaking discourse works against interdisciplinarity or improving collaboration between disciplines and evidences a particular perception of the meaning of place and placemaking and digital media's role in these endeavors.

The Meaning of Place and Digital Media

In NEA and grant-related documents, creative placemaking upholds a boundaried sense of place. The first item listed under suggestions for how to become involved with creative placemaking instructs potential placemakers to first "pick a place." The primary meaning of place promoted in creative placemaking documents is akin to a site or geographic locale. In describing the "four basic parts" that encompass the mission of ArtPlace and NEA's creative placemaking, the executive director of ArtPlace America explains how to identify a place for this sort of work: "There is a group of people who live and work in the same place. It can be a block, a neighborhood, a town, a city, or a region, but you need to be able to draw a circle around it on a map."[56] While this definition recognizes that people make place, there is also the sense that place is a concrete container—that place is self-evident through shared geographic boundaries and is inherently physical or legible on any given map. This definition builds on the oft-cited quote from the 2010 Creative Placemaking report, where a sense of place is described as "the physical and social character" of a given location as local or localized. In ArtPlace America's description of creative placemaking, the organization emphasizes that the focus of their initiatives is "all about the local" as a geographic entity.[57] These perspectives work against a mobile or extroverted sense of place where the meaning and characteristics of place are not intrinsic to a particular site but socially constructed and composed of intersecting mobile and global entities and networks.

In community arts literature, the concept of place is framed as a hyperlocal, humanized, "concrete and communitarian antidote to the abstracting and consumerist culture of neoliberal modernity."[58] Danielle Wyatt identifies "place" in Markusen and Gadwa Nicodemus's creative placemaking report as something that has been disseminated or scared off by "structural change and residential uprooting" that leaves storefronts vacant and downtown districts empty. The antidote, then, is to reinvest in storefronts and districts through the arts to foster a sense of community attachment to place and to each other. The NEA definition of place has been most noticeably critiqued as overly dependent on the built environment at the expense of people as social and cultural producers of place. However, place is also introduced as an entity constructed through exchange. Inherent in this definition of place is that the built environment and bounded places have been formed over time through a series of cultural, legislative, and above all else, economic exchanges.

The sense of place evoked in these documents is fragile and fleeting but also intentionally produced by organizations, cultural institutions, and the aggregation of lived experiences and interactions with a given location. The sense of place and the role of the community in producing a sense of place are highly organized and strategic. Place and sense of place are thought to be constructed and branded by professionals or community members who are guided by experts. Any sense of place preexisting the arrival of self-proclaimed creative placemakers is read as historic but latent, untapped, or incoherent and in need of a unified identity in order to be heard and understood. In addition, the work of creative placemaking foundations and practitioners adheres to the unwritten idea that place is experienced through orchestrated and planned events, exhibitions, and performances. The outcomes-oriented projects carve out circumscribed spaces in which a sense of place is recognized and celebrated. Place is seen as a rescued outcome rather than a messy, open-ended process. In this sense of place that urges and thrives on coherency it becomes difficult for alternative or contradictory understandings of place attachment and place identity to coexist simultaneously.

These understandings of place and placemaking position digital media technologies and practices in an awkward relationship with creative placemaking initiatives. Digital media, as it is imagined within creative placemaking, falls into the categories of structural change, flexible or mobile geographies, abstract spaces, and neoliberal consumer culture. These forces are read as directly counteracting a sense of place, disembedding people, and distracting them from each other. Creative placemakers who do not engage with digital media and those who employ websites and social media for promotional and outreach purposes understand digital affordances in terms of reach and transmission rather than ritual and communication and that digital media use produces "networked individualism" or "mobile privatization" rather than working toward common or communal experiences of the world. The rootedness of place in bounded locales and a cartographic sense of the local are read in opposition to the uprooting and border-crossing exchanges that digital media provide, implying that global or transborder connections lead to local disconnections.[59]

The insistence on place as physical site dictates and explains why the majority of creative placemaking funding was awarded to installations and built environments. The coupling of place and a discrete physical site reifies perspectives that physical presence and physical place not only matter but perhaps matter more than other forms of colocation and social interaction. The constructed prominence of a local sense of place as an entity that is not only physical but that structural changes and advanced capitalism have erased or concealed is mapped onto perspectives that resemble Joshua Meyrowitz's suggestions about electronic mediation: where we are no longer dictates possibilities for knowledge and experience.

Eric Gordon and Adriana de Souza e Silva's net locality, or the idea that digital media use has fundamentally altered and expanded the meaning of proximity, local contexts, local knowledge, and experiences, is approached cautiously by creative placemakers. The few funded projects that incorporate digital media to make place more accessible or emotionally and experientially "proximate" through "information-flows into traditional spatial situations" are celebrated as innovative and immersive for changing traditional spatial situations and built environments.[60] For example, Brian Corrigan, founder of OhHeckYeah, explains some of the goals he hopes to accomplish by layering and opening up public space and the built environment through digital media: "I think it's interesting to think of a theater district of not necessarily having theaters inside the buildings, but breaking down the walls to actually have the theater on the street . . . and doing it in such an immersive kind of way and an interactive way that we're literally using these video games as theater and we're reinventing what the stage is."[61] Corrigan's reinvention of space echoes classic ideas of the city as a theater where strangers negotiate copresence and engage in unexpected encounters in the form of a street ballet or drama. However, he sees digital media and play as what makes this performance and experience of the city possible. The immersion and interaction with video games create new situations for people to engage within public space, integrating embodiment, installation, and performance with the poetics of place.

Digital media projects funded by creative placemaking initiatives recognize the power of everyday people in the street to create senses of place attachment, identity, community, and belonging. In digital placemaking projects the social production of place and placemaking activities is reinvested in the street and in the hands of the public through the incorporation of digital media. Creative placemaking projects that incorporate digital media are invested in unlocking the potential and performance of place by paying attention to an "ecology of foci," or a variety of people, spaces, and stories simultaneously.[62] Projects that focus primarily on renewing or changing the built environment of physical structures within shared public space are often guided by singular strategic focuses and outcomes.

Fred Kent and Cynthia Nikitin note that there has been a noticeable shift in the realm of public arts creation and administration. The authors describe this shift as a gesture away from static, textbook outcomes toward "flexibility, changeability, and evolution" in the work produced and the process of producing public art where designers, artists, and planners work with communities.[63] Emphasis on collaboration and community participation in all aspects of public art and public planning and in the design of flexible, mutable, evolving projects delineates a space where digital media can be utilized to enact more widespread involvement and participation. Repositioning digital media within narratives of creative placemaking repurpose collective media use and collaborative play as expansions of the event-based and pop-up projects that are already promoted through creative placemaking. Digital placemaking projects can serve as vehicles for more integrative approaches to creative placemaking and evolved understandings of community participation, which have been critiqued as inadequate in previously funded projects.

The artists and organizations that propose digital media projects note that altering previously held imaginations of place through overlapping and nonlinear spatial and temporal contexts is valuable. However, valuing flexibility or mobility counteracts the coherence of place promoted by creative placemaking calls for proposals and mission statements. The overarching search for a coherent, unified meaning and sense of place among community members that can be showcased in a single mural or exhibition not only limits processes of placemaking but also assigns particular values to digital media. In the following section, I identify and analyze the divergent ways in which digital placemaking practitioners and creative placemaking organizations and funders interpret the value of digital media in the social production of place.

Value of Digital Media

In addition to demands for creative placemaking to be more inclusive and attentive to diverse community members and needs, creative placemaking has also been critiqued as overly indebted to economic development and the creative economy. The call for creative placemaking to disconnect from financial economies and outcomes measured through economic impact can also be seen in the discursive construction of digital media within creative placemaking literature. Within creative placemaking discourse, digital media is celebrated as creating economic value within industrial sectors but is condemned as distracting from productive activity in domestic and public life.

During interviews about their project, Anula Shetty and Michael Kuetemeyer, creators of Time Lens, encourage other artists to take advantage of mobile phones and apps as tools of creative expression and not to relinquish these media to the corporate sphere.[64] The urging to rescue or reappropriate digital and mobile media from being understood as commercialized and corporatized tools that produce financial value implies that apps and user-generated content need to be reconsidered by creative placemakers for artistic and social value. While digital media is seen as valuable in the realm of Silicon Valley and the growth of innovation and trade, there is a disinterest or avoidance of integrating alternate perspectives about the role of digital media in everyday life and public space. Shetty and Kuetemeyer's comment about the threat of the corporate sphere can be read as a move toward recontextualizing and revaluing digital media within creative placemaking and artistic production more generally.

The concretization and continued funding of creative placemaking efforts have shifted the meaning and practice of arts-driven placemaking from a context built on social exchange and cultural value to one that is more explicitly concerned with generating financial capital and economic outcomes as markers of successful urban improvement initiatives. In addition to thinking about mobile media and apps as vehicles for artistic expression and community engagement, creative placemakers need to shift from a corporate imagination of digital media as having economic value to other forms of social and artistic value within creative placemaking. Creative placemakers could reconsider perceived affordances and properties of digital media such as reach, mobility, temporal structure, and interactivity as re-placeing rather than displacing and as qualities that understand digital technologies as operating beyond lucrative tools of promotion, branding, and industry prowess.[65]

Scott McQuire has written at length about the potential for digital public art to promote polysemic understandings of place, public encounters that foster social skills for interacting with others and "becoming public," and spark curiosity and engagement with urban place and urban communities.[66] However, creative placemaking literature and efforts internalize the affordances and outcomes of digital media in public space quite differently. While the "reach" of digital media has been perceived in creative placemaking as a tool of widespread and cost-efficient promotion and distribution of professional materials, these media can be reinterpreted as inclusive and collaborative tools for inviting diverse experiences and knowledge about place from diasporic or mobile community members. Shifts and overlays of temporal and spatial structures that are influenced by user mobility, rhythms of the city, and synchronous communication that alter senses of "near" and "now" can be intentionally incorporated into art practices and productions as vehicles for deep engagement with place rather than being read as cannibalizing audience attention. Interactivity, although employed as a buzzword to describe a variety of digital and nondigital projects, can be further explored as means to gain immersive and embodied experiences with place through textual as well as social interactivity and can include the diverse populations who have contributed to the meaning of place over time.

There are striking differences between the perception of digital media among creative placemaking initiatives and civic media projects. Although these types of projects often overlap in purpose and intended outcomes, projects geared toward civic efficacy have recognized digital media affordances like reach, interactivity, and mobility as meaningful ways to engage communities in collaborative processes of place attachment and urban renewal and in addressing issues facing local communities. Scholars and community activists regard digital media as useful storytelling tools that bond community members to the places where they live.[67] In regard to civic placemaking, Giota Alevizou, Katerina Alexiou, Dave Harte, Shawn Sobers, Theodore Zamenopoulos, and Jerome Turner note the ways in which digital media provide agency and efficacy to communities through the ability to tell and share stories of their individual and collective lives as well as issues and inequities that affect them.[68] Digital storytelling has been shown to bring together diverse ethnic communities within neighborhoods and build on community members' preference for the internet as the primary channel for access to news, information, and local stories.[69] Immigrant rights movements and immigrant communities have worked to cultivate a sense of belonging, engage community members, build allegiances with local and distant allies, and coordinate civic actions through ICTs such as social media and mobile phones.[70] Digital games and online spaces have been created to educate community members about planning decisions and changes to their built environment and to solicit alternative plans, build trust among community members, and generate input from people who are typically left out of or disengaged from planning processes.[71]

The aforementioned projects, although they are invested in creative, community-based productions and understandings of place, fall outside the purview of creative placemaking. These initiatives are not formally arts-driven, nor do they state economic outcomes as their primary goal. However, the intended ambitions of these projects echo creative placemaking sentiments: bringing community members together in a collaborative process of making place through creative expression and practice in order to shape the social and physical character of a local environment for the benefit of its residents. Understanding digital media in ways that echo civic media projects that encourage learning and social economies of storytelling and information sharing in the service of place attachment, identity, and belonging could serve as models for how creative placemaking discourse can pivot to recognize the affordances of digital media as beneficial to arts-driven placemaking processes.

Conclusion

Re-placeing the city is a minority perspective within creative placemaking funding agencies and, thus, among award-winning practitioners as well. Although some artists and community organizations utilize digital media to creatively and artistically express forgotten or underrecognized experiences of place or to overlay traditional spatial situations with playful encounters, the majority of initiatives regard the value of digital media in terms of economic development and marketing. Organizations that play a dominant, active role in shaping the meaning of creative placemaking tend to consider digital media as displacing and distracting rather than enriching or engaging. A shift in perspective and the incorporation of digital media as creative rather than commercial could help recognize experiences of place attachment and place identity that are emerging alongside digital media use in everyday life. Although some critics call for an end to creative placemaking endeavors,[72] a reconceptualization of the role of digital media in these endeavors might help creative placemakers formulate new imaginations of community involvement and investment in re-placeing the city. The reinterpretation of digital media as creative, artistic, and playful fosters an opportunity for creative placemaking practitioners to reconceptualize placemaking as more people-centered and less geographically bounded.

Digital media can be especially useful in ameliorating some of the equity issues voiced by creative placemaking participants and arts organizations, namely that the community is not being listened to in a comprehensive and inclusive way. An overreliance on digital media for community dialogues can potentially create other significant equity issues that allow for unequal participation among community members due to uneven digital media access and literacy. However, there are creative, inclusive ways to counteract some of these divides as seen in projects like Time Lens, where guides and sets of instructions are distributed to aid in collecting digital stories, as well as OhHeckYeah, where people gather at central locations to collectively interact with shared technology with their bodies, faces, and gestures. Professional creative placemakers need to appreciate a wider range of placemaking processes and the distributed meanings of place as integral values. They also need to reconsider the simultaneity of presence, information spaces, and social situations that digital media can produce as valuable rather than as a debilitating variable in need of control.

Conclusion

More frequently than ever before, collective and individual placemaking involves routine engagement with digital media texts and practices. As the amount of accessible information about place proliferates, so, too, does the desire to "know one's place" within space and society. The notion of "spatial reality" has become more personalized, customized, and shareable and at the same time more cartographic, quantifiable, and legible. Noted in several of the case studies presented in this book, digital technologies and practices are, in fact, key elements employed in humanizing the environment of urban spaces. Somewhat paradoxically, the return to place, urban embodiment, and embeddedness is activated and maintained through mediated, symbolic, and networked technologies and practices. I have encouraged readers to think of digitally mediated placemaking not as a paradox but as something that populations across the globe habitually and strategically do in their performances of place.

Throughout this book I have called attention to place and placemaking as integral to analyses of digital media use and relationships between media, bodies, and urban environments. Scholars of geography, communication and media studies, architecture and urban planning agree that most people live in a world where omnipresent digital and location-aware technologies mediate our interactions in locations where networked spaces and physical environments are intertwined.[1] These researchers have investigated what people do with digital technologies in public spaces and how mobile and digital media contribute to new forms of knowing and experiencing space and place. For example, Mizuko Ito has observed that place, and where one locates oneself, has become a hybrid of physical and digital copresent contexts filled with collocated and remote social contact. Mobile phone use, in this case, "augments the properties of a particular place" by customizing and personalizing place and constructing new ways of being together.[2] Expanding on this perspective, scholars argue that mobile media encourage a relational sense of place, which may lead to the parochialization of public space through engagement with mobile social networks.[3] On the other hand, geographers such as Matthew A. Zook, Mark Graham, Martin Dodge, and Rob Kitchin have noted the ways in which software, code, algorithms, online mapping, and rankings influence and direct the ways that people interact with their local environment, where digital media govern spatiality and mobility.[4]

Building on these studies, I have argued that people consciously employ and actively seek out digital media (such as mobile phones, wireless and fiber-optic networks, ubiquitous computing and navigation technologies, and location-based social media) in order to create and negotiate a new sense of place within urban environments. Instead of merely layering or coexisting within physical and virtual urban spaces, I propose that networked urban subjects are actively re-placing the city through their digital media use. Furthermore, the sense of place produced through digital placemaking emphasizes the event of making mutable, mobile, and participatory places rather than places as pause. Evidenced throughout this book, making place with digital media highlights place as a performative process. As Henri Lefebvre famously observed, space is not simply read but *made*. The chapters in this book present examples and frameworks for rethinking colloquial connotations of digital media and place as well as entry points for analyzing how and why place is made and what types of places are socially and technologically produced through our imaginations of and engagement with digital media.

Re-placing the city was not shown to be an exclusively bottom-up or grassroots process. The physical and discursive constructions of smart cities discussed in chapter 1 can be read as strategic digital placemaking practices. Urban developers and municipal officials envision opportunities and face challenges in incorporating digital media technologies and infrastructures into built environments. In the case of smart-from-the-start cities, public officials, urban developers, architects, and planners harnessed digital technologies and discourses about ubiquitous computing to construct underinhabited smart cities as bounded and rooted places rather than abstract spaces under construction. Smart-from-the-start cities continue to proliferate. Many are still not fully inhabited, and edifices remain adorned with cranes and scaffolding. However, smart-city developers continue to produce these cities as unique places through the presence and promise of digital connectivity.

In chapter 2, people experienced the implementation of fiber-optic networks as a move toward transforming the meaning of urban place. In the case of Google Fiber for Communities, proponents regarded the installation of a gigabit network as an urban upgrade that would make their city exceptional, offering amenities and quality of life unlike other places. Evident in this case study was how previous experiences of place and mobility influenced decisions to adopt gigabit service and shaped affective relationships with this new digital infrastructure. This chapter highlighted digital placemaking efforts activated through network implementation processes and deployment models and the role of infrastructure projects in re-placeing the city.

The study of wayfinding tactics and navigation technologies in chapter 3 revealed that technology users assess social and physical conditions in association with screened representations of the city. As a result of their navigation technology use, several participants understood the city as a place to be explored and approached the city as familiar or manageable and with an increased willingness to take risks. Navigation technology users' demands of their smartphones and GPS systems were inherently social. Aside from arriving on time and being able to enjoy the journey without worrying about directions or getting lost, participants wanted to acquire a local knowledge of place through their navigation systems: safe routes and secure mobility as well as the foundation for spatial knowledge that created an intimate sense of place.

In the analysis of locative and social media use in chapter 4, participants utilized digital media technologies to perform their social and physical place within the city. Through their production of geo-coded annotations, check-ins, and selfies, urban networked subjects enacted a sense of belonging and mutual ownership of the city. Digital media users augmented their sense of the city as humanized as well as polysemic. A sense of place within the city was not erased by their activities; instead participants represented themselves as social agents in the production of place.

Finally, chapter 5 analyzed creative placemaking policies and funding practices, highlighting resistance to digital media use within professional placemaking practices. While funded initiatives and discourses around creative placemaking efforts juxtaposed digital media and sense of place as opposing forces, the few practitioners who utilized digital media for storytelling and community engagement realized rewarding results. In this chapter, I suggested that a reconceptualization of digital media and its affordances within creative placemaking projects and funding opportunities could more directly mobilize and benefit communities as well as counter critiques of lack of community engagement within creative placemaking initiatives.

The examples presented in each chapter—place promotion, urban transformation, wayfinding tactics, self-presentation, and creative placemaking—reflect anxieties and attempts to reproduce a sense of place and/or a sense of self within the city. Some of the preceding chapters showcase efforts to cultivate and sell the particularities of place to global and regional audiences through the mobilization and implementation of enhanced digital infrastructures. Other chapters examine the desire to know, archive, and express one's "place" within rapidly changing or unfamiliar physical, economic, social, and cultural environments.

My logic in selecting case studies that seem to share more differences than similarities is to demonstrate that the wide range of activities being undertaken by urban planners as well as social media users can and should be conceived of and critiqued as placemaking activities. The case studies in each chapter illustrate the range of scales, technologies, and actors engaged in re-placeing the city. These geographically distant locales and distinct populations exhibit the same overarching desire to create meaningful, inhabited places within mobile situational geographies. However, each chapter presents a different situational geography that is disrupted and then stabilized through digital media use. In this book, I claim that socio-technical practices of re-placeing the city extend beyond a particular bounded locale to integrate a variety of sites through a common phenomenon. Practices of re-placeing the city are not exclusive to certain cities or populations but represent cultural practices and experiences that permeate everyday interactions with digital media within many different sites and cultural contexts.

Beyond the City

Although this book focuses on urban space and place, re-placeing is not exclusive to urban environments. Rural and suburban social media users create and harness place identity in performances of the spatial self and locational capital online. Searching for hashtags such as #outinthecountry, #countrylife, or #suburbia on Instagram yields millions of posts by people performing polysemic interpretations of and personal attachments to the places they visit and live. Rural, suburban, and exurban experiences of digital infrastructures are equally dependent on sense of place. I have written elsewhere about how my own relationships with broadband access are shaped by rurality,[5] but there are many more stories to be told about re-placeing in locations besides cities.

In addition to analyzing re-placeing in rural or suburban environments, this book barely scratches the surface of the significance of re-placeing within migration studies, tourism studies, or natural environments. For example, in chapters 3 and 4 I briefly analyze touristic practices in regard to navigation and social media, but it is often through tourism that re-placeing becomes highly visible. Tourists' photographic activities of documenting souvenirs of place and presence in place are re-mediated and shared widely on blogs, annotated maps, and social media platforms. In addition, digital platforms and services that coordinate "local" travel experiences such as Airbnb Experiences or EatWith further complicate the positionality of resident and tourist or what it means to be "a local." Far from cities, these travel practices have become both highly controversial as well as informative for agencies such as national parks services and environmental sustainability organizations, for example. Recent studies have suggested that geo-coded posts on Twitter, Flickr, and Instagram can help assess the popularity of routes and locations within national parks and serve as evidence that people form strong feelings of place attachment via social media that can be leveraged into environmental stewardship.[6] However, some park rangers and journalists argue that social media texts exponentially increase the popularity of certain locations, leading to overvisitation and careless iPhone photographers that squander natural landscapes and stress ecosystems.[7] Examining tourists' use of digital media through the lens of re-placeing can expand analyses of place attachment and place identity to understand cultural norms around the conspicuous consumption and branding of place, the social construction of "local" or "authentic" places, and the reasons repeated images of certain places are sought after and commodified online. Reading these images and texts as efforts to re-place space may reveal new methods for mobilizing citizens in regard to place-based issues such as migration and belonging in place, historic preservation, neighborhood and city management, participatory planning, and environmental stewardship.

Participating in Place

Placemaking is too often defined by its objectives and outcomes rather than the methods, ideologies, and particularities of its process. Throughout this book, I suggest that we ought to be more attentive to the processes of placemaking as well as the types of places we enact. Although placemaking has been professionalized in the work of urban planners, real estate developers, interior decorators, and architects, placemaking has also become commonly understood as a collaborative, community, or human-centered approach to the planning and design of shared spaces. Traditionally, placemaking has been understood as both the production of built environments and the "settlement" or construction of certain locations to be lived in in meaningful ways. David Stea and Mete Turan offer a combination of these perspectives by defining placemaking as the multiscalar "act of cultural incorporation, broadly conceived, into built form."[8] This emphasis on built environment situates public placemaking within the realm of urban planning, architecture, and urban design as well as the domain of the trained professional or credentialed expert. Highly publicized placemaking efforts typically manifest in physical additions to the built environment such as parks, benches and modular seating areas, food carts and retail districts, or spaces for public art and gatherings.

Alternate interpretations have further emphasized the connection between placemaking and culture, noting that placemaking is a process of shared, continuous, quotidian practices: "the ongoing labor of people that makes, transforms, and cares for places."[9] This version of placemaking aims to cultivate shared values and collective processes of recognizing and coproducing specific physical, cultural, and social experiences in a particular place. Democratized views of placemaking have expanded the variety of activities that qualify as making place, from lasting changes in physical spaces to singular or ephemeral events or repetitive, intimate, microprocesses that are continually done and undone. This includes actions to facilitate diversity and pleasurable unexpected encounters and to potentially improve a local population's or community's quality of life, economic prosperity, or aesthetic characteristics.

Placemaking has also been characterized by its excavation of local narratives and cultural figures, public recognition of communities and demographic populations, or the official celebration of unique cultures and character of a given location. Bolstered by perspectives of celebrated urbanists such as Jane Jacobs and William Whyte, there have been marked shifts from understanding placemaking as exclusively top-down to occurring within the sociability and vernacular creativity of pedestrian life. Consequently, placemaking includes tactics undertaken by residents in order to reshape or appropriate preexisting spaces.

Drawing on these perspectives, Lynda H. Schneekloth and Robert G. Shibley explain that placemaking is "world making" because each action "embodies a vision of who we are and offers a hope of what we want to be as individuals and as groups who share a place in the world."[10] I also regard placemaking (its processes and products) as empirically, cognitively, and somatically powerful. Placemaking not only produces and silences certain interactions between culture and environment but through iterative grassroots as well as professional practices, it also produces and reproduces ontologies, imaginations, and possibilities for being in the world. The examples in this book revisit the poetics of placemaking to examine the social decisions and imaginations that inform how we participate in place and the heterogeneous ways in which digital media become effective and controversial placemaking tools. However, the cases presented in this book can also be understood as moments where people can intervene in the socio-technical production of place for better or for worse.

Placemaking activities are generally thought to produce positive intended outcomes. Numerous reports, news articles, and press releases have highlighted the ways in which placemaking efforts have fostered community efficacy and identity, created new community traditions, increased local profit among small businesses, and encouraged more interaction with and use of public spaces. These efforts imply that a sense of place is an essential and desirable aspect of everyday life, so much so that if a notable sense of place doesn't already exist within a given location, one must be created. However, the social production of place occurs for a variety of reasons and is orchestrated or implemented by different actors within diverse contexts and situations. For example, a real estate developer might produce a sense of place to sell a property or district as unique for a specific target market or audience. A neighborhood organization might produce a sense of place to build cohesion and investment among neighbors. Some individuals might choose to foster a particular sense of place to feel at home, safe, and rooted in their environment or to accrue social or financial capital within social networks or media markets. In each of these situations, distinct affordances of digital media may be idealized or employed to coordinate or influence performances of place.

Across all projects and practices discussed in this book, digital media users recognize and inhabit the space of humanistic use and the space of top-down exchange processes simultaneously. The references to neoliberalism and commodification in the analysis of these projects are meant to indicate the ways in which these spaces (humanistic and capitalistic) are not separate; instead, they are jointed and made accessible and understandable through digital technology use and implementation. The "abstract space" of state control, economic value, and advanced capitalism become intertwined with the "absolute space" of vernacular knowledge, symbolic imaginations, and the self in the use of commercial platforms, the construction of places for profit or economic development, or the generic repetition and economies of value assigned to circulated expressions of place.

Within these relationships, the assertion of the "right to the city" from the bottom up emerges as a key point of struggle and contestation in the making of place through digital media. Urban studies and geography scholars have discussed ongoing tensions and collaborations between people who plan urban spaces and those who move through and engage with them. To complicate matters, top-down interpretations and meanings of the city are not the only visions of urban place that are circulated publicly. The activities, events, and discourses involved in digital placemaking often serve as a series of instances where place-based realities and spatial experiences are articulated and where geographic articulations of power become audible to larger communities and public spheres. Unlike overt forms of placemaking that rely on professional constructions of physical spaces, the instances where traces of situated power-geometries are recognized and articulated through digital media can be individual, banal, and subtle. Digital texts about places such as user-generated and geo-coded photographs and maps, shared recommendations or tips, and storytelling projects and crowdsourced narratives are highly visible opportunities to engage with and analyze digital placemaking practices. But we can also study the social production of place and the processes of placemaking in and adjacent to digital media. Studying how people utilize forms and practices of digital media that leave traces of their activity and presence but don't necessarily produce observable or circulated media texts to analyze should be sites and situations for future research into re-placeing and digital placemaking.

Future Research

Aside from the non-use and after-access experiences of Kansas City communities' interactions with Google Fiber, I have had the opportunity to interview and survey only a limited sample of digital media non-users. However, I have found that re-placeing the city and digital placemaking practices are integral to their experiences of the city as well. The few navigation technology non-users I interviewed for chapter 3 began to articulate the ways in which other people's technology use affected their own mobility and perception of space and place. Some participants noted that networked urban subjects had certain expectations about non-users' knowledge of and access to the city. People who didn't own a mobile phone or chose not to use digital navigation systems described some of the ways in which networked subjects' experience of the city as augmented or layered did not map onto their own. One participant explained how she was forced to buy a pay-as-you-go cell phone if she wanted to continue to housesit for her friends. Another participant noted that his friends expected him to have access to or acquire directions to locations while on the go. A few participants expressed that they felt "out of the loop" or did not have access to a holistic sense of the city because they did not have a smartphone. I do not mean to imply that non-users or those who choose to opt out of using digital technologies are inherently disadvantaged. Instead, I'm suggesting that the relationship of non-users to social, technological, and physical spaces of the city are equally complex and worthy of further interrogation and that practices of re-placement could be explored in these contexts as well.

It is imperative that scholars of urban spaces and digital media investigate the plethora of localized or rescaled ways in which specific populations and urban developers actually experience (and understand their experiences of) being, seeing, and knowing digital media and urban environments. Scholars who are interested in questions of space and place should continue to examine the ways in which urban spaces are being re-marked and reinformed as *places* in conjunction with digital mediascapes and practices. Re-placeing provides a framework that can and should be applied to analyzing the ways that distinct communities activate and interact with digital placemaking in culturally specific ways that reflect their subjective experiences and social hierarchies, including how particular communities are disproportionately affected by the re-placeing strategies of others. Situated within the "spatial turn" in media studies, this book perpetuates these discussions within humanities and cultural studies debates by emphasizing the activities and power struggles within digital performances. A cultural studies approach to digital placemaking makes explicit the vernacular digital experiences of urban space by looking at the manner in which digital placemaking is *actually* incorporated into practices and expressions of everyday life. Embedded in these uses and experiences of digital media in the city are many different visions of the future of urban computing and ways of knowing, constructing, and resisting how the city works and acts.

I've suggested that we must engage with the politics and realities of place and placemaking to fully understand how we experience digital media in our everyday lives. But what is at stake in doing so? Adopting place as a lens for understanding digital media imaginaries and use illustrates how urban planners and developers, city managers and municipal officials, and creative placemakers adhere to preexisting, sometimes outmoded assumptions of urban informatics. Models such as strategies for smart-city programming, promises of domestic high-speed networks, and the role of the arts in the production of place carry traces of residual as well as emerging ideologies about the meaning and experience of place as well as the role that digital media play in placemaking. These models and strategies do not always recognize or carefully consider the changing understandings of place and placemaking experienced by digital media users and non-users. At stake in the co-construction of place and digital media is outlining the social productions and processes that inscribe who and what activities belong in urban space and how they are supported or sidelined by social, physical, and technological infrastructures.

Digital media, in some ways, are akin to the boulevards in Baron Haussmann's reinvention of Paris in the power they yield to reshape urban space and urban life. As Harvey describes, Haussmann's grand boulevards became lined with shops and cafes, attracted tourism, and celebrated the creative productions of the fashion industry and its consumption by fashionable flaneurs who strolled these massive throughways to see and be seen.[11] The boulevards connected disparate sections of the city, collapsing neighborhoods and altering neighborhood life in the name of innovation in order to increase efficient flows of goods and services and to manage a population experiencing rapid growth. These techno-scientific arteries for more robust traffic flow and mobility doubled as places for public performances of sociality and consumption as well as locational capital. Boulevards helped to rebrand Paris as the City of Lights and promoted not only a particular image of the city and a renewed sense of place but also the visibility and selective inclusion of some communities and activities over others. As the case studies in this book illustrate, digital media are employed toward similar placemaking ends: place promotion and branding, streamlined efficiency and smart growth, and a platform for performances of identity, exploration, and self-expression while they simultaneously connect and segment the city. Now the boulevards are also lined with sensors, antennae, cameras, and mobile phones that influence potential routes and mobilities and experiences of place—sometimes even in contrast to the programmed space and activities of the physical streets.

The right to intervene in and contribute to the social production of urban space now includes the right to re-place the city and to exercise individual and collective agency in reshaping and participating in processes of urbanization through digital media. By realizing the potential of digital media in placemaking processes and how re-placeing operates at different scales within everyday life, citizens and communities can arbitrate the meaning of place and coordinate or democratize actions that contribute to the social production of cities and city life. Re-placeing is a new lens through which to read and critically examine what we already do with digital media. However, it is important to recognize the ways in which these digital placemaking practices are currently not always a right but a privilege. With this in mind, re-placeing is also an approach that helps digital media users and non-users envision what we *could* do to make productions of place through digital media more heeded and valued as well as more equitable and just.

ACKNOWLEDGMENTS

I've been thinking about the intersections between digital media and urban space for quite some time, and there are many people and places that have influenced this thinking. It wasn't until graduate school that I attempted to research and concretize any thoughts on this topic. Michael Curtin, Kris Olds, Rob Howard, Michele Hilmes, and Jonathan Gray provided feedback at integral moments that helped shape many of the ideas that appear in this book. I feel incredibly fortunate to have taken classes and had discussions with Lisa Nakamura during this time as well. Her encouragement and support for pursuing this project at its very early stages and her service as a mentor within a field of study that was entirely new to me as an MA student have had a lasting impact to say the least.

I've had the opportunity to present concepts and chapters from this book as works in progress in colloquia and seminars at a variety of schools and programs at the University of Kansas and elsewhere, and I am thankful for all the thoughtful suggestions and critiques I've received. Research and writing of this book was generously supported by the University of Kansas New Faculty General Research Fund and the Research Excellence Fund. The book proposal writing workshop at the Hall Center for the Humanities helped jumpstart the writing process for this manuscript while my writing buddies Maya Stiller, Celka Straughn, Marisa Ford, and (office spouse) Jessa Lingel were instrumental in sustaining momentum from proposal to publication. I am also grateful to Lisha Nadkarni at NYU Press, Adrienne Shaw, and the anonymous reviewers for their interest in and careful reading of this manuscript.

I extend my thanks to the numerous research participants and interviewees (many of whom were anonymous and some named) who contributed to this project. I am indebted to you for openly sharing your perspectives and taking time out of your busy schedules to tour field sites, walk through architectural models, and speak with me about your experiences planning and using digital media within urban spaces.

Without your opinions and perspectives, this project could never have been completed.

The process of researching, writing, and publishing a book can take years, and my parents and friends have always been a constant source of support and encouragement. However, living with someone who is writing a book (or two) deserves its own special form of recognition. I'm continually inspired by Ben Schwab's tenacity and intellectual rigor and have benefitted from his exceptional critical insight. Reading sections of this manuscript only scratch the surface of his contributions to this book. *Efharisto poli* and *te amo*.

I especially want to acknowledge the role that my grandparents played in shaping this project. All four of my grandparents arrived in New York City after enduring the worst of humanity and always dreamed of where they were going without ever forgetting where they'd been. Through memories of distant cities that will never be the same again and stories about people I will never know, they showed me how places and communities are steeped in implicit narratives of love and loss and how vast metropolises and small towns can be sites of constant symbolic, cultural, and political struggle. Through their accomplishments, experiences, and recollections, I began to understand how powerful place is in the creation of identity and how important cultivating a "sense of place" can be.

APPENDIX

Timeline of Google Fiber in Kansas City, 2010–2015

February 2010	Google announces that it will build an experimental one-gigabit-per-second (Gbps) fiber-optic network in a select number of US cities. The company launches a competition for cities to bid on Google Fiber services.
March 2010	The Google Fiber competition ends, and the company begins reviewing applications. During the monthlong campaign for Google services, the company receives more than 1,100 requests from communities across the United States and approximately 194,000 from individuals.
March 2011	Kansas City, Kansas, is chosen as the winning city.
May 2011	The winning bid expands to include the neighboring city of Kansas City, Missouri.
February 2012	Google begins fiber infrastructure installation in KCK and KCMO.
March 2012	Google receives approval from Kansas and Missouri governments to provide video services as well as fiber-optic networks.
April 2012	Despite delays, Google announces that it has installed more than one hundred miles of backbone fiber in KCK and KCMO.
June 2012	The newly created Mayor's Bi-State Innovation Team publishes a digital roadmap for utilizing Google Fiber titled "Playing to Win in America's Digital Crossroads."
July 2012	Google launches fiber-optic internet service in KCK and KCMO. Preregistration for Google Fiber's gigabit network begins. In order to acquire Google Fiber, neighborhoods (called "fiberhoods" in Google campaigns) must qualify by preregistering at least 5 percent of their residents for a ten-dollar fee per household. Neighborhoods that qualify for service will also have Google Fiber installed in public buildings such as libraries, schools, and hospitals. Two days after preregistration opens, more than 20 percent of eligible neighborhoods in KCMO qualify for fiber. There are several KCK and urban core neighborhoods where no one signs up. Prices for installation and services are announced. Google Fiber TV and internet service are priced at $120 per month. For seventy dollars per month 1 Gbps internet service is available (priced similarly to area competitors, but with faster speeds). A "free" option is offered, which provides 5 Mpbs download and 1 Mbps upload speeds to at-home customers for a one-time $300 construction fee with service guaranteed at no cost for approximately seven years. Preregistration for the "free" service is still required.

September 2012	The first round of preregistration ends, and residents are able to sign up for Google Fiber service. Google releases maps of neighborhoods that qualify for gigabit service. Of the 202 neighborhoods that could potentially receive service, twenty-two neighborhoods do not qualify. Many of the households that do not participate in the preregistration process are identified as lower-income neighborhoods that have lacked affordable or any internet access. Google notes that preregistration will reopen in 2013.
October-November 2012	The first "fiberhood" installation begins in Hanover Heights, Kansas, followed by a second KCK fiberhood (Dub's Dread). The first KCMO fiberhood, Crown Center, is slated for installation in the spring of 2013. The Mayor's Bi-State Innovation Team establishes KC Digital Drive to initiate strategies outlined in KC's digital road map, including digital inclusion efforts.
March 2013	Google Fiber expands to more neighborhoods in KCK and KCMO as well as the adjacent town of Olathe, Kansas.
April 2013–May 2013	Google Fiber is to be deployed in Austin, Texas, and Provo, Utah, as well as Kansas City suburbs.
June 2013–August 2013	Google Fiber expands to more neighborhoods in Kansas City. In August the Greater Kansas City Community Foundation announces the creation of the Kansas City Digital Inclusion Fund to support nonprofits and community organizations working to ameliorate digital divides.
November 2014	Small businesses in Kansas City can now sign up for Google Fiber service.
January 2015	Google announces that it will build fiber-optic networks and provide gigabit service in Charlotte, North Carolina; Atlanta, Georgia; Nashville, Tennessee; and Raleigh-Durham, North Carolina, with several other cities to follow in coming months.
July 2015	Google announces that it will provide free internet service to low-income communities in all Google Fiber markets as part of US Department of Housing and Urban Development's ConnectHome initiatives.
February 2016	ConnectHome installation begins in Kansas City.

NOTES

INTRODUCTION

1 Shuhei Hosokawa, "The Walkman Effect," *Popular Music* 4 (1984): 167.

2 Hosokawa, 167.

3 Margaret Morse, "An Ontology of Everyday Distraction: The Freeway, the Mall, and Television," in *Logics of Television: Essays in Cultural Criticism*, ed. Patricia Mellencamp (Bloomington: Indiana University Press, 1990), 193.

4 Joshua Meyrowitz, *No Sense of Place: The Impact of Electronic Media on Social Behavior* (Oxford: Oxford University Press, 1985).

5 Edward Relph, *Place and Placelessness* (London: Sage, 1976), 90. Relph also blames increased mobility (changing homes, travel and tourism, highways) and mass culture for these effects and adheres to the idea that places lose their special or unique character, producing a superficial sense of place or what Nigel Thrift refers to as "almost places."

6 Donna Jeanne Haraway, *Simians, Cyborgs, and Women: The Reinvention of Nature* (London: Free Association, 1991); N. Katherine Hayles, *How We Became Posthuman: Virtual Bodies in Cybernetics, Literature, and Informatics* (Chicago: University of Chicago Press, 1999); N. Katherine Hayles, *How We Think: Digital Media and Contemporary Technogenesis* (Chicago: University of Chicago Press, 2012); Mark B. N. Hansen, *Bodies in Code: Interfaces with Digital Media* (New York: Routledge, 2006).

7 Rowan Wilken, "Mobilizing Place: Mobile Media, Peripatetics, and the Renegotiation of Urban Places," *Journal of Urban Technology* 15, no. 3 (December 1, 2008): 39–55; Scott McQuire, *Geomedia: Networked Cities and the Future of Public Space* (Cambridge: Polity, 2016).

8 Michael Bull, "No Dead Air! The iPod and the Culture of Mobile Listening," *Leisure Studies* 24, no. 4 (January 1, 2005): 343–55.

9 Ellen Goodman, "The Latest Rage," *Boston Globe*, March 21, 1999.

10 Sherry Turkle, *Alone Together: Why We Expect More from Technology and Less from Each Other* (New York: Basic Books, 2011); David Riesman, with Nathan Glazer and Reuel Denney, *The Lonely Crowd: A Study of the Changing American Character*, abridged and revised ed. (New Haven, NJ: Yale University Press, 2001).

11 Debra Benita Shaw, "Streets for Cyborgs: The Electronic Flâneur and the Posthuman City," *Space and Culture* 18, no. 3 (August 1, 2015): 231.

12 Robert Luke, "The Phoneur: Digital Pedagogies of the Wireless Web," in *Communities of Difference: Culture, Language, Technology*, ed. Peter Trifonas (New York: Palgrave MacMillan, 2005), 185–204.

13 David Morley, *Home Territories: Media, Mobility and Identity* (New York: Routledge, 2000), 13.

14 David Harvey, "From Space to Place and Back Again: Reflections on the Condition of Postmodernity," in *Mapping the Futures: Local Cultures, Global Change*, ed. Jon Bird, Barry Curtis, Tim Putnam, George Robertson, and Lisa Tickner, Futures: New Perspectives for Cultural Analysis (London: Routledge, 1993), 3–29; Yi-Fu Tuan, "Space and Place: Humanistic Perspective," in *Philosophy in Geography*, ed. Stephen Gale and Gunnar Olsson, Theory and Decision Library 20 (Dordrecht: Springer Netherlands, 1979), 387–427; Tim Cresswell, *Place: A Short Introduction* (Malden, MA: Wiley-Blackwell, 2004).

15 Anthony Giddens, *The Consequences of Modernity* (Redwood City, CA: Stanford University Press, 1990), 79–80.

16 Lee Humphreys and Tony Liao, "Foursquare and the Parochialization of Public Space," *First Monday* 18, no. 11 (November 27, 2013), www.firstmonday.org; Janne Lindqvist, Justin Cranshaw, Jason Wiese, Jason Hong, and John Zimmerman, "I'm the Mayor of My House: Examining Why People Use Foursquare: A Social-Driven Location Sharing Application" (CHI '11: Proceedings of the SIGCHI Conference on Human Factors in Computing Systems, Vancouver, BC, May 7–12, 2011), 2409–18; Jordan Frith, "Turning Life into a Game: Foursquare, Gamification, and Personal Mobility," *Mobile Media & Communication* 1, no. 2 (2013): 248–62; Adriana de Souza e Silva and Daniel M. Sutko, eds., *Digital Cityscapes: Merging Digital and Urban Playspaces* (New York: Peter Lang, 2009); Henriette Cramer, Mattias Rost, and Lars Erik Holmquist, "Performing a Check-In: Emerging Practices, Norms and 'Conflicts' in Location-Sharing Using Foursquare" (MobileHCI '11: Proceedings of the 13th International Conference on Human Computer Interaction with Mobile Devices and Services, Stockholm, Sweden, August 30–September 2, 2011), 57–66; Jason Farman, *Mobile Interface Theory: Embodied Space and Locative Media* (New York: Routledge, 2012); Christian Licoppe and Yoriko Inada, "Emergent Uses of a Multiplayer Location-Aware Mobile Game: The Interactional Consequences of Mediated Encounters," *Mobilities* 1, no. 1 (March 1, 2006): 39–61; Mimi Sheller and John Urry, eds., *Mobile Technologies of the City* (New York: Routledge, 2006); Richard Ling and Birgitte Yttri, "Hyper-Coordination via Mobile Phones in Norway," in *Perpetual Contact: Mobile Communication, Private Talk, Public Performance*, ed. James E. Katz and Mark Aakhus (Cambridge: Cambridge University Press, 2002), 139–69.

17 Lee Humphreys, *The Qualified Self: Social Media and the Accounting of Everyday Life* (Cambridge, MA: MIT Press, 2018).

18 Nicky Gregson and Gillian Rose, "Taking Butler Elsewhere: Performativities, Spatialities and Subjectivities," *Environment and Planning D: Society and Space* 18, no. 4 (2000): 447.

19 Erika Polson, "A Gateway to the Global City: Mobile Place-Making Practices by Expats," *New Media & Society* 17, no. 4 (April 1, 2015): 629–45.

20 Cresswell, *Place*.

21 Doreen B. Massey, *Space, Place and Gender* (Minneapolis: University of Minnesota Press, 1994); Tim Cresswell, *In Place/Out of Place: Geography, Ideology, and Transgression* (Minneapolis: University of Minnesota Press, 1996); Henri Lefebvre, *The Production of Space* (Cambridge, MA: Blackwell, 1991); Gill Valentine, "Living with Difference: Reflections on Geographies of Encounter," *Progress in Human Geography* 32, no. 3 (June 2008): 323–37; Gill Valentine, "The Geography of Women's Fear," *Area* 21, no. 4 (December 1989), 385–90; Mei-Po Kwan, "Time, Information Technologies, and the Geographies of Everyday Life," *Urban Geography* 23, no. 5 (2002): 471–82.

22 Lynda H. Schneekloth and Robert G. Shibley, "Implacing Architecture into the Practice of Placemaking," *Journal of Architectural Education* 53, no. 3 (February 2000): 132.

23 Michel de Certeau, *The Practice of Everyday Life* (Berkeley: University of California Press, 2011), 37.

24 Steve Harrison and Paul Dourish, "Re-place-ing Space: The Roles of Place and Space in Collaborative Systems" (Proceedings of the ACM Conference on Computer-Supported Cooperative Work CSCW '96, Boston, MA, November 16–20, 1996), 67–76.

25 Cresswell, *Place*, 29.

26 Cresswell, *In Place/Out of Place*, 3.

27 Pier Carlo Palermo and Davide Ponzini, *Place-Making and Urban Development: New Challenges for Contemporary Planning and Design* (New York: Routledge, 2015).

28 Doreen B. Massey, "Power-Geometry and a Progressive Sense of Place," in *Mapping the Futures*, ed. Jon Bird, Barry Curtis, Tim Putnam, George Robertson, and Lisa Tickner (London: Routledge, 1993).

29 David Bordwell, "Historical Poetics of Cinema," in *The Cinema Text: Methods and Approaches*, ed. R. Barton Palmer, Georgia State Literary Studies 3 (New York: AMS, 1989), 369–98.

30 Jonathan Skinner, "Editor's Statement," *Ecopoetics* 1 (2001): 5–8.

31 Barney Warf and Santa Arias, *The Spatial Turn: Interdisciplinary Perspectives* (London: Taylor & Francis, 2008).

32 Shaw, "Streets for Cyborgs," 239.

33 Barry Brown and Mark Perry, "Of Maps and Guidebooks: Designing Geographical Technologies," *SIGGROUP Bulletin* 22, no. 3 (December 2001): 28–32.

34 Etienne Wenger, *Communities of Practice: Learning, Meaning, and Identity* (New York: Cambridge University Press, 1998).

35 Edward S. Casey, "Between Geography and Philosophy: What Does It Mean to Be in the Place-World?," *Annals of the Association of American Geographers* 91, no. 4 (2001): 684.

36 Daniel Latorre, "Digital Placemaking—Authentic Civic Engagement," Project for Public Spaces (blog), September 22, 2011, http://www.pps.org.

37 Emily Sun, "The Importance of Play in Digital Placemaking" (Ninth International AAAI Conference on Web and Social Media, Oxford, UK, May 26–29, 2015), www.aaai.org; Allison Powell, Brian Hendrick, Arpan Ganguli, Tatevik Sargsyan, Shagun Shah, and Eca Tkavc-Dubokovic, "Digital Rendezvous: Experiences of Students, Staff, and Alumni on a Campus Memory Map" (Ninth International AAAI Conference on Web and Social Media, Oxford, UK, May 26–29, 2015), www.aaai.org; Yong-Chan Kim and Sandra J. Ball-Rokeach, "Community Storytelling Network, Neighborhood Context, and Civic Engagement: A Multilevel Approach," *Human Communication Research* 32, no. 4 (October 1, 2006): 411–39; Sandra J. Ball-Rokeach, Yong-Chan Kim, and Sorin Matei, "Storytelling Neighborhood: Paths to Belonging in Diverse Urban Environments," *Communication Research* 28, no. 4 (August 2001): 392–428; Jan Seeburger, Marcus Foth, and Dian W. Tjondronegoro, "Digital Design Interventions for Creating New Presentations of Self in Public Urban Places," in *Citizen's Right to the Digital City: Urban Interfaces, Activism, and Placemaking*, ed. Marcus Foth, Martin Brynskov, and Timo Ojala (Singapore: Springer, 2015), 1–21; Erika Polson, *Privileged Mobilities: Professional Migration, Geo-Social Media, and a New Global Middle Class* (New York: Peter Lang, 2015).

38 Maria Manta Conroy and Jennifer Evans-Cowley, "E-participation in Planning: An Analysis of Cities Adopting On-Line Citizen Participation Tools," *Environment and Planning C* 24, no. 3 (2006): 371; Moozhan Shakeri, Richard Kingston, and Nuno Pinto, "Towards a Community Support System; Social Media Culture, Games and Planning Tools" (Ninth International AAAI Conference on Web and Social Media, Oxford, UK, May 26–29, 2015), www.aaai.org; Eric Gordon, Engagement Lab, Emerson College, accessed November 20, 2015, http://elab.emerson.edu/.

39 For example, see Sheila Roberts, "An Incomplete Replacing: The White South African Expatriate," in *Displacements: Cultural Identities in Question*, ed. Angelika Bammer (Bloomington: Indiana University Press, 1994), 172–81. Re-placeing has been applied to understanding networks of exchange or shifting geographies of networks such as the geography of British financial spaces. Removing or resurrecting physical environments has been understood as re-placeing, such as the postcolonial re-placement and/or destruction of monuments and buildings. It has also been seen as ascribing, uniting, or mapping place onto memories and personal or collective narratives and histories, which undoes or reconsiders previous understandings of certain locations (e.g., Jewish experiences and memories in post–World War II Europe or the work of the Truth and Reconciliation Commission in South Africa).

40 Harrison and Dourish, "Re-place-ing Space," 67–76.

41 Mizuko Ito, "Mobile Phones, Japanese Youth and the Re-placement of Social Contact," chap. 9 in *Mobile Communications: Re-negotiation of the Social Sphere*, ed. Richard Ling and P. E. Pedersen (London: Springer, 2005).

42 Matthew A. Zook and Mark Graham, "Mapping DigiPlace: Geocoded Internet Data and the Representation of Place," *Environment and Planning B: Planning and Design* 34, no. 3 (June 1, 2007): 466–82; Stephen D. N. Graham, "Software-Sorted Geographies," *Progress in Human Geography* 29, no. 5 (October 1, 2005): 562–80; Mimi Sheller, "Infrastructures of the Imagined Island: Software, Mobilities, and the Architecture of Caribbean Paradise," *Environment and Planning A* 41, no. 6 (June 1, 2009): 1386–403; Nigel Thrift and Shaun French, "The Automatic Production of Space," *Transactions of the Institute of British Geographers* 27, no. 3 (2002): 309–35; Rob Kitchin and Martin Dodge, *Code/Space: Software and Everyday Life* (Cambridge, MA: MIT Press, 2011).

43 Alexander R. Galloway, *The Interface Effect* (Cambridge: Polity, 2012).

44 Lori Emerson, *Reading Writing Interfaces* (Minneapolis: University of Minnesota Press, 2014).

45 Ulf Hannerz, *Cultural Complexity: Studies in the Social Organization of Meaning* (New York: Columbia University Press, 1992); George E. Marcus, *Ethnography through Thick and Thin* (Princeton, NJ: Princeton University Press, 1998); Robert K. Yin, *Case Study Research Design and Methods*, 5th ed. (Thousand Oaks, CA: Sage, 2014); Karen Fog Olwig and Kirsten Hastrup, *Siting Culture: The Shifting Anthropological Object* (New York: Routledge, 1997); Jenna Burrell, "The Field Site as a Network: A Strategy for Locating Ethnographic Research," *Field Methods* 21, no. 2 (2009): 181–99; Jessa Lingel, "Networked Field Studies: Comparative Inquiry and Online Communities," *Social Media + Society* 3, no. 4 (October 2017).

46 Kathryn Zickuhr, "Location-Based Services," Pew Research Center, September 12, 2013, www.pewinternet.org.

47 Ann Markusen and Anne Gadwa, "Creative Placemaking" (Washington, DC: National Endowment for the Arts, 2010), www.arts.gov.

CHAPTER 1. THE SMART CITY

1 Amy Glasmeier and Susan Christopherson, "Thinking about Smart Cities," *Cambridge Journal of Regions, Economy and Society* 8, no. 1 (2015): 3–12.

2 Michael Batty, "How Disruptive Is the Smart Cities Movement?," *Environment and Planning B: Planning and Design* 43, no. 3 (May 1, 2016): 442.

3 Luc Sante, "Smart City," *New York* 28, no. 5 (January 30, 1995): 34.

4 Sante, 36.

5 Albert Lepawsky, "City Plan: Metro Style," *Journal of Land & Public Utility Economics* 16, no. 2 (May 1940): 137–50.

6 Stephen Graham and Simon Marvin, "Planning Cybercities? Integrating Telecommunications into Urban Planning," *Town Planning Review* 70, no. 1 (1999): 105.

7 Associated Press, "High-Tech Concepts to Shape 'Smart Cities' for Japanese," *Journal of Commerce*, August 7, 1987, 5A.

8 Taylor Shelton, Matthew Zook, and Alan Wiig, "The 'Actually Existing Smart City,'" *Cambridge Journal of Regions, Economy and Society* 8, no. 1 (March 1, 2015): 13–25.

9   Glasmeier and Christopherson, "Thinking about Smart Cities"; P. H. Harris, "The Technopolis Phenomenon—Smart Cities, Fast Systems, Global Networks," *Behavioral Science*, no. 38 (1992): 2.

10 Rob Kitchin, "Making Sense of Smart Cities: Addressing Present Shortcomings," *Cambridge Journal of Regions, Economy and Society* 8, no. 1 (March 1, 2015): 131–36.

11 Aaron Back, "IBM Launches a 'Smart City' Project in China," Technology, *Wall Street Journal, Eastern Edition*, September 17, 2009.

12 The Internet of Things (IoT) has become a buzzword that refers to a network of connected devices, where everyday objects and appliances are connected to the internet. Staff, "Advantech, Intel Plan for Smart Cities and the Internet of Things," *Control (1049-5541)* 26, no. 12 (December 18, 2013): 24–26.

13 Vito Albino, Umberto Berardi, and Rosa Maria Dangelico, "Smart Cities: Definitions, Dimensions, Performance, and Initiatives," *Journal of Urban Technology* 22, no. 1 (January 2015): 3–21.

14 Albino, Berardi, and Dangelico.

15 Albino, Berardi, and Dangelico.

16 J. Logan and H. Molotch, *"The City and Growth Machine" Urban Fortunes: The Political Economy of Place* (Berkeley: University of California Press, 1987); Shelton, Zook, and Wiig, "The 'Actually Existing Smart City.'"

17 Shelton, Zook, and Wiig.

18 Nadine Post, "Livable City Gets Smarter," *ENR: Engineering News-Record* 267, no. 17 (December 12, 2011): 32.

19 Ben Leitschuh, "Resource Finder," *Planning* 81, no. 11 (December 2015): 46.

20 Anna Kordunsky, "Overcoming the Sustainability Challenge: An Interview with Guruduth Banavar," in "The Future of the City," special issue, *Journal of International Affairs* 65, no. 2 (Spring/Summer 2012): 147–53.

21 Robin Meadows, "San Francisco and Paris Get Smart," *Frontiers in Ecology and the Environment* 11, no. 4 (2013): 172; Kordunsky.

22 Sofia Shwayri, "From the New Town to the Ubiquitous Ecocity: A Korean New Urban Type?," *Traditional Dwellings and Settlements Review* 26, no. 1 (2014): 79–80; Post, "Livable City Gets Smarter."

23 Philip Siekman, "The Smart Car Is Looking More So instead of Giving Up, as Some Industry Gossips Predicted, DaimlerChrysler Is Betting Heavily on a Tiny Car Built in an Innovative French Factory," *Forbes*, April 15, 2002, http://archive.fortune.com; "Daimler Increases Production of Smart EV," *Automotive Engineer* 36, no. 7 (September 2011): 5.

24 Margaret Tan, "Creating the Digital Economy: Strategies and Perspectives from Singapore," *International Journal of Electronic Commerce* 3, no. 3 (Spring 1999): 105–22.

25 Post, "Livable City Gets Smarter."

26 Kordunsky, "Overcoming the Sustainability Challenge"; Jonathan Donner, *After Access: Inclusion, Development, and a More Mobile Internet* (Cambridge, MA: MIT Press, 2015).

27 Shefali Anand, "In India, a GIFT from Modi Is Still Waiting to Be Opened Up," Property Report, *Wall Street Journal, Eastern Edition*, July 29, 2015.

28 Edward C. Relph, *The Modern Urban Landscape: 1880 to the Present* (Baltimore, MD: Johns Hopkins University Press, 1987).

29 Post, "Livable City Gets Smarter."

30 Jeong Wha-Huh, Songdo U-Life, 2009.

31 Bert Williams, "Going Wireless," *American City & County* 129, no. 3 (March 2014): 15.

32 Tim Bunnell, *Malaysia, Modernity and the Multimedia Super Corridor: A Critical Geography of Intelligent Landscapes* (London: Routledge, 2004).

33 Laura Schatz and Laura C. Johnson, "Smart City North: Economic and Labour Force Impacts of Call Centres in Sudbury, Ontario," *Work Organisation, Labour & Globalization* 1, no. 2 (Summer 2007): 116–30.

34 Neil Brenner and Christian Schmid, "Towards a New Epistemology of the Urban?," *City* 19, nos. 2–3 (2015): 151–82.

35 For more examples of smart-city technologies prototyped and advertised in South Korean U-cities, see Germaine Halegoua, "The Policy and Export of Ubiquitous Place: Investigating South Korean U-Cities," in *From Social Butterfly to Engaged Citizen: Urban Informatics, Social Media, Ubiquitous Computing, and Mobile Technology to Support Citizen Engagement*, eds. Marcus Foth, Laura Forlano, Christine Satchell, and Martin Gibbs (Cambridge, MA: MIT Press, 2011), 315–34.

36 Saul Austerlitz, "Urban Planners Working to Generate without Becoming Degenerate," *National*, April 13, 2012.

37 Gale International, POSCO E&C, and KPF, *New Songdo City* (Kohn Pedersen Fox, 2004), 90.

38 PlanIT, "Living PlanIT: What We Do," accessed May 23, 2016, www.living-planit.com.

39 Kasmira Jefford, "My Blueprint for the Smart City: Build It Exactly like an iPhone; Green Pioneers; Steve Lewis of Living Planit Is Thinking Big, Says Kasmira Jefford," Business, *Sunday Times* (London), January 23, 2011.

40 Relph, *The Modern Urban Landscape*, 83.

41 Anthony M. Townsend, *Smart Cities: Big Data, Civic Hackers, and the Quest for a New Utopia* (New York: W. W. Norton, 2013).

42 Adam Greenfield, *Against the Smart City*, 1.3 ed. (New York: Do Projects, 2013).

43 PlanITValley, "Living PlanIT CEO Steve Lewis Speaking about PlanIT Valley and Building Sustainable Cities," video, January 22, 2011, www.youtube.com/watch?v=JcotR99syGQ.

44 Shwayri, "From the New Town to the Ubiquitous Ecocity."

45 IBM Social Media, "Smarter Cities—Speech by IBM CEO Sam Palmisano at The Atlantic Council," video, May 6, 2009, www.youtube.com/watch?v=31zKQhpoKo8.

46 Helen Knight, "The City with a Brain," *New Scientist* 208, no. 2781 (October 9, 2010): 1.

47 Masdar City, "About Masdar City," 2016, www.masdar.ae.

48 IBM Social Media, "Smarter Cities."

49 Gale International, POSCO E&C, and KPF, *New Songdo City*.

50 Federico Cugurullo, "How to Build a Sandcastle: An Analysis of the Genesis and Development of Masdar City," *Journal of Urban Technology* 20, no. 1 (January 2013): 23–37.

51 PlanIT, "Living PlanIT."

52 Post, "Livable City Gets Smarter."

53 Gale International, POSCO E&C, and KPF, *New Songdo City*, 6.

54 Gale International, POSCO E&C, and KPF.

55 Gale International, POSCO E&C, and KPF, 37.

56 Cugurullo, "How to Build a Sandcastle," 30.

57 PlanIT Valley, "Living PlanIT CEO Steve Lewis."

58 Shannon Mattern, "Instrumental City: The View from Hudson Yards," *Places Journal*, April 26, 2016, https://placesjournal.org.

59 Cugurullo, "How to Build a Sandcastle."

60 Gale International, POSCO E&C, and KPF, *New Songdo City*, 11.

61 Gale International, POSCO E&C, and KPF, 27.

62 Masdar, "About Masdar City."

63 Masdar.

64 Masdar City, "Masdar City: Innovative Sustainable Development Brochure," 2015, http://masdar.ae/.

65 Masdar City.

66 Cugurullo, "How to Build a Sandcastle."

67 Susan DeFreitas, "In Portugal, a Smart City from the Ground Up," EarthTechling (blog), June 6, 2012, http://earthtechling.com.

68 Gale International, POSCO E&C, and KPF, *New Songdo City*, 21.

69 Michael Fahy, "Masdar City Ramps up Expansion with New Wave of Building Activity," *National*, October 26, 2015.

70 Parky at the Pictures, "Parky at the Pictures (In Cinemas 27/1/2011)," *Oxford Times*, January 27, 2011.

71 Masdar City, "About Masdar City."

72 Will Doig, "Science Fiction No More: The Perfect City Is under Construction," Salon, April 28, 2012, www.salon.com.

73 Arjen Oosterman, "Notes from the Telepresent," *Volume* 34 (Winter 2012).

74 Rachel Keeton, "New Songdo City," *Volume* 34 (Winter 2012).

75 Surabhi Pancholi, Tan Yigitcanlar, and Mirko Guaralda, "Societal Integration That Matters: Place Making Experience of Macquarie Park Innovation District, Sydney," *City, Culture and Society* 13 (June 2018): 13–21; Tan Yigitcanlar, Mirko Guaralda, Manuela B. Taboada, and Surabhi Pancholi, "Place Making for Knowledge Generation and Innovation: Planning and Branding Brisbane's Knowledge Community Precincts," *Journal of Urban Technology* 23, no. 1 (January 2, 2016): 115–46.

76 Lucy Williamson, "Tomorrow's Cities: Just How Smart Is Songdo?," *BBC News*, September 2, 2013, www.bbc.com.

77 Graham and Marvin, "Planning Cybercities?," 105.

78 Greenfield, *Against the Smart City*; Graham and Marvin; M. Christine Boyer, *CyberCities: Visual Perception in the Age of Electronic Communication* (Princeton, NJ: Princeton Architectural Press, 1996); Stephen Graham and Alessandro Aurigi, "Virtual Cities, Social Polarization and the Crisis in Urban Public Space," *Journal of Urban Technology* 4, no. 1 (1997): 19–52.

79 Edgar Pieterse, *City Futures: Confronting the Crisis of Urban Development* (Chicago: University of Chicago Press, 2008), 108.

80 Mattern, "Instrumental City."

81 Scott McQuire, *The Media City: Media, Architecture, and Urban Space* (London: Sage, 2008), 138.

82 Jane Wakefield, "Tomorrow's Cities: What's It like to Live in a Smart City?," *BBC News*, September 23, 2013, www.bbc.com.

83 William H Whyte, *The Social Life of Small Urban Spaces* (New York: Project for Public Spaces, 1980), www.pps.org.

84 Cugurullo, "How to Build a Sandcastle," 35.

85 Doig, "Science Fiction No More"; Mark Shepard, ed., *Sentient City: Ubiquitous Computing, Architecture, and the Future of Urban Space* (Cambridge, MA: MIT Press, 2011).

86 Kordunsky, "Overcoming the Sustainability Challenge," 149.

87 Kordunsky, 150.

88 Williamson, "Tomorrow's Cities."

89 Williamson.

90 Cugurullo, "How to Build a Sandcastle"; Fahy, "Masdar City Ramps Up Expansion."

91 Anand, "In India, a Gift from Modi."

92 Anand.

93 Graham and Marvin, "Planning Cybercities?," 110.

94 Jennifer Gabrys, "Programming Environments: Environmentality and Citizen Sensing in the Smart City," *Environment and Planning D: Society and Space* 32, no. 1 (February 1, 2014): 30–48.

95 Jane Wakefield, "Tomorrow's Cities: Do You Want to Live in a Smart City?," *BBC News*, August 19, 2013, www.bbc.com.

96 Gabrys, "Programming Environments."

97 Sheila Jasanoff and Sang-Hyun Kim, "Containing the Atom: Sociotechnical Imaginaries and Nuclear Power in the and South Korea," *Minerva* 47 (2009): 119–146.

98 Jasanoff and Kim, 120; emphasis in original.

99 Pier Carlo Palermo and Davide Ponzini, *Place-Making and Urban Development: New Challenges for Contemporary Planning and Design* (New York: Routledge, 2015).

100 Yi-Fu Tuan, "Space and Place: Humanistic Perspective," in *Philosophy in Geography*, ed. Stephen Gale and Gunnar Olsson, Theory and Decision Library 20 (Dordrecht: Springer Netherlands, 1979), 387–427.

101 Maroš Krivý, "Towards a Critique of Cybernetic Urbanism: The Smart City and the Society of Control," *Planning Theory*, April 27, 2016.

102 Anthony Townsend, "Smart Cities: What If the Smart Cities of the Future Are Chock Full of Bugs?," *Places*, October 7, 2013, https://placesjournal.org; Doig, "Science Fiction No More"; Wakefield, "Tomorrow's Cities"; Drew Hemment and Anthony Townsend, eds., *Smart Citizens* (Manchester: Future Everything, 2013).

103 Anne Balsamo, *Designing Culture* (Durham, NC: Duke University Press, 2011).

CHAPTER 2. THE CONNECTED CITY

 1 In 2011 Kansas City, Kansas, and Kansas City, Missouri, won a Google-hosted competition to have the company install a one-gigabit fiber-optic network in their cities. See appendix for a detailed timeline of Google Fiber in Kansas City from 2010 to 2016.

 2 In November 2015 the McDonald's qualified for $100 per month for one year under the Small Business Early Access Program (the program was launched in November 2014) even though the restaurant is located in an area that did not qualify as a fiberhood. The site doesn't qualify for the Community Connections program as it is not a public or nonprofit institution. As of writing this book, the McDonald's still has not signed up for Google Fiber service.

 3 Frank Morris, "Another First for Kansas City: Free Google Fiber for Low-Income Housing Residents," KCUR, accessed February 5, 2016, http://kcur.org.

 4 Geoffrey C. Bowker, Karen Baker, Florence Millerand, and David Ribes, "Toward Information Infrastructure Studies: Ways of Knowing in a Networked Environment," in *International Handbook of Internet Research*, ed. Jeremy Hunsinger, Lisbeth Klastrup, and Matthew M. Allen (Dordrecht: Springer Science & Business Media, 2010); Brian Larkin, "The Politics and Poetics of Infrastructure," *Annual Review of Anthropology* 42, no. 1 (2013): 327–43.

 5 Jonathan Donner, *After Access: Inclusion, Development, and a More Mobile Internet* (Cambridge, MA: MIT Press, 2015), 50–51.

 6 Larkin, "The Politics and Poetics of Infrastructure," 329.

 7 Lucy Suchman, Jeanette Blomberg, Julian E. Orr, and Randall Trigg, "Reconstructing Technologies as Social Practice," *American Behavioral Scientist* 43, no. 3 (November 1, 1999): 392–408; Bill Kirkpatrick, "Play, Power, and Policy: Putting John Fiske Back into Media Policy" (Fiske Matters: A Conference on John Fiske's Continuing Legacy for Cultural Studies, Madison, WI, June 11–12, 2010).

 8 Helga Tawil-Souri, "Cellular Borders: Dis/Connecting Phone Calls in Israel-Palestine," in *Signal Traffic: Critical Studies of Media Infrastructures*, ed. Lisa Parks and Nicole Starosielski (Urbana: University of Illinois Press, 2015), 157–82; Sarah Harris, "Service Providers as Digital Media Infrastructure: Turkey's Cybercafe Operators," in *Signal Traffic: Critical Studies of Media Infrastructures*, ed. Lisa Parks and Nicole Starosielski (Urbana: University of Illinois Press, 2015), 205–24.

 9 Lisa Parks, "Media Infrastructures and Affect," *Flow* 19, no. 12 (2014), http://flowtv.org.

10 Parks.

11 Parks; Christian Sandvig, "The Internet as Infrastructure," in *The Oxford Handbook of Internet Studies*, ed. W. Dutton (Oxford: Oxford University Press, 2013), 86–108.

12 Sako Musterd and Zoltán Kovács, *Place-Making and Policies for Competitive Cities* (Hoboken, NJ: John Wiley & Sons, 2013).

13 Catherine A. Middleton, Andrew Clement, and Graham Longford, "ICT Infrastructure as Public Infrastructure: Exploring the Benefits of Public Wireless Networks," SSRN Scholarly Paper (Rochester, NY: Social Science Research Network, August 15, 2006), http://papers.ssrn.com.

14 Tom Vanderbilt, "Walker in the Wireless City," *New York Times*, November 24, 2002, www.nytimes.com.

15 Harvey Jassem, "Municipal Wi-Fi Comes to Town," in *Displacing Place: Mobile Communication in the Twenty-First Century*, ed. Sharon Kleinman (New York: Peter Lang, 2007), 21–37.

16 Craig J. Settles, *Building the Gigabit City*, vol. 1 (Los Gatos, CA: Smashwords, 2013).

17 Gwen Shaffer, "Frame-Up: An Analysis of Arguments for and against Municipal Wireless Initiatives," *Public Works Management & Policy* 11, no. 3 (January 1, 2007): 210.

18 François Bar and Namkee Park, "Municipal Wi-Fi Networks: The Goals, Practices, and Policy Implications of the U.S. Case," *Communication & Strategies* 61, no. 1 (2006): 110.

19 Andrea H. Tapia and Julio Angel Ortiz, "Network Hopes Municipalities Deploying Wireless Internet to Increase Civic Engagement," *Social Science Computer Review* 28, no. 1 (February 1, 2010): 93–117.

20 Tapia and Ortiz; Sharon Strover, Gary Chapman, and Jody Waters, "Beyond Community Networking and CTCs: Access, Development, and Public Policy," *Telecommunications Policy* 28, nos. 7–8 (2004): 465–85.

21 Harvey C. Jassem, "Municipal Wi-Fi: The Coda," *Journal of Urban Technology* 17, no. 2 (August 1, 2010): 3; David Shein, "Municipal Wireless: A Primer for Public Discussion," the Center for Advancing the Study of Cyber Infrastructure, Rochester Institute of Technology, 2005, http://scholarworks.rit.edu.

22 "City to Buy What's Left of Wireless Philadelphia for $2 Million" (Philadelphia), *Inquirer*, December 16, 2009, accessed February 29, 2016, www.philly.com.

23 Joshua Breitbart, "The Philadelphia Story," New America Foundation, Open Technology Institute, December 11, 2007, www.newamerica.org.

24 Sascha Meinrath, "The Future of Municipal Wireless: The Two State of Pennsylvania," New America Foundation, Open Technology Institute, February 6, 2008, www.newamerica.org; Sascha Meinrath, "The Philadelphia Story: Learning from a Municipal Wireless Pioneer," New America Foundation, Open Technology Institute, December 11, 2007, www.newamerica.org.

25 Tapia and Ortiz, "Network Hopes Municipalities."

26 Laura Forlano, "Wi-Fi Geographies: When Code Meets Place," *Information Society* 25 (2009): 344–52; Laura Forlano, "Anytime? Anywhere?: Reframing Debates

around Municipal Wireless Networking," in "Wireless Networking for Communities, Citizens and the Public Interest," special issue, *Journal of Community Informatics* 4, no. 1 (2008).

27 Alison Powell and Leslie Regan Shade, "Going Wi-Fi in Canada: Municipal and Community Initiatives," *Government Information Quarterly* 23 (2006): 381–403.

28 Google Blog, "Introducing Our Google Fiber for Communities Website," July 13, 2010, http://googleblog.blogspot.com.

29 Google Blog, "Super Fast Fiber for Kansas City," July 26, 2012, http://googlefiber-blog.blogspot.com.

30 Google, "Google Fiber Comes to Kansas City, MO," video, May 16, 2011, https://www.youtube.com/watch?v=TmSuNyOpsXU.

31 "KC Digital Roadmap," Open Data KC, February 20, 2015, accessed March 7, 2016, https://data.kcmo.org.

32 "KCMO Is Evolving into a Smart City," City of Kansas City, accessed March 7, 2016, http://kcmo.gov.

33 "Smart City Advisory Board Meeting—Project Summary Presentation," Open Data KC, August 31, 2015, accessed March 7, 2016, https://data.kcmo.org.

34 For example, a Facebook invitation for a December 15, 2015, meeting at Thou Mayest Coffee Roasters in the Crossroads District read, "The Office of Innovation is hosting Urban Momentum: Where Conversation Meets Innovation. The City will provide an update on the Smart City project, chat with community partners, and talk about how we can work together to make this project robust and move Kansas City forward. Please join us at 4:00 for smart city conversation at Thou Mayest (upstairs), followed by networking and socializing downstairs at the 5:00 hour."

35 Michael Indergaard, *Silicon Alley: The Rise and Fall of a New Media District* (New York: Routledge, 2004).

36 As the Detroit Digital Justice Coalition "About" page explains, "DiscoTechs feature interactive, multimedia workshops designed to demystify, engage, and inform the community about issues of Internet use and ownership, and our communications rights on and offline." "Discovering Technology," Detroit Digital Justice Coalition, www.alliedmedia.org.

37 Google Blog, "Super Fast Fiber for Kansas City."

38 Google, "Google Fiber Launch Announcement in Kansas City, July 2012," video, July 26, 2012, www.youtube.com/watch?v=6uZVqPuq81c.

39 There have been 239 of these events in Kansas City as of March 9, 2016.

40 One sign-up event description reads, "Fiber Fall Family Day: Bring the whole family for an afternoon of fun with Google Fiber. Enjoy treats from the candy bar, take your picture in the photobooth, or join us for some family-friendly games. You'll even get a chance to leave with your very own yard sign." November 7, 2015. Both announcements from https://fiber.google.com.

41 The description of the event listed under Kansas City Pride Fest on the Google Fiber events page for June 6, 2015, reads, "Google Fiber is excited to participate in

the KC PrideFest. Visit our tent to dance with the team in our interactive booth while also learning about Google Fiber and how to sign up for service."

42 Public use sites were selected by the city to receive free Google Fiber connection, but these spaces had to be located in a fiberhood. Therefore, beyond individual household connection, it was beneficial for the community and neighborhood that residents sign up for service.

43 Sally Wyatt, Graham Thomas, and Tiziana Terranova, "They Came, They Surfed, They Went Back to the Beach: Conceptualizing Use and Non-use of the Internet," chap. 2 in *Virtual Society?: Technology, Cyberbole, Reality*, ed. Steve Woolgar (Oxford: Oxford University Press, 2002): 23–40; Neil Selwyn, Stephen Gorard, and John Furlong, "Whose Internet Is It Anyway? Exploring Adults' (Non)Use of the Internet in Everyday Life," *European Journal of Communication* 20, no. 1 (March 1, 2005): 5–26; Laura Portwood-Stacer, "Media Refusal and Conspicuous Non-consumption: The Performative and Political Dimensions of Facebook Abstention," *New Media & Society* 15, no. 7 (December 5, 2012): 1041–57; Ben Light, *Disconnecting with Social Networking Sites* (London: Palgrave Macmillan, 2014); Jed R. Brubaker, Mike Ananny, and Kate Crawford, "Departing Glances: A Sociotechnical Account of 'Leaving' Grindr," *New Media & Society* 18, no. 3 (July 7, 2014): 373–90.

44 Laura Portwood-Stacer, "Media Refusal and Conspicuous Non-consumption: The Performative and Political Dimensions of Facebook Abstention," *New Media & Society* 15, no. 7 (December 5, 2012): 1041-1057; Jan van Dijk and Kenneth Hacker, "The Digital Divide as a Complex and Dynamic Phenomenon," *Information Society* 19, no. 4 (September 1, 2003): 315–26.

45 Google employees and digital inclusion activists noted that this practice skewed initial metrics on active fiberhoods. Although fiberhoods were registered, the number of registrations within a fiberhood did not always correlate to the number of active residences within the neighborhood.

46 Google and Mayor's Bi-State Innovation Team, "The State of Internet Connectivity in KC: Neighborhood-Based Research Findings," June 22, 2012, 4.

47 Google and Mayor's Bi-State Innovation Team.

48 The Kansas City study also found that of the 17 percent who did not use the internet on a daily basis, approximately half of them didn't think that the lack of internet use was a disadvantage in the categories of accessing health information, locating government services, learning new things, and accessing local community news and other news media. However, 41 percent did see their lack of internet use as a disadvantage in regard to job hunting, which was the largest percentage reported in terms of perceived disadvantage.

49 The Verge, "Detours: Google Fiber and Kansas City's Grassroots Broadband Revolution, 2013," video, September 11, 2013, www.youtube.com/watch?v=NojmZW_ZoJ8.

50 Students take quizzes and tutorials through GCFLearnFree (https://edu.gcflearnfree.org). They are also encouraged to set up a Gmail address if they don't have

an email account already in order to sign up for services like GCFLearnFree or government, health, job, and educational services and sites.

51 The instructor told me that this man, a senior citizen, attends class almost every session and uses the internet to search for anything that's on his mind—this day was disability and disability law.

52 Interactions in other Connecting for Good and public library computer labs differed. Students and young families also attend these open computer sessions to play games online, stream media, create music, watch videos, and use the computers and internet access for more creative and playful activities as well as activities that necessitate consistent, robust internet connections and use more bandwidth.

53 Google, "Google Fiber: About," July 27, 2012, https://web.archive.org.

54 Donner, *After Access*, 137.

55 Adriana de Souza e Silva, Daniel M. Sutko, Fernando A Salis, and Claudio de Souza e Silca, "Mobile Phone Appropriation in the Favelas of Rio de Janeiro, Brazil," *New Media & Society* 13, no. 3 (May 1, 2011): 411–26.

56 Nancy Scola, "In Kansas City, Few Poor People, Renters Sign Up for Google Fiber," *Washington Post*, October 6, 2014, www.washingtonpost.com.

57 Mei-Po Kwan, "Feminist Visualization: Re-Envisioning GIS as a Method in Feminist Geographic Research," *Annals of the Association of American Geographers* 92, no. 4 (2002): 645–61; Mei-Po Kwan, "Beyond Space (As We Knew It): Toward Temporally Integrated Geographies of Segregation, Health, and Accessibility: Space-Time Integration in Geography and GIScience," *Annals of the Association of American Geographers* 103, no. 5 (September 2013): 1078–86; Kim Sawchuk, "Impaired," chap. 39 in *The Routledge Handbook of Mobilities*, ed. Peter Adey, David Bissell, Kevin Hannam, Peter Merriman, and Mimi Sheller (New York: Routledge, 2014).

58 Mike Rogoway, "Google Fiber: The Digital Divide Won't Be Crossed Digitally," Government Technology, December 8, 2014, www.govtech.com.

59 Mei-Po Kwan, "Time, Information Technologies, and the Geographies of Everyday Life," *Urban Geography* 23, no. 5 (2002): 471–82.

60 "KCMO Is Evolving into a Smart City."

61 Brian Ellison and Luke X. Martin, "Google Fiber in KC, Five Years Later," KCUR, April 1, 2016, http://kcur.org.

62 Karen E. Fisher and Charles M. Naumer, "Information Grounds: Theoretical Basis and Empirical Findings on Information Flow in Social Settings," in *New Directions in Human Information Behavior*, ed. Amanda Spink and Charles Cole, Information Science and Knowledge Management 8 (Dordrecht: Springer Netherlands, 2006), 93–111.

63 Representatives from Connecting for Good told me that they, along with other digital inclusion organizations, approached Google with the proposition of signal sharing early on in the campaign but that Google didn't agree with this plan.

64 Cook Network Consultants, "Google Fiber Reshapes Kansas City: While Its People Try Very Hard to Rewrite Its Future," in *The Cook Report on Internet Pro-*

tocol: Technology, Economics, and Policy (Ewing, NJ: Cook Network Consultants, February 2015), 6.

65 Elfreda A. Chatman, "A Theory of Life in the Round," *Journal of the American Society for Information Science* 50, no. 3 (1999): 207–17.

66 The last suggestion was eventually downvoted but received the most comments (three comments) of appreciation and added ideas by fellow forum members. All these ideas were submitted by members of DeWitt Creativity Group, web designers and developers, members of the start-up community, technology entrepreneurs, Gigabit Challenge winners, and community members who did not indicate their affiliations.

67 Mike Liimata, "E-community Center for Rosedale Area," KC Gig Ideas—KC Digital Drive, November 5, 2011, https://web.archive.org.

68 Lisandra R. Carmichael, Charles R. McClure, Lauren H. Mandel, and Marcia A. Mardis, "Broadband Adoption: Practical Approaches and Proposed Strategies for Measuring Selected Aspects of Community-Based Broadband Deployment and Use," *International Journal of Communication* 6 (October 2012), accessed February 29, 2016, http://ijoc.org; Sascha Meinrath, "Two Perspectives on the National Broadband Plan: A Conversation with Craig Settles and Blair Levin," New America, accessed February 29, 2016, www.newamerica.org; "Mission Statement & Principles," CLIC: Coalition for Local Internet Choice (blog), accessed February 29, 2016, www.localnetchoice.org.

69 Bincy Ninan-Moses, "Allied Media Projects and the Detroit Digital Justice Coalition: Building a Healthy Digital Ecosystem in Detroit," New America, December 6, 2011, www.newamerica.org.

70 Georgia Bullen, Hollie Russon-Gilman, and Laurenellen McCann, "Think Local First," New America, May 12, 2014, www.newamerica.org.

71 Christina Dunbar-Hester, *Low Power to the People: Pirates, Protest, and Politics in FM Radio Activism* (Cambridge, MA: MIT Press, 2014).

CHAPTER 3. THE FAMILIAR CITY

1 Adapted from the understanding of tripartite spatial layering through use of mobile communication technologies by Mizuko Ito, Daisuke Okabe, and Ken Anderson, "Portable Objects in Three Global Cities: The Personalization of Urban Places," chap. 3 in *The Reconstruction of Space and Time: Mobile Communication Practices*, ed. Rich Ling and Scott Campbell (New Brunswick, NJ: Transaction, 2007).

2 See "Young Adults Are Especially Likely to Use Their Phone for Navigation—Either by Car, Public Transit, or Taxi," in Aaron Smith, "U.S. Smartphone Use in 2015," Pew Research Center: Internet, Science & Technology, April 1, 2015, accessed October 20, 2015, www.pewinternet.org.

3 Scott M. Freundschuh and Max J Egenhofer, "Human Conceptions of Spaces: Implications for GIS," *Transactions in GIS* 2, no. 4 (December 1997): 361–75.

4 Scott McQuire, *Geomedia, Networked Cities and the Politics of Urban Space: Networked Cities and the Future of Public Space* (Cambridge: Polity, 2016).

5 Katharine S. Willis and Jens Geelhaar, "Information Places: Navigating Interfaces between Physical and Digital Space," chap. 14 in *Urban Informatics*, ed. Marcus Foth (Hershey, PA: ICS Global, 2008).

6 Toru Ishikawa, Hiromichi Fujiwara, Osamu Imai, and Atsuyuki Okabe, "Wayfinding with a GPS-Based Mobile Navigation System: A Comparison with Maps and Direct Experience," *Journal of Environmental Psychology* 28, no. 1 (March 2008): 74–82; Willis and Geelhaar, "Information Places"; Katharine S. Willis, Christoph Hölscher, Gregor Wilbertz, and Chao Li, "A Comparison of Spatial Knowledge Acquisition with Maps and Mobile Maps," *Computers, Environment, and Urban Systems* 33 (2009): 100–110; Andrew J. May, Tracy Ross, Steven H. Bayer, and Mikko J. Tarkiainen, "Pedestrian Navigation Aids: Information Requirements and Design Implications," *Personal Ubiquitous Computing* 7 (2003): 331–38; Stefan Munzer, Hubert D. Zimmer, Maximilian Schwalm, Jörg Baus, and Ilhan Aslan, "Computer-Assisted Navigation and the Acquisition of Route and Survey Knowledge," *Journal of Environmental Psychology* 26 (2006): 300–308.

7 Rowan Wilken, "Mobilizing Place: Mobile Media, Peripatetics, and the Renegotiation of Urban Places," *Journal of Urban Technology* 15, no. 3 (December 1, 2008): 39–55; Rowan Wilken and Gerard Goggin, *Mobile Technology and Place* (London: Routledge, 2012).

8 Nanna Verhoeff, *Mobile Screens: The Visual Regime of Navigation* (Amsterdam: Amsterdam University Press, 2012).

9 Jason Farman, "Mapping the Digital Empire: Google Earth and the Process of Postmodern Cartography," *New Media & Society* 12, no. 6 (September 1, 2010): 869–88; Sybille Lammes, "Digital Mapping Interfaces: From Immutable Mobiles to Mutable Images," *New Media & Society* 19, no. 7 (January 22, 2016): 1019–33.

10 Matthew A. Zook and Mark Graham, "The Creative Reconstruction of the Internet: Google and the Privatization of Cyberspace and Digiplace," *Geoforum* 38, no. 6 (2007): 1322–43; Matthew A. Zook and Mark Graham, "Mapping DigiPlace: Geocoded Internet Data and the Representation of Place," *Environment and Planning B: Planning and Design* 34, no. 3 (June 1, 2007): 466–82.

11 C. Chesher, "Navigating Sociotechnical Spaces: Comparing Computer Games and Sat Navs as Digital Spatial Media," *Convergence: The International Journal of Research into New Media Technologies* 18, no. 3 (August 1, 2012): 315–30; McQuire, *Geomedia, Networked Cities and the Politics of Urban Space.*

12 Paul Dourish, "Re-space-ing Place: Place and Space Ten Years On" (Proceedings of the ACM Conference on Computer-Supported Cooperative Work CSCW, Banff, Alberta, 2006), 8.

13 Edward C. Tolman, "Cognitive Maps in Rats and Men," *Psychological Review* 55, no. 4 (1948): 189–208.

14 Stanley Milgram, "The Experience of Living in Cities," *Science* 13 (March 1970): 1461–68.

15 Janet Vertesi, "Mind the Gap: The London Underground Map and Users' Representations of Urban Space," *Social Studies of Science* 38, no. 1 (February 1, 2008): 7–33; Frank Bentley, Henriette Cramer, Santosh Basapur, and William Hamilton, "Drawing the City: Differing Perceptions of the Urban Environment" (ACM SIGCHI Conference on Human Factors in Computing Systems, Austin, TX, May 5–10, 2012).

16 Fredric Jameson, *Postmodernism, or, the Cultural Logic of Late Capitalism* (Durham, NC: Duke University Press, 1991), 51.

17 Jameson, 51.

18 Michael Chanan, "Going South: On Documentary as a Form of Cognitive Geography," *Cinema Journal* 50, no. 1 (2010): 147–54; Carlos Gallego, "Topographies of Resistance: Cognitive Mapping in Chicano/a Migrant Literature," *Arizona Quarterly: A Journal of American Literature, Culture, and Theory* 70, no. 2 (2014): 21–53; Eric Gordon, "Mapping Digital Networks: From Cyberspace to Google," *Information, Communication & Society* 10, no. 6 (December 1, 2007): 885–901; Wendy Hui Kyong Chun, *Programmed Visions* (Cambridge, MA: MIT Press, 2011).

19 Roger M. Downs, David Stea, and Kenneth E. Boulding, eds., *Image and Environment: Cognitive Mapping and Spatial Behavior*, new ed. (New Brunswick, NJ: Aldine Transaction, 2005).

20 Kathryn Zickuhr and Aaron Smith, "28% of American Adults Use Mobile and Social Location-Based Services," Pew Research Center: Internet & Technology, September 6, 2011, www.pewinternet.org.

21 Marcia J. Bates, "Fundamental Forms of Information," *Journal of the American Society for Information Science and Technology* 57, no. 8 (2006): 1033–45.

22 Bates.

23 Other users also referenced Street View in this way: "Sometimes if I do not understand the direction, I like that I can use the Street View and walk my way through it virtually to give me an idea of where I will be." And, "I think it helps a lot, because it allows you to see where you're going before you even go there. You can even use the Street View to see what the building your looking for looks like."

24 N. Katherine Hayles, *How We Think: Digital Media and Contemporary Technogenesis* (Chicago: University of Chicago Press, 2012), 81.

25 Hayles, 1.

26 Troels Fibæk Bertel, "'It's Like I Trust It So Much That I Don't Really Check Where It Is I'm Going before I Leave': Informational Uses of Smartphones among Danish Youth," *Mobile Media & Communication* 1, no. 3 (September 1, 2013): 299–313.

27 Clare L. Twigger-Ross and David L. Uzzell, "Place and Identity Processes," *Journal of Environmental Psychology* 16 (1996): 205–20.

28 Jordan Frith, *Smartphones as Locative Media* (Cambridge: Polity, 2015).

29 Milgram, "The Experience of Living in Cities," 1462.

30 Georg Simmel, "The Metropolis and Mental Life," chap. 20 in *Georg Simmel on Individuality and Social Forms*, ed. Donald N. Levine (Chicago: University of Chicago Press, 1971).

31 Freundschuh and Egenhofer, "Human Conceptions of Spaces."

32 Gary H. Winkel, "The Perception of Neighborhood Change," in *Cognition and Social Behavior and the Environment*, ed. John H. Harvey (New York: Erlbaum, 1981).

33 For an analysis of these marketing campaigns, see Germaine R. Halegoua, "New Mediated Spaces and the Urban Environment" (PhD diss., University of Wisconsin–Madison, 2012).

34 Jessa Lingel, "Information Tactics of Immigrants in Urban Environments," *Information Research* 16, no. 4 (2011).

35 It was not solely females who expressed these concerns but males too: "It makes me feel dangerous [in danger]" (Asian male, 18). "I'm a South Korean, and English is not my native language, so when I'm in South Korea, I feel confident to find the place, but in States [the United States], sometimes I do not feel confident because of language barrier and culture stuffs" (Asian male, 28).

36 Heidi Rae Cooley, *Finding Augusta: Habits of Mobility and Governance in the Digital Era* (Hanover, NH: Dartmouth College Press, 2014).

37 Gayatri Chakravorty Spivak, *The Post-Colonial Critic: Interviews, Strategies, Dialogues*, ed. S. Harasym (New York: Routledge, 1990), 41.

38 Erika Polson, "A Gateway to the Global City: Mobile Place-Making Practices by Expats," *New Media & Society* 17, no. 4 (April 1, 2015): 629–45.

39 McQuire, *Geomedia, Networked Cities and the Politics of Urban Space*.

40 Zook and Graham, "The Creative Reconstruction of the Internet"; Caitlin Dewey, "You Probably Haven't Even Noticed Google's Sketchy Quest to Control the World's Knowledge," *Washington Post*, May 11, 2016, www.washingtonpost.com.

41 Zook and Graham, "Mapping DigiPlace."

42 Cooley, *Finding Augusta*.

43 Henri Lefebvre, *Rhythmanalysis: Space, Time, and Everyday Life* (New York: Continuum, 2004).

44 Jason Farman, *Mobile Interface Theory: Embodied Space and Locative Media* (New York: Routledge, 2012).

45 Wendy Hui Kyong Chun, *Programmed Visions*, 71; emphasis in original.

46 Participants noted that they rarely veered from or adjusted the directions provided by their navigation devices. For example, they rarely took shortcuts across parking lots while driving or cut across fields on foot.

47 David Harvey, "The Right to the City," *New Left Review* 2, no. 53 (October 2008): 23–40.

48 Rob Kitchin and Scott Freundschuch, "Cognitive Mapping," chap. 1 in *Cognitive Mapping: Past, Present, and Future*, eds. Rob Kitchin and Scott Freundschuch (New York, Routledge, 2000).

CHAPTER 4. THE SOCIAL CITY

1 Elizabeth Wilson, *The Sphinx in the City* (Berkeley: University of California Press, 1992).

2 A. Walker and R. K. Moulton, "Photo Albums: Images of Time and Reflections of Self," *Qualitative Sociology* 12, no. 2 (1989): 155–82.

3 Esther Milne, *Letters, Postcards, Email: Technologies of Presence* (New York: Routledge, 2010); Todd Alden, "And We Lived Where Dusk Had Meaning," in *Real Photo Postcards*, ed. Laetitia Wolff (Princeton, NJ: Princeton Architectural Press, 2005), 6–10; Robert Bogdan, *Real Photo Postcard Guide: The People's Photography*, 1st ed. (Syracuse, NY: Syracuse University Press, 2006).

4 Lee Humphreys, *The Qualified Self: Social Media and the Accounting of Everyday Life* (Cambridge, MA: MIT Press, 2018).

5 Stéphane Roche, "Geographic Information Science II: Less Space, More Places in Smart Cities," *Progress in Human Geography*, May 19, 2015.

6 danah boyd, "Social Network Sites as Networked Publics: Affordances, Dynamics, and Implications," chap. 2 in *A Networked Self: Identity, Community, and Culture on Social Network Sites*, ed. Zizi Papacharissi (New York: Routledge, 2011).

7 Edward S. Casey, "Between Geography and Philosophy: What Does It Mean to Be in the Place-World?," *Annals of the Association of American Geographers* 91, no. 4 (2001): 684; emphasis in original.

8 John Cheney-Lippold, *We Are Data: Algorithms and the Making of Our Digital Selves* (New York: NYU Press, 2017); Safiya Umoja Noble, *Algorithms of Oppression: How Search Engines Reinforce Racism* (New York: NYU Press, 2018).

9 Zizi Papacharissi, *A Networked Self: Identity, Community, and Culture on Social Network Sites* (New York: Routledge, 2011), 307.

10 Joshua Meyrowitz, *No Sense of Place: The Impact of Electronic Media on Social Behavior* (Oxford: Oxford University Press, 1985).

11 Adriana de Souza e Silva and Jordan Frith, *Mobile Interfaces in Public Spaces: Locational Privacy, Control, and Urban Sociability* (New York: Routledge, 2012), 163; Cara Wallis, *Technomobility in China: Young Migrant Women and Mobile Phones* (New York: New York University Press, 2013).

12 Heidi Rae Cooley, *Finding Augusta: Habits of Mobility and Governance in the Digital Era* (Hanover, NH: Dartmouth College Press, 2014).

13 Eric Gordon and Adriana de Souza e Silva, *Net Locality: Why Location Matters in a Networked World* (Malden, MA: Wiley-Blackwell, 2011).

14 Harold M. Proshansky, Abbe K. Fabian, and Robert Kaminoff, "Place-Identity: Physical World Socialization of the Self," *Journal of Environmental Psychology* 3, no. 1 (March 1, 1983): 57–83; Setha M. Low and Irwin Altman, "Place Attachment," in *Place Attachment*, ed. Irwin Altman and Setha M. Low, Human Behavior and Environment 12 (Boston: Springer, 1992), 1–12; Dolores Hayden, *The Power of Place: Urban Landscapes as Public History* (Cambridge, MA: MIT Press, 1995); Jason Farman, *Mobile Interface Theory: Embodied Space and Locative Media* (New York: Routledge, 2012).

15 Didem Ozkul and Lee Humphreys, "Record and Remember: Memory and Meaning-Making Practices through Mobile Media," *Mobile Media & Communication* 3, no. 3 (September 2015): 351–65.

16 Raz Schwartz and Germaine R. Halegoua, "The Spatial Self: Location-Based Identity Performance on Social Media," *New Media & Society* 17, no. 10 (April 9, 2014): 1643–60.

17 Ingrid Richardson and Rowan Wilken, "Parerga of the Third Screen: Mobile Media, Place, and Presence," in *Mobile Technology and Place*, ed. Rowan Wilken and Gerard Goggin (New York: Routledge, 2012), 181–97.

18 Sarah Pink, "Sensory Digital Photography: Re-thinking 'Moving' and the Image," *Visual Studies* 26, no. 1 (March 2011): 4–13.

19 Casey, "Between Geography and Philosophy," 685.

20 Rob Sullivan, *Geography Speaks: Performative Aspects of Geography* (Farnham, UK: Ashgate, 2011), 64.

21 Humphreys, *The Qualified Self*.

22 Larissa Hjorth and Ingrid Richardson, *Gaming in Social, Locative and Mobile Media* (Basingstoke, UK: Palgrave Macmillan, 2014).

23 Counts Media Inc., "YA Overview History," Counts Media (blog), accessed in 2006, www.countsmedia.com.

24 Sam Toman, "[murmur] Whispers Sweet Something in Your Ear," Sceneandheard, September 30, 2003, accessed in 2006, www.sceneandheard.ca.

25 M. Christine Boyer, *The City of Collective Memory* (Cambridge, MA: MIT Press, 1994), 52.

26 Germaine R. Halegoua, "New Mediated Spaces and the Urban Environment" (PhD diss., University of Wisconsin–Madison, 2012).

27 Mike Crang and Stephen Graham, "Sentient Cities: Ambient Intelligence and the Politics of Urban Space," *Information, Communication, and Society* 10, no. 6 (December 2007): 789–817.

28 Srilata Zaheer and Lilach Nachum, "Sense of Place: From Location Resources to MNE Locational Capital," *Global Strategy Journal* 1, nos. 1–2 (May 1, 2011): 96–108; Paul Temple, *The Physical University: Contours of Space and Place in Higher Education* (New York: Routledge, 2014).

29 Mariane Hirsch, *Family Frames: Photography, Narrative and Postmemory* (Cambridge: Harvard University Press, 1997).

30 Doreen B. Massey, *For Space* (London: Sage, 2005), 124.

31 Farman, *Mobile Interface Theory*.

32 Larissa Hjorth, "Relocating the Mobile: A Case Study of Locative Media in Seoul, South Korea," *Convergence: The International Journal of Research into New Media Technologies* 19, no. 2 (May 2013): 246; Pink, "Sensory Digital Photography."

33 Matthew W. Wilson, "Location-Based Services, Conspicuous Mobility, and the Location-Aware Future," in "Spatialities of Aging," special issue, *Geoforum* 43, no. 6 (November 2012): 1266–75.

34 Lee Humphreys and Tony Liao, "Foursquare and the Parochialization of Public Space," *First Monday* 18, no. 11 (November 27, 2013), http://firstmonday.org.

35 De Souza e Silva and Frith, *Mobile Interfaces in Public Spaces*, 172.

36 Lee Humphreys, "Connecting, Coordinating, Cataloguing: Communicative Practices on Mobile Social Networks," *Journal of Broadcasting & Electronic Media* 56, no. 4 (October 1, 2012): 494–510; Janne Lindqvist, Justin Cranshaw, Jason Wiese, Jason Hong, and John Zimmerman, "I'm the Mayor of My House: Examining Why People Use Foursquare: A Social-Driven Location Sharing Application" (CHI '11: Proceedings of the SIGCHI Conference on Human Factors in Computing Systems, Vancouver, BC, May 2–12, 2011), 2409–18.

37 Hjorth and Richardson, *Gaming in Social, Locative and Mobile Media*; Jordan Frith, "Turning Life into a Game: Foursquare, Gamification, and Personal Mobility," *Mobile Media & Communication* 1, no. 2 (2013): 248–62.

38 Henriette Cramer, Mattias Rost, and Lars Erik Holmquist, "Performing a Check-In: Emerging Practices, Norms and 'Conflicts' in Location-Sharing Using Foursquare" (MobileHCI '11: Proceedings of the 13th International Conference on Human Computer Interaction with Mobile Devices and Services, Stockholm, Sweden, August 30–September 2, 2011), 57–66.

39 Mimi Sheller, "Mobile Conviviality," *Flow Journal*, November 5, 2012, www.flow-journal.org.

40 Louise Barkhuus, Barry Brown, Marek Bell, and Scott Sherwood, "From Awareness to Repartee: Sharing Location Within Social Groups" (ACM SIGCHI Conference on Human Factors in Computing Systems, CHI '08, Florence, Italy, April 5–10, 2008), 497–506.

41 De Certeau, *The Practice of Everyday Life* (Berkeley: University of California Press, 2011), 97.

42 Josh Constine, "Instagram Hits 1 Billion Monthly Users, up from 800M in September," TechCrunch, June 20, 2018, https://techcrunch.com.

43 Theresa M. Senft and Nancy K. Baym, "Selfies Introduction: What Does the Selfie Say? Investigating a Global Phenomenon," *International Journal of Communication* 9 (May 15, 2015): 19.

44 Jon M. Wargo, "'Every Selfie Tells a Story . . .': LGBTQ Youth Lifestreams and New Media Narratives as Connective Identity Texts," *New Media & Society* 19, no. 4 (October 23, 2015): 2.

45 Barbara Harrison, "Snap Happy: Toward a Sociology of 'Everyday' Photography," in *Seeing Is Believing? Approaches to Visual Research*, ed. Christopher Pole, Studies in Qualitative Methodology 7 (Bingley, UK: Emerald, 2004), 23–39.

46 Katrin Tiidenberg, *Selfies: Why We Love (and Hate) Them* (Bingley, UK: Emerald, 2018).

47 David Nemer and Guo Freeman, "Empowering the Marginalized: Rethinking Selfies in the Slums of Brazil," *International Journal of Communication* 9 (May 15, 2015): 1832.

48 Wargo, "'Every Selfie Tells a Story,'" 8.

49 Aaron Hess, "The Selfie Assemblage," *International Journal of Communication* 9 (May 15, 2015): 18.

50 Hess.

51 Larissa Hjorth and Sarah Pink, "New Visualities and the Digital Wayfarer: Recon-
    ceptualizing Camera Phone Photography and Locative Media," *Mobile Media &
    Communication* 2, no. 1 (2014): 42.

52 Henri Lefebvre, *The Production of Space* (Oxford: Blackwell, 1991).

53 Casey, "Between Geography and Philosophy."

54 Sullivan, *Geography Speaks*.

55 Miriam Redi, Daniele Quercia, Lindsay Graham, Samuel D Gosling, "Like
    Partying? Your Face Says It All. Predicting the Ambiance of Places with Profile
    Pictures" (Proceedings of the Ninth International AAAI Conference on Web and
    Social Media, Oxford, England, May 26–29, 2015) 347–56.

56 Jess Zimmerman, "Barbie's Instagram Is Superficial and Inauthentic. So Is Yours,"
    Guardian, September 9, 2015; Claire O'Reilly, "The Fall of the Instashammers,"
    Sun (England), December 6, 2015.

57 "White Saviour Barbie's World of Orphanage Selfies and Charity Startups," Life
    and Style, *Guardian*, April 28, 2016.

58 Liz Connor, "Hipster Barbie Perfectly Mimics East Londoners on Instagram,"
    London Life, *Evening Standard*, September 14, 2015, www.standard.co.uk.

59 Jess Cartner-Morley, "Insta-Barbie Pokes Fun at Hipsterdom," Analysis, *Mail &
    Guardian*, September 18, 2015.

60 Alice Marwick, *Status Update: Celebrity, Publicity and Branding in the Social Me-
    dia Age* (New Haven, CT: Yale University Press, 2015).

61 Peter van Ham, "Place Branding: The State of the Art," *Annals of the American
    Academy of Political and Social Science* 616 (2008): 126–49.

62 James Meese, Martin Gibbs, Marcus Carter, Michael Arnold, Bjorn Nansen,
    and Tamara Kohn, "Selfies at Funerals: Mourning and Presencing on Social
    Media Platforms." *International Journal of Communication* 9, no. 0 (May 15,
    2015); Lee Humphreys, *The Qualified Self: Social Media and the Accounting of
    Everyday Life* (Cambridge, MA: MIT Press, 2018); Hess, "The Selfie Assem-
    blage."

63 Madeleine Davies, "Selfies at Serious Places Is the Most Cringeworthy Tumblr
    of All Time," Jezebel, accessed June 30, 2016, http://jezebel.com; Arwa Mahdawi,
    "Thumbs-Up at a Holocaust Memorial: A Clear Breach of Selfie Etiquette," *Guard-
    ian*, accessed June 30, 2016. www.theguardian.com.

64 Mark Hensch, "Holocaust Museum: Stop Playing Pokémon Go Here," Hill, July 12,
    2016, http://thehill.com.

65 Sara Ahmed, *The Cultural Politics of Emotion* (New York: Routledge, 2013).

66 Zizi Papacharissi, "Affective Publics and Structures of Storytelling: Sentiment,
    Events and Mediality," *Information, Communication & Society* 19, no. 3 (March 3,
    2016): 307–24.

67 Papacharissi.

68 Wallis, *Technomobility in China*.

69 Helen Kennedy, Thomas Poell, and José van Dijck, "Data and Agency," *Big Data & Society* 2, no. 2 (December 2015).

70 Sung-Yueh Perng, Rob Kitchin, and Leighton Evans, "Locative Media and Data-Driven Computing Experiments," *Big Data & Society* 3, no. 1 (June 1, 2016); Rob Kitchin, "Data-Driven, Networked Urbanism," SSRN, August 10, 2015, http://papers.ssrn.com; Rob Kitchin and Tracey P. Lauriault, "Towards Critical Data Studies: Charting and Unpacking Data Assemblages and Their Work," SSRN, July 30, 2014, http://papers.ssrn.com.

71 Ernesto Ramirez, "How to Map Your Moves Data," Quantified Self (blog), March 14, 2014, http://quantifiedself.com.

72 Kate Crawford, Jessa Lingel, and Tero Karppi, "Our Metrics, Ourselves: A Hundred Years of Self-Tracking from the Weight Scale to the Wrist Wearable Device," *European Journal of Cultural Studies* 18, nos. 4–5 (2015): 494.

73 Farman, *Mobile Interface Theory*; Richardson and Wilken, "Parerga of the Third Screen."

74 Tamar Sharon and Dorien Zandbergen, "From Data Fetishism to Quantifying Selves: Self-Tracking Practices and the Other Values of Data," *New Media & Society* 19, no. 11 (March 9, 2016): 1695–1709.

75 Kennedy, Poell, and van Dijck, "Data and Agency."

76 Perng, Kitchin, and Evans, "Locative Media and Data-Driven Computing Experiments."

77 Perng, Kitchin, and Evans; Nadav Hochman and Lev Manovich, "Zooming into an Instagram City: Reading the Local through Social Media," *First Monday* 18, no. 7 (July 2013), http://firstmonday.org.

78 Raz Schwartz and Nadav Hochman, "The Social Media Life of Public Spaces: Reading Places through the Lens of Geotagged Data," chap. 4 in *Locative Media*, ed. Rowan Wilken and Gerard Goggin (New York: Routledge, 2014).

79 Justin Cranshaw, Raz Schwartz, Jason Hong, and Norman Sadeh, "Livehoods," Livehoods, accessed July 5, 2016, http://livehoods.org.

80 Wilson, "Location-Based Services, Conspicuous Mobility, and the Location-Aware Future."

81 Farman, *Mobile Interface Theory*, 73.

82 danah boyd and Kate Crawford, "Critical Questions for Big Data," *Information Communication & Society* 15, no. 5 (2012): 662–79.

83 Kitchin, "Data-Driven, Networked Urbanism."

84 Although Lefebvre describes the city as a place of encounters elsewhere, see Henri Lefebvre, *Writings on Cities* (Oxford: Blackwell, 2000).

85 M. Christine Boyer, *CyberCities: Visual Perception in the Age of Electronic Communication* (Princeton, NJ: Princeton Architectural Press, 1996); Edward Soja, *Postmetropolis: Critical Studies of Cities and Regions* (Oxford: Wiley-Blackwell, 2000).

CHAPTER 5. THE CREATIVE CITY

1 Tim Cresswell, *Place: A Short Introduction* (Wiley-Blackwell, 2004), 39.

2 Ann Markusen and Anne Gadwa, "Creative Placemaking" (Washington, DC: National Endowment for the Arts, 2010), www.arts.gov.

3 Markusen and Gadwa.

4 One of the original authors of the report has identified at least eight slightly different definitions of creative placemaking. However, all definitions include the arts as a key component of economic development and improved quality of life. See Anne Gadwa Nicodemus, "Creative Placemaking 2.0," *GIA Reader* 23, no. 2 (Summer 2012), www.giarts.org, for examples of various definitions.

5 Christina Sturdivant, "D.C. Announces Plans for 15 Citywide, Pop-Up Art Projects," DCist, May 5, 2016, http://dcist.com.

6 Christina Sturdivant, "Creative Placemaking—Bridging Communities through the Arts," East City Art, May 1, 2014, www.eastcityart.com.

7 Ann Markusen and Anne Gadwa, "Creative Placemaking," 3.

8 Anne Gadwa Nicodemus, "Creative Placemaking 101 for Community Developers," LISC Institute for Comprehensive Community Development, May 27, 2014, www.instituteccd.org.

9 "About ArtPlace," ArtPlace, April 16, 2015, www.artplaceamerica.org.

10 Jamie Bennett, "Creative Placemaking? What Is It That You Do?," ArtPlace, July 23, 2015, www.artplaceamerica.org.

11 Jenna Moran, Jason Schupbach, Courtney Spearman, and Jennifer Reut, *Beyond the Building: Performing Arts & Transforming Place* (Washington, DC: National Endowment for the Arts, 2015), 8.

12 "5 Questions for Carol Coletta, President, ArtPlace," *Philanthropy News Digest* (blog), October 29, 2011, http://pndblog.typepad.com.

13 Markusen and Gadwa, "Creative Placemaking."

14 Anne Gadwa Nicodemus, "Fuzzy Vibrancy: Creative Placemaking as Ascendant US Cultural Policy," *Cultural Trends* 22, nos. 3–4 (December 2013): 213–22; Ann Markusen, "Fuzzy Concepts, Proxy Data: Why Indicators Would Not Track Creative Placemaking Success," *International Journal of Urban Sciences* 17, no. 3 (November 1, 2013): 291–303.

15 "5 Questions for Carol Coletta, President, ArtPlace"; Gadwa Nicodemus, "Fuzzy Vibrancy."

16 According to an ArtPlace mission statement, the organization runs a national grants program, has invested in six community planning and development organizations, supports initiatives to retain and recruit creative placemaking practitioners, conducts research, and promotes success stories (from "About ArtPlace").

17 "About CIRD," Citizens' Institute on Rural Design, accessed July 20, 2016, www.rural-design.org.

18 Gadwa Nicodemus, "Fuzzy Vibrancy"; Gadwa Nicodemus, "Creative Placemaking 2.0."

19 Gadwa Nicodemus, "Creative Placemaking 101 for Community Developers."

20 Gadwa Nicodemus, "Fuzzy Vibrancy."

21 Bennett, "Creative Placemaking?"

22 Roberto Bedoya, "Placemaking and the Politics of Belonging and Dis-belonging," *GIA Reader* 24, no. 1 (Winter 2013), www.giarts.org; Debra Webb, "Placemaking and Social Equity: Expanding the Framework of Creative Placemaking," *Artivate: A Journal of Entrepreneurship in the Arts* 3, no. 1 (2013): 35–48.

23 Gadwa Nicodemus, "Fuzzy Vibrancy."

24 Moran et al., "Beyond the Building."

25 Susan Tate, "The Ninth Street Corridor Project: From the Studios to the Streets." *ArtPlace*, April 13, 2015www.artplaceamerica.org.

26 Nikki Wentling, "'Poetic' Lighting, Sound Art, Rocks: East Ninth Committee Signs off on Streetscape Design," *Laurence Journal-World*, March 30, 2016, www2.ljworld.com.

27 "East 9th St. Placekeepers," East 9th St. Placekeepers, accessed July 9, 2016, https://eastninth.net.

28 Stephen Pritchard, "Place Guarding: Activist & Social Practice Art-Direct Action against Gentrification Full# AAG2016 Paper," Coloring in Culture (blog), accessed July 19, 2016, https://colouringinculture.wordpress.com.

29 "HAA Dogpile! Artists of Transported + Renewed Weigh In," Glasstire (blog), December 1, 2014, http://glasstire.com.

30 Moran et al., "Beyond the Building."

31 Gadwa Nicodemus, "Fuzzy Vibrancy."

32 Bedoya, "Placemaking and the Politics of Belonging and Dis-belonging."

33 "Creative Communities and Arts-Based Placemaking," Project for Public Spaces (blog), accessed July 20, 2016, www.pps.org.

34 Abigail Satinsky, "Is Social Practice Gentrifying Community Arts?," Bad at Sports (blog), 2013, http://badatsports.com; Steve Panton, "Art That Knows Its Place," *Infinite Mile: A Journal of Art and Culture(s) in Detroit*, 12 (2014), https://infinitemiledetroit.com.

35 Moran et al., "Beyond the Building."

36 Jennifer S. Evans-Cowley, "Planning in the Age of Facebook: The Role of Social Networking in Planning Processes," *GeoJournal* 75, no. 5 (2010): 407–20.

37 The People's Emergency Center in Philadelphia has proposed to partner with arts organizations, several predominantly African American neighborhoods, and the Sixteenth Police District to include public art installations and performances such as "digital street art," "play structure builds," pop-up art events, and puppetry shows "that will engage neighbors in dialogue and creative exchange to make a safer neighborhood." The University of Oklahoma proposed to create a Placemaking Toolset where maps and information about creative placemaking and the arts can be found in both Spanish and English. From "2016 List of ArtPlace Finalists," ArtPlace, accessed July 12, 2016, www.artplaceamerica.org.

38 Jacob Poushter, "Smartphone Ownership and Internet Usage Continues to Climb in Emerging Economies," Pew Research Center's Global Attitudes Project (blog), February 22, 2016, www.pewglobal.org.

39 ZERO1's biennial is an outgrowth of the Interactive Media Festival that took place in Los Angeles during the 1990s. It was organized by Andy Cunningham, a Silicon Valley public relations strategist and the International Symposium for the Electronic Arts in 2006.

40 Markusen and Gadwa, "Creative Placemaking," 45.

41 "Silicon Valley Inside/Out," National Endowment for the Arts, accessed July 13, 2016, www.arts.gov.

42 Kevin Montgomery, "Dropbox Dudes Tried to Kick Children Off a Soccer Field," Gawker, October 10, 2014, http://valleywag.gawker.com; Julia Carrie Wong, "Dropbox, Airbnb, and the Fight over San Francisco's Public Spaces," New Yorker, October 23, 2014, www.newyorker.com; Ryan Bort, "The Tech Industry Is Stripping San Francisco of Its Culture, and Your City Could Be Next," Newsweek, October 1, 2015, www.newsweek.com.

43 Isaac D. Kremer, "Creative Placemaking to Transform a Park in Milwaukee," Main Street America, May 6, 2016, www.preservationnation.org.

44 Andre McMillan, "Creative Assets Map," ArtPlace, July 16, 2012, www.artplaceamerica.org.

45 Not included in this categorization of digital media projects are organizations that slated digital media or interactive art projects within a curated exhibition or festival. For example, an outdoor performance space in Miami wanted to include "virtual reality events" alongside dance, cinema, spoken word, and music performances in an upcoming festival. See "YoungArts: Outside the Box" project proposal by the National YoungArts Foundation https://www.artplaceamerica.org.

46 Jason Farman, ed., The Mobile Story: Narrative Practices with Locative Technologies (New York: Routledge, 2014).

47 Vic Vela, "Meet Brian Corrigan, Denver's 'Oh Heck Yeah' Phenom," Confluence, July 24, 2013, www.confluence-denver.com.

48 "Iron Triangle Interactive Art," National Endowment for the Arts, accessed July 11, 2016, www.arts.gov.

49 For one example, see Mode Set, "OhHeckYeah Street Arcade—Opening Night, 2014 on Vimeo," Vimeo, 2014, https://vimeo.com.

50 Peter Mello, "Waterfire's Learning Lab," ArtPlace, July 23, 2012, www.artplaceamerica.org.

51 Roxanne Fry, "Community Foundation of Northern Colorado: Arts @ the Feed & Grain," ArtPlace, November 1, 2013, www.artplaceamerica.org.

52 Julie Decker, "The Northern Initiative," ArtPlace, November 15, 2012, www.artplaceamerica.org.

53 Maggie Bryde, "MiKE," ArtPlace, February 5, 2012, www.artplaceamerica.org.

54 Bryde.

55 Jill Fantauzzacoffin, Joanna Berzowska, Ernest A. Edmonds, and Ken Goldberg, "The Arts, HCI, and Innovation Policy Discourse: Invited Panel" (ACM CHI '12 Extended Abstracts on Human Factors in Computing Systems, Austin, Texas, May 5–10, 2012), 1111–14.

56 Bennett, "Creative Placemaking?"

57 "About ArtPlace."

58 Danielle Wyatt, "Unsettling the Badlands: Community Art and the Governance of Place" (PhD diss., RMIT University, 2012), http://researchbank.rmit.edu.

59 Eric Gordon and Adriana de Souza e Silva, *Net Locality: Why Location Matters in a Networked World* (Malden, MA: Wiley-Blackwell, 2011), 85.

60 Eric Gordon, "Network Locality: Local Knowledge and Politics in a Network Culture," *First Monday* 13, no. 10 (October 6, 2008), http://firstmonday.org.

61 Vela, "Meet Brian Corrigan."

62 Gordon, "Network Locality," 93.

63 Fred Kent and Cynthia Nikitin, "Collaborative Placemaking: Good Public Art Depends on Good Public Spaces," *Public Art Review* 45 (Fall/Winter 2011): 17–17.

64 Juliana Reyes, "Watch a Chinatown Street Change over Time," Technical.ly Philly, June 25, 2014, http://technical.ly/philly.

65 Nancy K. Baym, *Personal Connections in the Digital Age* (Cambridge: Polity, 2010).

66 Scott McQuire, *Geomedia, Networked Cities and the Politics of Urban Space: Networked Cities and the Future of Public Space* (Cambridge: Polity, 2016).

67 Yong-Chan Kim and Sandra J. Ball-Rokeach, "Community Storytelling Network, Neighborhood Context, and Civic Engagement: A Multilevel Approach," *Human Communication Research* 32, no. 4 (October 1, 2006): 411–39; Sandra J. Ball-Rokeach, Yong-Chan Kim, and Sorin Matei, "Storytelling Neighborhood: Paths to Belonging in Diverse Urban Environments," *Communication Research* 28, no. 4 (August 2001): 392–428; Giota Alevizou, Katerina Alexiou, Dave Harte, Shawn Sobers, Theodore Zamenopoulos, and Jerome Turner, "Civic Cultures and Modalities of Place-Making," chap. 9 in *The Creative Citizen Unbound: How Social Media and DIY Culture Contribute to Democracy, Communities and the Creative Economy*, ed. Ian Hargreaves and John Hartley (Bristol, UK: Policy, 2016).

68 Alevizou et al.

69 Nien-Tsu N. Chen, Fan Dong, Sandra J. Ball-Rokeach, Michael Parks, and Jin Huang, "Building a New Media Platform for Local Storytelling and Civic Engagement in Ethnically Diverse Neighborhoods," *New Media & Society* 14, no. 6 (September 1, 2012): 931–50.

70 Sasha Costanza-Chock, "Digital Popular Communication: Lessons on Information and Communication Technologies for Social Change from the Immigrant Rights Movement," *National Civic Review* 100, no. 3 (2011): 29–35.

71 Eric Gordon and Jessica Baldwin-Philippi, "Playful Civic Learning: Enabling Lateral Trust and Reflection in Game-Based Public Participation," *International Journal of Communication* 8 (February 26, 2014): 28.

72 Pritchard, "Place Guarding."

CONCLUSION

1 Eric Gordon and Adriana de Souza e Silva, *Net Locality: Why Location Matters in a Networked World* (Malden, MA: Wiley-Blackwell, 2011); Scott McQuire, *The Media City: Media, Architecture, and Urban Space* (London: Sage, 2008); Malcolm McCullough, *Digital Ground: Architecture, Pervasive Computing, and Environmental Knowing* (Cambridge, MA: MIT Press, 2004); Rob Kitchin and Martin Dodge, *Code/Space: Software and Everyday Life* (Cambridge, MA: MIT Press, 2011).

2 Mizuko Ito, "Mobiles and the Appropriation of Place," *Receiver Magazine*, 2003, 3.

3 Lee Humphreys and Tony Liao, "Foursquare and the Parochialization of Public Space," *First Monday* 18, no. 11 (November 27, 2013), http://firstmonday.org; Rowan Wilken, "Mobilizing Place: Mobile Media, Peripatetics, and the Renegotiation of Urban Places," *Journal of Urban Technology* 15, no. 3 (December 1, 2008): 39–55.

4 M. Zook and M. Graham, "The Creative Reconstruction of the Internet: Google and the Privatization of Cyberspace and DigiPlace," *Geoforum* 38 (2007): 1322–43; Kitchin and Dodge, *Code/Space: Software and Everyday Life.*

5 Germaine Halegoua, "My First Year on the 'Rural' Side of the Digital Divide," Cyborgology (blog), November 2, 2015, https://thesocietypages.org.

6 Henrikki Tenkanen, Enrico Di Minin, Vuokko Heikinheimo, Anna Hausmann, Marna Herbst, Liisa Kajala, and Tuuli Toivonen, "Instagram, Flickr, or Twitter: Assessing the Usability of Social Media Data for Visitor Monitoring in Protected Areas," *Nature—Scientific Reports* 7 (2017), www.nature.com; Georgina G. Gurney, Jessica Blythe, Helen Adams, W. Neil Adger, Matthew Curnock, Lucy Faulkner, Thomas James, and Nadine A. Marshall, "Redefining Community Based on Place Attachment in a Connected World," *PNAS* 114, no. 38 (September 19, 2017): 10077–82.

7 Brent Knepper, "Instagram Is Loving Nature to Death," the Outline, November 7, 2017, https://theoutline.com; Ryan Thompson, "How Colorado's Outdoors Are Being Loved to Death—A KUNC Special Report," KUNC, September 1, 2016, www.kunc.org.

8 David Stea and Mete Turan, *Placemaking: Production of Built Environment in Two Cultures* (Aldershot, UK: Avebury, 1993), 6.

9 Lynda H. Schneekloth and Robert G. Shibley, *Placemaking: The Art and Practice of Building Communities* (New York: Wiley, 1995).

10 Schneekloth and Shibley, 191.

11 David Harvey, "The Right to the City," *New Left Review* 2, no. 53 (October 2008): 23–40.

INDEX

p. 3

ABOUT THE AUTHOR

Germaine R. Halegoua is Associate Professor in the Department of Film and Media Studies at the University of Kansas. She studies digital media and place, urban and community informatics, and cultural geographies of digital media and is the co-editor of *Locating Emerging Media*.